Modern Critical Views

Chinua Achebe
Henry Adams
Aeschylus
S. Y. Agnon
Edward Albee
Raphael Alberti
Louisa May Alcott
A. R. Ammons
Sherwood Anderson
Aristophanes
Matthew Arnold
Antonin Artaud
John Ashbery
Margaret Atwood
W. H. Auden
Jane Austen
Isaac Babel
Sir Francis Bacon
James Baldwin
Honoré de Balzac
John Barth
Donald Barthelme
Charles Baudelaire
Simone de Beauvoir
Samuel Beckett
Saul Bellow
Thomas Berger
John Berryman
The Bible
Elizabeth Bishop
William Blake
Giovanni Boccaccio
Heinrich Böll
Jorge Luis Borges
Elizabeth Bowen
Bertolt Brecht
The Brontës
Charles Brockden Brown
Sterling Brown
Robert Browning
Martin Buber
John Bunyan
Anthony Burgess
Kenneth Burke
Robert Burns
William Burroughs
George Gordon, Lord
  Byron
Pedro Calderón de la Barca
Italo Calvino
Albert Camus
Canadian Poetry: Modern
  and Contemporary
Canadian Poetry through
  E. J. Pratt
Thomas Carlyle
Alejo Carpentier
Lewis Carroll
Willa Cather
Louis-Ferdinand Céline
Miguel de Cervantes

Geoffrey Chaucer
John Cheever
Anton Chekhov
Kate Chopin
Chrétien de Troyes
Agatha Christie
Samuel Taylor Coleridge
Colette
William Congreve & the
  Restoration Dramatists
Joseph Conrad
Contemporary Poets
James Fenimore Cooper
Pierre Corneille
Julio Cortázar
Hart Crane
Stephen Crane
e. e. cummings
Dante
Robertson Davies
Daniel Defoe
Philip K. Dick
Charles Dickens
James Dickey
Emily Dickinson
Denis Diderot
Isak Dinesen
E. L. Doctorow
John Donne & the
  Seventeenth-Century
  Metaphysical Poets
John Dos Passos
Fyodor Dostoevsky
Frederick Douglass
Theodore Dreiser
John Dryden
W. E. B. Du Bois
Lawrence Durrell
George Eliot
T. S. Eliot
Elizabethan Dramatists
Ralph Ellison
Ralph Waldo Emerson
Euripides
William Faulkner
Henry Fielding
F. Scott Fitzgerald
Gustave Flaubert
E. M. Forster
John Fowles
Sigmund Freud
Robert Frost
Northrop Frye
Carlos Fuentes
William Gaddis
Federico García Lorca
Gabriel García Márquez
André Gide
W. S. Gilbert
Allen Ginsberg
J. W. von Goethe

Nikolai Gogol
William Golding
Oliver Goldsmith
Mary Gordon
Günther Grass
Robert Graves
Graham Greene
Thomas Hardy
Nathaniel Hawthorne
William Hazlitt
H. D.
Seamus Heaney
Lillian Hellman
Ernest Hemingway
Hermann Hesse
Geoffrey Hill
Friedrich Hölderlin
Homer
A. D. Hope
Gerard Manley Hopkins
Horace
A. E. Housman
William Dean Howells
Langston Hughes
Ted Hughes
Victor Hugo
Zora Neale Hurston
Aldous Huxley
Henrik Ibsen
Eugène Ionesco
Washington Irving
Henry James
Dr. Samuel Johnson and
  James Boswell
Ben Jonson
James Joyce
Carl Gustav Jung
Franz Kafka
Yasonari Kawabata
John Keats
Søren Kierkegaard
Rudyard Kipling
Melanie Klein
Heinrich von Kleist
Philip Larkin
D. H. Lawrence
John le Carré
Ursula K. Le Guin
Giacomo Leopardi
Doris Lessing
Sinclair Lewis
Jack London
Robert Lowell
Malcolm Lowry
Carson McCullers
Norman Mailer
Bernard Malamud
Stéphane Mallarmé
Sir Thomas Malory
André Malraux
Thomas Mann

Modern Critical Views

Katherine Mansfield
Christopher Marlowe
Andrew Marvell
Herman Melville
George Meredith
James Merrill
John Stuart Mill
Arthur Miller
Henry Miller
John Milton
Yukio Mishima
Molière
Michel de Montaigne
Eugenio Montale
Marianne Moore
Alberto Moravia
Toni Morrison
Alice Munro
Iris Murdoch
Robert Musil
Vladimir Nabokov
V. S. Naipaul
R. K. Narayan
Pablo Neruda
John Henry Newman
Friedrich Nietzsche
Frank Norris
Joyce Carol Oates
Sean O'Casey
Flannery O'Connor
Christopher Okigbo
Charles Olson
Eugene O'Neill
José Ortega y Gasset
Joe Orton
George Orwell
Ovid
Wilfred Owen
Amos Oz
Cynthia Ozick
Grace Paley
Blaise Pascal
Walter Pater
Octavio Paz
Walker Percy
Petrarch
Pindar
Harold Pinter
Luigi Pirandello
Sylvia Plath
Plato

Plautus
Edgar Allan Poe
Poets of Sensibility & the
  Sublime
Poets of the Nineties
Alexander Pope
Katherine Anne Porter
Ezra Pound
Anthony Powell
Pre-Raphaelite Poets
Marcel Proust
Manuel Puig
Alexander Pushkin
Thomas Pynchon
Francisco de Quevedo
François Rabelais
Jean Racine
Ishmael Reed
Adrienne Rich
Samuel Richardson
Mordecai Richler
Rainer Maria Rilke
Arthur Rimbaud
Edwin Arlington Robinson
Theodore Roethke
Philip Roth
Jean-Jacques Rousseau
John Ruskin
J. D. Salinger
Jean-Paul Sartre
Gershom Scholem
Sir Walter Scott
William Shakespeare
  Histories & Poems
  Comedies & Romances
  Tragedies
George Bernard Shaw
Mary Wollstonecraft
  Shelley
Percy Bysshe Shelley
Sam Shepard
Richard Brinsley Sheridan
Sir Philip Sidney
Isaac Bashevis Singer
Tobias Smollett
Alexander Solzhenitsyn
Sophocles
Wole Soyinka
Edmund Spenser
Gertrude Stein
John Steinbeck

Stendhal
Laurence Sterne
Wallace Stevens
Robert Louis Stevenson
Tom Stoppard
August Strindberg
Jonathan Swift
John Millington Synge
Alfred, Lord Tennyson
William Makepeace Thackeray
Dylan Thomas
Henry David Thoreau
James Thurber and S. J.
  Perelman
J. R. R. Tolkien
Leo Tolstoy
Jean Toomer
Lionel Trilling
Anthony Trollope
Ivan Turgenev
Mark Twain
Miguel de Unamuno
John Updike
Paul Valéry
Cesar Vallejo
Lope de Vega
Gore Vidal
Virgil
Voltaire
Kurt Vonnegut
Derek Walcott
Alice Walker
Robert Penn Warren
Evelyn Waugh
H. G. Wells
Eudora Welty
Nathanael West
Edith Wharton
Patrick White
Walt Whitman
Oscar Wilde
Tennessee Williams
William Carlos Williams
Thomas Wolfe
Virginia Woolf
William Wordsworth
Jay Wright
Richard Wright
William Butler Yeats
A. B. Yehoshua
Emile Zola

Modern Critical Views

JOHN BERRYMAN

Edited and with an introduction by
Harold Bloom
Sterling Professor of the Humanities
Yale University

CHELSEA HOUSE PUBLISHERS
New York ◊ Philadelphia

10 9 8 7 6 5 4 3 2 1

Library of Congress Cataloging-in-Publication Data
John Berryman.
    (Modern critical views)
    Bibliography: p.
    Includes index.
    1. Berryman, John, 1914–1972—Criticism and
interpretation. I. Bloom, Harold. II. Series.
PS3503.E744Z597   1988   811'.54   87–27728
ISBN 1-55546-310-X

Contents

Editor's Note   vii

Introduction   1
  Harold Bloom

Cagey John: Berryman as Medicine Man   5
  William Wasserstrom

Berryman's Long Dream   21
  Denis Donoghue

A Cursing Glory: John Berryman's *Love & Fame*   35
  Ernest C. Stefanik

Recovery: The Struggle between Prose and Life   49
  David Kalstone

How to Read Berryman's *Dream Songs*   53
  Edward Mendelson

John Berryman: The Question of Imperial Sway   71
  John Bayley

After Mr. Bones: John Berryman's Last Poems   89
  Joel Conarroe

Near the Top a Bad Turn Dared   101
  Diane Ackerman

The Yeatsian Mask: John Berryman   111
  Jerome Mazzaro

Berryman's Sonnets: In and Out of the Tradition   133
  David K. Weiser

Berryman Saved from Drowning   149
   Elizabeth Kaspar Aldrich

Chronology   165

Contributors   169

Bibliography   171

Acknowledgments   175

Index   177

Editor's Note

This book brings together a representative selection of the best criticism available upon the writings of the American poet John Berryman. The critical essays are reprinted here in the chronological order of their original publication. I am grateful to Bruce Covey for his assistance in editing this volume.

My introduction ponders the influence relation between W. B. Yeats and Berryman. William Wasserstrom begins the chronological sequence of criticism with a deeply informed overview of Berryman's poetic career, from its sources to its achieved shamanistic stance. In another generous survey, the Irish critic Denis Donoghue praises *The Dream Songs* as "all perception, surrounded by feeling."

Ernest C. Stefanik defends *Love & Fame* as a pilgrimage from despair to "Christian acceptance," while David Kalstone describes *Recovery*, Berryman's only novel, as a "harrowing departure" because it seems to divorce "exposure, truth about the self" from "literary merit."

The Dream Songs are judged by Edward Mendelson to "remain the most courageous and interesting poetic experiment of their decade," while the Oxford critic John Bayley goes further and joins Berryman to Robert Lowell as poets exercising imperial sway. Somewhat less imperially, Joel Conarroe writes a deft appreciation of *Love & Fame* and *Delusions, Etc.* In Diane Ackerman's briefer appreciation, Berryman is praised for "the courage to face ontological precipices."

Jerome Mazzaro, blending erudition and insight, arrives at a balanced view of both the Yeatsian and Freudian aspects of Berryman. *Berryman's Sonnets,* a problematic work in his development, are read by David K. Weiser as the representation of "an underlying conflict between inner impulses and outer norms." In this book's final essay, Elizabeth Kaspar Aldrich brilliantly interprets *Homage to Mistress Bradstreet* as Berryman's great crisis-poem, commemorating a poetic crisis she judges him to have surmounted.

Introduction

"I began work in verse-making as a burning, trivial disciple of the great Irish poet William Butler Yeats, and I hope I have moved off from there." That is John Berryman in 1965, and he added: "Then came Yeats, whom I didn't so much wish to resemble as to *be.*" Then came Auden, by Berryman's own testimony. "Winter Landscape" was cited by Berryman as his first poem in his own voice, and *Homage to Mistress Bradstreet* as his true breakthrough. That there are breakthroughs in the development or unfolding of a strong poet cannot be denied; the burden for literary criticism always must be to determine which poets inevitably compel the canon to make place for them. Roethke in his two best volumes achieved strength and then fell away from it. Robert Lowell, concerning whom I seem to be the only dissenter in our nation, did not achieve it, either in the manner of Eliot and Tate, or in that of W. C. Williams. Berryman I find the largest puzzle of his poetic generation, though I believe he will be judged at last only by *The Dream Songs.* To compare them, as some admirers do, to *Song of Myself,* is palpably an error; they are neither of that mode nor anywhere close to that astonishing eminence.

Berryman, like Lowell, continues to be overpraised in Britain, where both are associated with Anne Sexton and Sylvia Plath. This is hardly fair to Berryman, but British critics such as John Bayley and A. Alvarez seem to like their American poets to be suicidal, mentally ill, and a touch unruly, "beyond the Gentility Principle," as Alvarez phrases it. Wallace Stevens, in the judgment of Bayley, is inferior to Berryman and Lowell, which is roughly akin to my proclaiming that Alice Meynell and Charlotte Mew wrote better poems than Thomas Hardy, which I am not about to proclaim. Perhaps Berryman has some permanent poems, but they are hard to locate if you start out with his admirers' hyperbolical guides, which have little actual relation to the terrain of the work itself.

Yeats never left Berryman, who made extraordinary efforts to stop *sounding* like Yeats. That is a perfectly normal procedure in severe cases of poetic influence; Browning's remarkable diction and syntax resulted from his need to stop being Shelley, and the Browning dramatic monologue, with its purported objectivity, was a swerve away from the flamboyant subjectivity of the Shelleyan lyric, or the autobiographical romance of the *Alastor* variety. It would be wonderful if Berryman had become the American Browning, but alas he did not. *The Dream Songs* are not *Men and Women,* and *Love & Fame* is not *Asolando.* In the spirit of having named Lowell as our William Mason, and Plath as our Felicia Hemans, I could call Berryman our "Festus" Bailey or our Alexander Smith, creator of that other masterpiece of the Spasmodic School, *A Life Drama.* Berryman's similarity to Bailey and Smith is quite uncanny, and like Mason and Hemans in their eras, the Spasmodics had critical admirers as profusely enthusiastic as Alvarez, Bayley, Mendelson, and other loyal Berrymanians. Contemporary acclaim is sometimes a very bad indication of a poet's future canonicity.

The poem by Berryman I love best is the proper answer to me, or to anyone else who has the temerity to worry the issue of poetic survival. Here is the last stanza of his superb "A Professor's Song":

> Alive now-no-Blake would have written prose,
> But movement following movement crisply flows,
> So much the better, better the much so,
> As burbleth Mozart. Twelve. The class can go.
> Until I meet you, then, in Upper Hell
> Convulsed, foaming immortal blood: farewell.

Yes, yes indeed, a more than palpable hit, but there precisely is the maddening and necessary question: among the poets, whose blood is immortal? No one likes the question, poets least of all, but it has to be asked, and answered. The cost of belatedness is not a shrinking of literary space, but of the reader's time. I have had the experience of being denounced in this regard, in print and out, by a vociferous bevy of literary journalists, inchoate rhapsodes, and academic impostors, but they too must choose whom they will read in the time they have, and even they must recognize that we cannot reread everyone. Berryman's poetry does not repress this dilemma, no poetry wholly can, however implicitly the sorrow is addressed, and Berryman, even more than most of his contemporaries, was obsessed with this burden. Elizabeth Kaspar Aldrich is particularly shrewd in noting how central this anxiety was to Berryman's imagination. She quotes his splendid remark, from the same 1965 interview that acknowledged the influence of Yeats and Auden:

"A poem's force may be pivoted on a missing or misrepresented element in an agreed-upon or imposed design." Someone indeed is always missing, or misrepresented. Aldrich, who loves *Homage to Mistress Bradstreet* more than I do, though I must acknowledge it an ambitious and admirable poem, catches the precise function of crossing over that it fulfilled:

> The "more" that Berryman's poem attempts seems to me, finally, a foredoomed willing-into-being of a burdensome past (the "present" of Anne's world against which she rebels, to which she finally submits) the real burden of which is its quality of absence. Thus, extreme identification with his heroine represents an attempted appropriation of a past from which he is—by the very fact of a literary ancestor like Hawthorne—all the more displaced. But the very hopelessness of the effort is the extraordinary power of *Homage to Mistress Bradstreet*. This is a poem which celebrates impossibilities. The impossibility of living in the faithless void of the present time, the impossibility of being an American poet at all—these are celebrated in this most American of poems in verse Berryman equalled but never surpassed. And it is the nearly impossible intensity of the poet's emotion—need, rage, longing, grief—that this verse contains, and that his Muse/mistress/subject is able to embody. Anne Bradstreet could, paradoxically, embody for Berryman the very weaknesses and absences from which his poetic effort had hitherto suffered—his breakthrough, at what he described as enormous cost; thereafter, *The Dream Songs* and Henry.

I find this persuasive and poignant, though I am uneasy as to all that celebration of impossibilities. "The impossibility of being an American poet at all"—but we have had Whitman, Dickinson, Frost, Stevens, Marianne Moore, Hart Crane, R. P. Warren, Elizabeth Bishop, John Ashbery, James Merrill, A. R. Ammons and, if you will, Eliot, Pound, W. C. Williams and more. Are we to say of *The Dream Songs* also that the very hopelessness of the effort is their extraordinary power? Poetic ambition is vital to poetic strength, and is commendable, and perhaps (*pace* Allen Tate) the poetic will *can* perform the work of the imagination. Like *Homage, The Dream Songs* would move even the stoniest of critics, but the question cannot be one of pathos alone. Mad songs are a major lyric genre in our language, and Yeats excelled in them, in and for our century. Late Yeats always hovers nearby in *The Dream Songs,* by which I do not mean the Yeatsian *persona* of Crazy Jane and Tom the Lunatic but the mask of Yeats himself, the wild old wicked man, sometimes appearing as Ribh. What is absent in *The Dream Songs*, inevitably, is the strongest Yeats, the poet who could end almost his last poem by discarding all his own mythologies and personae, and cry aloud in a perfection of agnostic recognition of dying and death:

> O Rocky Voice
> Shall we in that great night rejoice?
> What do we know but that we face
> One another in this place?

Berryman, confronted by that, as all of us are, could only yield, as all of us yield. His own achieved mode, as here in the first stanza of *Dream Song* 88, remained Yeatsian, but without enough perhaps of a swerve into individual difference:

> In slack times visit I the violent dead
> and pick their awful brains. Most seem to feel
> nothing is secret more
> to my disdain I find, when we who fled
> cherish the knowings of both worlds, conceal
> more, beat on the floor,

The violent dead poet here, whose brain is picked, necessarily is Yeats. Berryman, who fled the living world while cherishing the knowings of both the living and the dead, conceals more than Yeats, beats on the floor (a trope taken from Yeats), and finds by rereading Yeats that his own deepest secrets are revealed there, to his own disdain. This has the power of sincerity, but not enough is missing, not enough is misrepresented, and the design is manifestly imposed.

WILLIAM WASSERSTROM

Cagey John: Berryman
as Medicine Man

*No doubt the situation of the writer in America has always
been difficult, his responsibilities always enormous. But they
are even more extreme now because everything seems to be
turning in on him at once. The mass society in which he
lives is becoming even more massive, more monolithic,
devious, and even more anxious to swallow him up whole. At
the same time, the under-forces he can sense at work are more
violent, more destructive, and more impossible to contain or
deny. And the certainties have become fewer. . . . Even the
dominant creed of modern America, that of psychoanalysis,
helps only to thrust the artist more deeply in on himself. So he
is left alone to play out by ear his art, his identity, and even
his society on the page in front of him.*

—A. ALVAREZ

With Theodore Roethke's death, Randall Jarrell's and Delmore Schwartz's,
three of the half dozen superbly endowed poets of the American middle
generation are now gone. Those who remain, John Berryman, Karl Shapiro,
Robert Lowell, survive in the state of touch-and-go. Although it is no longer
helpful to speak of this as a condition of the literary life in America, the matter is dramatic enough to warrant mention and to require, someday, sorting
out. Survival itself, however, despite disease and gloom, is impressive too.
And for all the cachet and power lately come to Lowell and to the Lowell
circle at *The New York Review of Books,* it is less Lowell's endurance than

From *The Centennial Review* 12, no. 3 (Summer 1968). © 1968 by The Centennial
Review.

Berryman's which must be celebrated. For it is Berryman's genius that contrives a poetry which blends the twin modes of work and purpose common to all American arts today—measure and balance on the one hand and, on the other, a scarcely controlled explosion of immoderate passion. In William Burroughs's fiction, Norman O. Brown's criticism and Berryman's verse, *77 Dream Songs,* we are confronted by accomplishment of quite a new kind, the attainment of New Apocalyptists, cooked and raw, a ritual ceremony of revelation so fierce and intricate that their work most perplexes those whom it most enchants.

Despite the attention lavished on Berryman's songs, despite a Pulitzer Prize and a unanimity of opinion on the poet's gifts, there are two opposing general views on Berryman's art. Some see artifice where others find innovation, footwork not choreography—as if these poems represented the mind of still another camp follower of apocalypse, a sort of death-of-god man or one of Warhol's Chelsea boys. Those who contend that the poems express a failure, not a feat of language, ascribe this to a defeat of the American artist's will to enact the role of a public poet in a society whose quality and tone must defeat any poet's will. Clotted in the act of utterance, it is said, Berryman does not fuse arcane learning and mother wit, formal speech and demotic. Rather, he resorts to idiosyncrasy and inversion, quirks and tics of diction which exhibit a mind at the end of its tether and do not display means to unlock those fetters which jail the mind.

Negative opinion at its harshest, Philip Toynbee's essay in *Encounter* (March 1965), turns on that critic's effort to "throw a certain doubt on Allen Tate's belief that Berryman's poetry 'cannot be imitated.'" Toynbee offers five samples of Berryman's method, remarks that these are "not consecutive, which does Mr. Berryman an injustice," then confesses that "what may prove to do him a greater injustice is that two of them were written by me, taking a few minutes for each verse." Although in six or twelve lines nearly anyone can seem to imitate almost anybody, the gambit would be more arresting if Toynbee were charier, warier, in its use. For a similar trick opens a later essay, a review of Mary Renault's *The Mask of Apollo* in *The New Republic,* and therefore tends to throw a certain doubt on the utility, for literary criticism, of a reviewer's gimmick.

Toynbee's essay is useful as a point of departure, not for its show of audacity but for its judgment, given in the form of a suspicion, that in the end "there will *not* emerge a sense of that inevitable union of means and meaning which we receive from all good poetry." For what in fact distinguishes Berryman's poetry is the invention of truly audacious means exactly suited to his meaning. Regard the four epigraphs which open the book. The initial one ("THOU DREWEST NEAR IN THE DAY") stands alone. Unidentified, it is followed, next page, by a trio of lines, the first also unascribed but written in Negro dialect ("GO IN, BRACK MAN, DE DAY'S YO' OWN"); the second (" . . . I AM THEIR MUSICK") is drawn from Lamentations 3:63. And the third ("BUT THERE IS ANOTHER METHOD") is taken from an unnamed work by the South African reformer and fantasist, Olive Schreiner. Short, flat, these seem to offer disjointed, not sibylline learning, and properly mystified, we know that a certain amount of detective work is in order.

What it yields is extraordinary. "GO IN, BRACK MAN" turns up as the epigraph in a book on the history of blackface minstrelsy in America, Carl Wittke's *Tambo and Bones* (1930). Olive Schreiner's comment is taken from a work which has long haunted Berryman, *Dreams* (1914), where Miss Schreiner defined two ways in which artists customarily depict "truth." The first, of which she disapproved, she named the "stage method": people behave as puppets of the creator's will, character is cut and dried, problems are devised so that solutions can be found. "But there is another method—the method of life we all lead. Here nothing can be prophesied. There is a strange coming and going of feet. Men appear, act and re-act upon each other, and pass away. When the crisis comes, the man who would fit it does not return. When the curtain falls, no one is ready. When the footlights are brightest, they are blown out: and what the name of the play is no one knows."

Olive Schreiner was a shrewder theorist than practitioner of literature: her notion of a "stage" method corresponds to the technique Abram Tertz condemns in the essay on socialist realism, and that "other" method corresponds to the technique Tertz approved, the literature of phantasmagoria. Hearing her speak about coming and going of feet, performances of the unnameable, we naturally think of Beckett. But it is not just a prescience of literary cunning which Berryman admires in Miss Schreiner. Both she and that other exemplary lady to whom Berryman has committed himself, Anne Bradstreet, are women in whom a passion for things of the spirit is suffused by a compassion for the life of flesh. Indeed, the color of spirit is in Berryman's view livid flesh. And it is Anne's skin "cratered" by smallpox, the "body a-drain" with its "pustules snapping," which he loves. That identical matters engage Olive Schreiner's sympathy too is evident in a dream-vision, "The Sunlight Lay Across My Bed," where the dreamer finds herself in a place inhabited by people who suffer all the least supportable forms of physical grief. Unaccountably, the more nastily bruised their bodies are, the more intense is the light they exude. "I had thought that blindness and maimedness were great evils," she says, marveling that in this "strange land" men convert pain into energy. Awaking, she realizes that her mission is to celebrate, without rant or romantic illusion or heroic pose, the vitality of life in men mutilated but unmastered by earth. This was the "music" she would henceforth sing: "I was glad the long day was before me."

Better equipped now to take up the clues offered by Berrman's epigraphs, we recognize in these a filigree of signs which specify a coherent pattern of purposes within the 77 songs. "I AM THEIR MUSICK" links the book, Lamentations, with Olive Schreiner's book, *Dreams*. "BUT THERE IS ANOTHER METHOD," which connotes a particular principle of literary creation, leads to the line from minstrelsy, "GO IN BRACK MAN, DE DAY'S YO' OWN," where dialect alone identifies exactly whose plight and passion and grief and pain are sung by whom on which stage in accord with what mode of performance. Applying a similar technique of argument to the dedicatory epigraph, "THOU DREWEST NEAR IN THE DAY," Lamentations 3:57, we infer that the cycle as a whole, for all its hodgepodge of association, is single-minded in pursuit of one theme: Fear not. "THOU DREWEST NEAR IN THE DAY THAT I CALLED UPON THEE: THOU SAIDST, FEAR NOT."

If all this sounds as much like an exercise in mathematical proof as criticism of verse, part of the reason is that Berryman has in fact introduced a system of arithmetic notation into his numbers and thereby turned the fact of number into a main issue within the very form of the verse. The 77 songs are distributed among three sections—26, 25, 26. With nine exceptions, each poem is 18 lines in length, arranged in three verse paragraphs each six lines long. The nine exceptions must be deliberate, for Berryman resorts to the most patent subterfuges of dilation in order to vary a pattern which could easily conform to standard. And the standard itself is very tidily signified by a cue, at once arithmetic and thematic, present in the central epigraph, Lamentations 3:63—the 77 *Dream Songs* offer three sections of poems, six verses per stanza, three stanzas per poem.

Berryman's taste for mystification is thus supported by a mystique of numerology—a mystique which is the more firmly bolstered by the poet's reliance on a biblical book which is itself gnomic in form and function. Not only does Lamentations mourn the fall of Old Jerusalem and therefore supply a paradigm for Berryman's lament, fall of our New Jerusalem, but also each of its sections develops an alphabetical acrostic. The third section, the one on which Berryman draws, is unique in that it elaborates three verses around its letter instead of the one verse per letter usual in the other sections. That is, Lamentations 3 has 66 verses; the other two sections have 22 verses each. There may be a touch of alphabetic play in the 77 songs, represented by the number of poems placed in each of its segments. But Berryman's ingenuity is spent on an exercise of wider range. For a more impressive intersection of form and meaning occurs when we restore, from Lamentations 3:63, that half which Berryman has left off: "Behold their sitting down, and their rising up: I am their musick." In this restoration we accomplish nothing less than the connection of minstrel show and holy text. Tambo and Bones rise and sit in response to questions from the Interlocutor who plays straight man to their end men. He is the one through whom the two speak. He is their music and they are of course his. Berryman, casting himself in the role of the interlocutor, in this way devises a secular language and music no less intricate than the sacred. The poet conceives a "method" which will recreate the downs and ups, the debasements which degrade and the passions which inspirit the lives of mutilated men, American Negroes, "Henry" and "Bones," who convert pain into song.

The place of minstrelsy on Berryman's stage cannot, however, be this neatly disposed of. For minstrelsy represents the climactic and synoptic solution to the poet's "long, often back-breaking search for an inclusive style, a style that could use his erudition," Robert Lowell says, and "catch the high, even frenetic, intensity of his experience, disgusts and enthusiasm." Before it is possible to decide whether or not this solution works, it is necessary to acquire a little of Berryman's erudition—that is, search out where diverse clues lead. The second Dream Song, for example, called "Big Buttons, Cornets: the Advance," leads to Daddy Rice, Thomas Dartmouth Rice, a white actor who in the 1820s and 1830s "sang and jumped 'Jim Crow,'" Berryman explains, in dedicating this song to the memory of that man. Impersonating a plantation Negro, dressed in patchy pants and ragged shoes (wearing, according to some reports, a vest with buttons made of five- and ten-dollar gold pieces), he wheeled and turned and jumped "windmill fashion." Throwing weight alternately on the heel of one foot and the toe of the other, he chanted comment on the movements of his dance:

> This is the style of Alabama
> What they hab in Mobile,
> And dis is Louisiana
> Whar de track upon de heel.

From Long Island to Indiana, from "Kentuck" to "ol Mississip," I "weel about, and turn about, and do jis so" and "Eb'ry time I weel about, I jump Jim Crow": Step and fetch it if you can! Because ways of jumping Jim Crow varied from place to place—"De Georgia step" went according to "de double rule of three"—part of the point of Rice's song and dance was to display nuance within the first wholly original and authentic form of folk art to be developed within the American experience. But whatever these steps and rules were, Rice's impersonations served as the model and mainspring for minstrels and minstrel shows of later decades. Shortly after Rice introduced his dance, in 1828, blackface actors banded together, first in pairs and later in diverse combinations which somehow implicate a rule of three: "two banjoists and one dancer; one banjoist and two dancers; one fiddler and two dancers; one banjoist, a dancer and a singer." Rice himself, dancing solo, remained the most popular of all blackface performers in Great Britain and the United States. He was able to fill the American Theatre on the Bowery even on the "Fifty-seventh night" of this "original and celebrated extravaganza . . . on which occasion every department of the house was thronged to an excess unprecedented in the records of theatrical attraction," according to an advertisement dated November 25, 1833.

Within ten years of this date the Virginia Minstrels had been formed. Four white men in blackface sat onstage in semicircle, turned partly toward the audience and partly toward one another, fiddle and banjo flanked by tambourine and bones. Their show was divided into two parts and both parts alternated ensemble play with solo act—song, skit, dance in no certain order. During the 1850s and later, at a zenith of popularity, the classic form of minstrelsy was fixed by two groups, Bryant's Minstrels and Christy's Band of Original Virginia Minstrels. Christy's three minstrels performed on banjo, violin, tambourine, bones, triangle—and "they all played double." Both this troupe and Bryant's presented a three-part entertainment which opened with a chorus and grand entrance. Then the interlocutor, in whiteface and full dress, said "Gentlemen be seated" and exchanged jokes with Tambo and Bones, dressed in blackface, swallow tails and striped trousers. Part 2, the olio, ended with a hoedown in which each member of the company did a solo turn. What happened in part 3 is not clear—or not clear to me, anyway, for specialists differ in their opinions. It was probably ragout again, spiced by skit, farce and sketch based on subjects drawn from plantation life.

Most of their stuff is lost, but the cakewalk remains alive still, a dance step which, LeRoi Jones contends in *Blues People,* originated as a Negro parody of white high manners in the manor house. Because the cakewalk seems to develop from black caricature of white custom, Jones wonders what response is appropriate to a white company which, unaware of self-mockery, offers Stepin Fetchit as straight burlesque of the black peasantry. "I find the idea of white minstrels in black-face satirizing a dance satirizing themselves a remarkable kind of irony—which, I suppose, is the whole point of minstrel shows." Amplifying this idea, Jones claims that parody in black minstrel shows was directed against whites. Wearing stagy blackface to cover their true color, Negro minstrels in the 1870s exploited the deepest resources of private and communal life—folk speech, song, dance, game and play—in order to devise a form of public entertainment which would please both sets of audiences. Whereas white minstrels in blackface merely exposed their own folly, Negro minstrels in blackface, anticipating Genet, created a black travesty of white burlesque and thereby cut deep into the double life of both races.

Black minstrels accomplished something really momentous, Jones thinks, by mocking white audiences with a music, true jazz and classic blues, until then unknown outside shantytown. And it is precisely in the use of similar materials that Berryman has introduced matter no less fateful for English prosody. Blues, which spring "from no readily apparent Western source," are customarily pieces in twelve bars: "each verse is of three lines, each line is about four bars long. The words of the song usually occupy about one-half of each line, leaving a space of two bars for either a sung answer or an instrumental response." Knowing that Berryman's epigraphs, for example, which are invariably halved, require the reader to supply that portion of the utterance which the poet has left off, we suspect that the form of blues and not its idiom alone—minstrelsy itself, not just its stereotypes—is subsumed within the very form of Berryman's verse. When the first line of the first Dream Song breaks, the effect is a sort of syncopation ("Huffy Henry hid   the day"). But the break elsewhere, as in Song 3, is intended to exact a voiced response from the reader:

> Rilke was a *jerk*.
> I admit his griefs & music
> & titled spelled all-disappointed ladies.
> A threshold worse than the circles
> where the vile settle & lurk,
> Rilke's. As I said,—

There are many examples. But it is in Song 2, the one dedicated to Daddy Rice, which crystallizes the full resourcefulness of Berryman's art. "Le's do a hoedown, gal," in the second stanza, prepares for the olio of the third stanza, where Henry goes into his act, does his solo speciality, enacts a black burlesque of white parody, performs a cakewalk—a masque in which Sir Bones speaks from behind his mask a satiric language taken from Negro rhyming slang, the kind of speech devised in order to hide true meaning from the Man, the enemy:

> —Sir Bones, or Galahad; astonishin
> yo legal & yo good. Is you feel well?

Honey dusk do sprawl.
—Hit's hard. Kinged or thing, though, fling & wing.
Poll-cats are coming, hurrah, hurray.
I votes in my hole.

Cakewalk and masque, blues and slang—these bits and echoes do indeed banish meaning. Berryman's sense is virtually gone. Paradoxically, its very disappearance must be taken as a sign of the poet's achievement. Compare Berryman's verses with those of "Old Pee Dee," a song popular but commonplace in the last century.

To Boston Part I den sail roun,
Dey said de Dickens was in town;
I ax dem who de Dickens was
Dey sed 'twas massa Pickwick Boz.
Ring de Hoop! an blow de horn!
Massa Dickens eat de corn,
Way down in de low ground feeld
3,4 mile from Pompey's hee.

Here too exterior meaning is banished and external sense is gone. Both Berryman's songs and minstrel songs disdain manifest statement and replace it in the manner of dreams, with a juxtaposition of images. A dream is tough to crack because it replaces a conscious conjunction of ideas with an unconscious disjunction of images which make sheerly irrational sense. A minstrel song is equally troublesome because it exploits both principles, conjunction and disjunction, so that its white (manifest) sense will be one thing and its black (latent) sense another. And black is at odds with white. In minstrelsy, then, Berryman found an exact analogue to dream. And in blues he found a music which permitted him to excise, deliberately, any connectives which might pull his work toward merely rational order. For it is not, as Leslie Fiedler remarks, Berryman's or Roethke's or Lowell's lucidity and logic we admire but "their flirtation with incoherence and disorder." And it is Berryman's distinction that he alone plunges deep into some public sources of the primitive American imagination in search of a tradition which represents long immersion in and mastery of disjunction and disorder.

What distinguishes a dream song, therefore, is not a coquetry or a clumsiness of art, as Toynbee argued, but a rather capital thing, the discovery that American minstrelsy long ago devised a formula which could transmit the mood of an idea and simultaneously conceal its reason. This discovery enabled Berryman to create what Lowell calls a "waking hallucination," the form which unites conscious design and unconscious drift. Design and drift are perhaps clearest seen in song 40 whose initial line, "I'm scared a lonely. Never see my son," an undisguised importation of Negritude, is drawn straight from the heart of misery incarnate in Sir Bones. The song itself mourns the lives of all who must "cry oursel's awake" yet who manage to convert grief into energy, energy into work, work to survive the lure of suicide and at last, each day, make "it all the way to that bed on these feet." This song plainly recalls the theme of Olive Schreiner's *Dreams*. Less plain but more vivid is its evocation of that great man of blues, Leadbelly, whose own music is curiously obsessed by exactly the same theme—interplay of sleeplessness and dream as his biographer Frederic Ramsey says—which absorbs Berryman. "Sleeplessness complements the dream," real and unreal are mixed, "seen and unseen come together," so that in the end the text and tone of Leadbelly's song can be best described as a "waking dream."

Whether or not Berryman knows Ramsey's memoir, doubtless he knows Huddie Leadbetter's music. Nor is there any doubt that he knows Charles Lamb's remark about the sanity of true genius: the poet dreams being awake, is not possessed by but has dominion over his subject. And surely Berryman knows the etymology of "vernacular"—from *verna*, slave born in his master's house. For in 1963, after many years' labor on a project whose working title, since 1955, has been *The Dream Songs*, Berryman said that the poems refer to somebody "apparently named Henry, or says he is. He has a tendency to talk about himself in the third person. His last name is in doubt. It is given at some point as Henry House and at other points as Henry Pussy-cat." Miss Schreiner, Leadbelly, Lamb—all are represented in this potpourri of songs by John the minstrel man who, possessed by his subject, the savageries which mutilate men in our nightmarish world, dreams up Henry, sans surname, caricature of the American black man, enslaved in his own house. Mixing formal speech and folk, high art and pop, John furnishes Henry with the very language and ritual, drawn from the history of the American white man, which first enabled white to imitate black and black to parody white. In this way the victim is not possessed by but achieves dominion over the tyrant; indeed, he transforms himself into the tyrant's savior. "I was a derision to all my people; *and* their song all the day," says Lamentations 3:14, in paraphrase of virtually everything I have so laboriously construed till now.

II

Realizing that *The Dream Songs* date from 1955 or earlier, recalling that this period coincides with the period following publication of Berryman's psychoanalytic study, *Stephen Crane* (1950), we are tempted to return to that little book in order to discover which of its ideas bear on these songs. For when Berryman says that the strongest influence on Crane's poetry was Olive Schreiner's "small book of allegories published in Boston . . . *Dreams,*" and says again that the parable and proverbial form of Crane's poetry is traceable to "the Bible and to Olive Schreiner's *Dreams,*" we know that we are placed amid two of Berryman's own sources of imagination and assume instantly that we must add a third, Crane himself.

Stephen Crane is a work both dense and diffuse. Pioneer in its use of Freud to untangle some knotty problems of motive in Crane's life and art, Berryman's work then seemed to refer to Crane alone. Today, reading Berryman's tortuous inquiry into Crane's habit of nomenclature ("the names authors give their characters seldom receive sufficient attention unless the significance of a name is immediately striking"), we are notified that Berryman's own choice of names cannot go unattended. Not all asides hide an issue of moment, of course, but this one rather obviously ties diverse things in a neat packet: "the discovery of Henry's whole identity, by him and by us, comprises the plot of the poem," says William Meredith, to whom Song 36 is dedicated.

The place of "Henry" in Crane's life, the role of "Henry" in Crane's art— these comprise the plot of Berryman's book. Crane's first hero, Berryman contends, "was the African explorer Henry Stanley. Henry is the name of the hero in *The Red Badge of Courage,* the name of *The Monster* and the name displaced at the catastrophe of The Blue Hotel, and we shall come shortly to a Prince Henry [Prince Henry of Prussia] . . . Stephen Crane seems to have had a middle name beginning with H which he dropped after 1893, and perhaps it was 'Henry'—a name very common in the family." Straining to make a strange point, Berryman wonders if Crane's friendship with Henry James in Sussex was not due in some way to an affinity of name.

Circumstantial stuff, surely; nevertheless the argument enables Berryman to concentrate on the fiction, *The Monster,* which most cogently reveals the special role of "Henry" in Crane's unconscious mind. The story is a "study of a society's fear, stupidity, persecution" of Henry Johnson, "Negro coachman of a small-town doctor." Brave and good, Henry is "mutilated while saving the doctor's little boy when the house burns." As a result he is rendered "faceless" and harmlessly insane. His fate represents a pattern of action, habitual in Crane's art, which Berryman calls the rescue-and-punishment theme: "for trying to rescue the boy, the Negro is punished with mutilation and idiocy, he becomes a 'monster' and has to hide his no-face." To have no face, to be veiled, understood psychoanalytically, is "to hide one's face, to be ashamed." Although Berryman is certain that "all three figures, father, Negro, son," represent components of Crane's own identity, it is Henry Johnson, veiled and shamed, who serves as "the chief Crane-mask." And shame, the presiding mood of Crane's repressed life, Berryman's psychoanalysis traces to "oedipal elements" in the writer's "rivalry against the father, the wish to *be* the father."

Although Crane's Henry and Berryman's are not equivalent—Berryman's relation with his own father is not in question—both figures serve as emblems of the black unconscious in American life on which Crane instinctively drew and in which Berryman along with, say, Norman Mailer or James Baldwin, now discover matter for exaltation. What is instinctive in Crane, in Mailer sloppy and in Baldwin vague, Berryman's psychoanalysis renders bare and sharp. As Freud provided him with the key to motive in Crane's art, so too did Freud furnish him with a dramatis personae of the inner life. According to rules set down in *The Ego and the Id,* ego is a "poor creature owing service to three masters and consequently menaced by three several dangers; from the external world, from the libido . . . and from the severity of the superego. Three kinds of anxiety correspond to these three dangers," and three kinds of action are performed by the ego as it struggles to dispel anxiety in order to fulfill its trio of functions: "to mediate between the world and the id, to make the id comply with the world's demands and . . . to accommodate the world to the id's desires."

From these permutations of the rule of three ("triads of Hegel," Berryman says in "Op. posth. no. 1," drawn from "upstairs and from down," from metaphysics and psychology, which bolster Henry's determination to serve as "the American Bard"), the poet derives his calculus of character. Instead of Henry, read ego. In place of id, visualize Bones, end man of minstrel shows, unruly in the beat of tambourine and rattle of bones, bobbing up and down, swaying to and fro, sputtering coarse sayings, shouts and hoarse laughter. Sometimes, like id, that olio of vulgar and irrepressible want, Bones's black need bursts his own and even, beyond disentangling, Berryman's bounds. At other times Henry goes into a cakewalk of mediation: Song 22, "Of 1826," compares the life of America today ("teenage cancer") with its life on July 4, 1826, the day when Adams, dying, gasped "Thomas Jefferson still lives" even as Jefferson, incredibly, that day lay dying too. Although Adams and Jefferson died, left us in the lurch, Henry lives. "I am Henry Pussycat! My whiskers fly!" Elsewhere Henry is all but obliterated by "them," superego rampant, those who in the name and age of Ike "took away his crotch."

> Henry hates the world. What the world to Henry did will not bear
> thought.

Pain so excruciating may not bear thought, but it does enable Henry to accomplish the one act which makes thought and life bearable, which synthesizes all fragments of the self, which helps the self to mediate, accommodate, comply and in this way avoid all menace of extinction. "Pulling Henry together," in the last songs of this sequence, "considering, like a madman," Henry "put forth a book." For all the agony his dreams portray, Henry is no house cat, no pussyfoot Uncle Tom who rattles a pair of bones for the general amusement. He is a tomcat with passion enough (cat house) and guts enough (outhouse) to make our bones rattle. In echo of Marianne Moore's account of poetry—an imaginary garden with real toads in it— Berryman conjures out of the materials of the unconscious an imaginary minstrel show with a real Jim Crow. Polymorph, magpie, jackdaw, cunning and chattering bird, Henry performs in song and dance a ritual of exorcism, a black rite of salvation inside the white skin of his maker whose identity he disguises with a burnt-cork mask. And if Henry can do it, reassemble his parts by turning, in Olive Schreiner's fashion, frightful nightmare into savage song, then "perhaps the unutterable midnights of the universe will have no power to daunt the colour of the soul."

III

Those are the words, derived from the final statement in Crane's story, *The Monster*, which Berryman chose to conclude his *Stephen Crane*. And I have imitated Berryman's rhetoric in order to underscore the constancy of his devotion to a consistent set of ideas and images. If, however, the whole affair is treated as a brilliant display of marvelous or misspent gifts, or if we assent to one pronouncement or another—"It is the quality of their journey, not their destination, which is their value"—then all we have is a charcuterie of rime. And that is not justification enough for thirty years' study and experiment in music and mathematics, history and psychology and myth, which prepared the way for Berryman's theory and performance of a masterwork. However impressive the quality of Berryman's journey may be, far more portentous is the place Henry hopes to go. For he is on his way somewhere, he remarks in Song 76, "Henry's Confession": "I saw nobody coming, so I went instead," says our Rescuer. With this song Berryman himself disappears. "Cagey John" has gone native and, like the composer John Cage, has chosen silence. Having adopted the mask and speech of a primitive, cagey John has pulled Joyce's trick and slipped away, vanished into his work. "Wif a book of his in either hand / he is stript down to move on." Joyce's trick it may be, but it is again Crane whom Berryman selects for his model, Crane's

Maggie, which Berryman cherishes because in no other work did an American author manage to remain so "persistently invisible behind his creation." Duplicating Crane's feat, cagey John disappears inside "his own mad books."

Inspired by Crane, sharing with Joyce the atavism of a lapsed Catholic who preserves outside theology a passion for trinity—sharing with Joyce too a conviction that the myth-making, dream-making and poetry-making faculties of imagination are at bottom one—cagey John undertakes to transmute secular art into a sacramental rite. For if myth can be said to reach deep down and far back into the history of race, then obviously it parallels the reach of minstrelsy, which goes deep into American racial history. And if the myth of minstrelsy enables Berryman to recreate some of the aims of primitive ritual drama, that form in which "art and life converge, life itself is seen as drama, roles are symbolically acted out" by means of "masks, poems, songs . . . and above all the dance," then the poet can be said to cast himself into the role of ur-poet, medicine man. "In constant danger of breakdown, of ceasing to function, or of functioning fantastically, in ways that were too private to elicit a popular response," the shaman's presence served his people as a daily "reminder that life often balances on the knife edge."

Although in each detail these views might well refer to Berryman, his poetry, his state of spirit, I have taken the remarks from an essay in anthropology—Stanley Diamond's "Plato and the Definition of the Primitive"—not in literary criticism. Almost any anthropological study of the primitive would do. For these ideas today are taken for conventional wisdom by members of a generation taught by Konrad Lorenz, Lévi-Strauss and Henrich Zimmer, to scour the savage world in order to determine what in the nature of man is original, what is artificial. And Berryman, who some years ago went on a State Department tour of the Far East, whose 77 songs include mention of lotos, Ganges, Bodhidharma and so on, apparently found in Eastern myths some old and subtle sanctions for the transformation of a minstrel show into an imitation of a sacred action designed to purge fear.

For when we recognize what myth it is which best coincides with Berryman's intentions, with the aims delicately implied in the leading epigraph, then we discover why Daddy Rice's dance opens the 77 *Dream Songs.* Far-fetched though the idea may seem, it is the dance of Shiva which Berryman hopes we will associate with Jim Crow. Shiva, according to Zimmer's account, is "The Black One," member of a trinity which includes Brahma the Creator, and Vishnu the Preserver. And his "flying arms and legs and the swaying of his torso," crowned by a "masklike" head, are accompanied by mystic utterance, at once holy speech and impenetrable silence, the syllable AUM, Shiva's dream song: "A—is the state of waking consciousness . . . U—is the state of dreaming consciousness . . . M—the state of dreamless sleep." Wearing the brahminical thread which adorns the three upper castes of India, the twice-born, those who inhabit the sphere of history and the realm of eternity, Shiva too dances in time to a double rule of three. Berryman seems to have connected this thread to two of Shiva's four arms, the one which holds a drum symbolizing the beat of time, and the one which is held aloft in the eternal gesture of comfort, of certitude, the gesture *abhaya-mudrā:* Fear not. Making these connections, *The Dream Songs* dispute and dispel the notion, more persuasive to British and Continental critics than American, that poetry cannot work as an agent of therapy or as the reliquary of culture or a surrogate for worship.

Having been exported to India by the American Department of State, Berryman has imported into his poetry those symbols of ritual drama which unite Brahma and Jehovah, The Dance of Shiva and *The Lamentations of Jeremiah,* in a single gesture. I must confess, however, that the role of Shiva in Berryman's art is, though plausible, uncertain. What is certain is that Berryman was drawn to the primitive, as *Stephen Crane* yields its final gloss, by way of Robert Graves.

> Robert Graves, one of the shrewdest, craziest, and most neglected students of poetry living, laid out a theory of the origins of poetry once. A savage dreams, is frightened by the dream, and goes to the medicine man to have it explained. The medicine man can make up anything, anything will reassure the savage, so long as the manner of its delivery is impressive; so he chants, perhaps he stamps his foot, people like rhythm, what he says becomes rhythmical, people like to hear things *again,* and what he says begins to rhyme. Poetry begins—as a practical matter, for *use.* It reassures the savage. Perhaps he only hears back again, chanted, the dream he just told the medicine man, but he is reassured: it is like a spell. And medicine men are shrewd: interpretation enters the chanting, symbols are developed and connected, the gods are invoked, poetry booms.

It was Graves, then, whose theory—joining primordial and present time, dream and song, song and dance, dance and rite, rite and rime—first invited Berryman to plunge into a study of the mythic origins and ritual ends of the arts of imagination. Making this theory his own, Berryman argued that Crane's poetry must be read as "a series of anti-spells." Today, Graves's skeleton of a theory has been fleshed out by cagey John, the invisible and silent man behind the stage on which a "Spellbound," raving, savage Henry and his shaman Bones reenact in dialogue "made-up stories/lighting the past of Henry," stories which cunningly transmute inchoate terror into a booming poetry of the anti-spell. For if a medicine man can be said to invent *poetry* when he casts a savage's dreams into chants which reassure the patient, then a poet can be said to invent a *cure* when he casts his song into the form of a dream which makes manifest the disintegration, death and, in "Op. Posth. no. 10," the reincarnation of a people: "Henry may be returning to our life / adult & difficult."

If, finally, it was Graves who set Berryman going, it is Lévi-Strauss's essay, "The Effectiveness of Symbols," which tells how far he has come. "In the schizophrenic cure the healer performs the acts and the patient produces his myth; in the shamanistic cure the healer supplies the myth and the patient performs the actions." Cagey John, the schizophrene, disintegrates, disappears then reappears in the mask of a minstrel man who jumps Jim Crow and thereby supplies the myth which will enable his blues people to understand the "lessen" Bones has up his "slave." Drawing his myth from minstrelsy, his parable from Olive Schreiner, his theory from Graves, his text from Lamentations—finding in Freud his cast of characters and in Crane the very model of a quintessential poet—Berryman savages America for its taste for blood.

Not just America, of course. For two songs, "The Translator—I" and "The Translator—II," not included among the 77, take up the trial of Joseph Brodsky, the Soviet poet and translator who in March 1964 was sentenced to five years' labor, psychiatric confinement, as a social parasite.

> Henry rushes not in here. The matter's their
>   matter,
> and Hart Crane drowned himself some over
>   money.

American hands are unclean too, bloody with the murder of poets. Suddenly he decides that it is "Henry's matter after all," the fate of that young man Brodsky

> Who only wanted to walk beside the canals
> talking about poetry & make it.

Deciding that Brodsky's is Henry's matter, Berryman causes Henry to advance some steps along his way, a way I take to represent a reversal of the rescue-and-punishment theme which Berryman contended was the obsession of

Crane's unconscious mind. Human matter is my matter, Henry's matter, defines the chief article of belief which underlies Berryman's making poetry and making poetry the instrument whereby the world might be healed and whole. We are in each others' hands who care, says the line which epitomizes Berryman's gist in *Homage to Mistress Bradstreet*. Fear not.

Berryman's testament. The marvel is that this old testament represents exactly the sort of conquest over prosody and politics to which both the Beats and Black Mountaineers, two chief schools of American experiment today, aspire. Allen Ginsberg chants foul and elegant words in jazzy and cantorial rhythms. And Charles Olson finds, in the heartbeat and breath of speech, a formula which—he hopes—will put body back into American English. All three in concert, Berryman the medicine man and Ginsberg the zaddik and Olson the guru, intoning the prophetic voice of poetry, share in common the will to transform and transmit primal human and American energy, by way of the poem, to the life of the people. Although all resort to "myth," none search that murky realm for quick consolation, none replace the bitter savor of character for the treacle of archetype. But it is Berryman alone who has confronted all imaginable demons, learned to speak their tongue and, like Luther, invented a devilish vernacular which must henceforth invade standard speech.

DENIS DONOGHUE

Berryman's Long Dream

John Berryman has now completed the long poem, *The Dream Songs*, begun in 1955. The first part of the dream was published in 1964 as *77 Dream Songs*. Songs 78–385, the middle and the end, are given now as *His Toy, His Dream, His Rest*.

In Song 354 Mr. Berryman writes three stanzas of sardonic meditation on the problem of the long poem. "The only happy people in the world," he sings, "are those who do not have to write long poems." An unwritten essay is called "The Care and Feeding of Long Poems." The poet planned to consult President Johnson on the problem, during his ten seconds in the receiving line at the White House. But the invitation reached him too late, an ocean away, in Ireland. So the problem persisted, until the poet resolved it in his own way. His own way; not Eliot's way in *Four Quartets,* Williams's way in *Paterson,* Pound's way in the *Cantos,* or Hart Crane's way in *The Bridge.* It comes to a question of form; how to be free and law-abiding at the same time. Or how to ensure that the whole poem is greater than the sum of its parts. In the twentieth century a poet feels incomplete, apparently, until he has written a long poem. He wants a mighty reach, a span, everything implied and encompassed, not merely one little poem and then another little poem. Mr. Berryman's answer was to conceive a diary, a dream diary, in which the dream would allow the poet every desirable kind of freedom, and law could be acknowledged in the movement of time, the insistence of years, decay, death. It is always an open question, how free a poet should be in his poem. Perhaps the answer is: as free as he needs to be. But in extreme cases the price is high.

From *Art International* 13, no. 3 (March 20, 1969). © 1969 by Denis Donoghue.

21

Mr. Berryman's case is extreme. On the understanding, perhaps, that one *Song of Myself* is enough, he decided to hand over his entire dream world to an invented character called Henry, not to be confused with John Berryman, author and poet. "The poem then, whatever its wide cast of characters, is essentially about an imaginary character (not the poet, not me) named Henry, a white American in early middle age sometimes in blackface, who has suffered an irreversible loss and talks about himself sometimes in the first person, sometimes in the third, sometimes even in the second; he has a friend, never named, who addresses him as Mr. Bones and variants thereof. Requiescat in pace." Amen, indeed. Mr. Berryman is hard on those readers who think that Henry Pussy-cat is just a pet name for John Berryman; he is impatient. Has he not assured us that H. P. and J. B. are two,—not one? Has he not arranged to send H. P. into death before the long dream is over, so that the last dream songs are sung by a Lazarus, come back to tell all? Is not this enough? Thus far, the case is simple. When we read of Henry on LSD, we do not think of Mr. Berryman as a devotee of acid. And so on. For my own part, I have no difficulty in accepting the invented character Henry as distinct from his maker in the *77 Dream Songs*. I might have confused them in the dark. But as the dreams continue in the new and last book, the identity of Henry as distinct from J. B. becomes harder to take. "Edgy Henry" begins to collapse into his poet, and the poem begins to sound like the *Song of Myself*. This would not matter if it were a different kind of poem.

On the first page of the first dream song we read, stanza 3:

> What he has now to say is a long
> wonder the world can bear & be.
> Once in a sycamore I was glad
> all at the top, and I sang.
> Hard on the land wears the strong sea
> and empty grows every bed.

Three voices, two lines each, speaking in one stanza. The first voice is objective, the poet introducing his character, giving the gist of his theme. The second voice may be received as Henry's voice, recalling the good times, sycamores and songs. But the third voice is different from either; it is generic, representative, apocalyptic, Mankind rather than any particular man, Henry or J. B. or anyone else. In this third voice the feeling is universal rather than local; it is consistent with the first and second voices, but distinct, as if its experience were the history of the world rather than the fate of a man. It is my understanding that these three voices are nearly as many as the poet requires for his long poem: the unidentified friend who addresses Henry occasionally as Mr. Bones uses an Al Jolson voice and a chocolate idiom to admonish his white American friend, but beyond that degree he is hardly distinguished from any other figure, silent, sympathetic, watchful. So the three voices are nearly enough.

It is my impression that Mr. Berryman first practised this procedure in an early story called "The Imaginary Jew" (1945). The Gentile hero, by a great reach of sympathy, becomes an imaginary Jew, fights the Jew's battles, accepts insult. At the end he says to himself:

> In the days following, as my resentment died, I saw that I had not been a victim altogether unjustly. My persecutors were right: I was a Jew. The imaginary Jew I was was as real as the imaginary Jew hunted down, on other nights and days, in a real Jew. Every murderer strikes the mirror, the lash of the torturer falls on the mirror and cuts the real image, and the real and the imaginary blood flow down together.

A Gentile who becomes an imaginary Jew by an act of sympathy is perhaps as complete as a modern man can be. The corresponding power in poetry is the dramatic imagination. Mr. Berryman is not a dramatist, but he is gifted in dramatic narrative, as in *Homage to Mistress Bradstreet,* where several voices are distinguished, each bearing its proper burden, its own history. The three voices heard in the first Song are also practised in the poem to Anne Bradstreet. Sometimes the words on the page carry Anne's voice, her experience, her character; sometimes different words, with a different rhythm and a different syntax, carry her husband's voice. And sometimes Anne's husband is enabled to speak, as Mr. Berryman says in a gloss, "at last, in the fortune of an echo of her—and when she is loneliest . . . as if she had summoned him; and only thus, perhaps, is she enabled to hear him." Often, in the same poem, what we hear is the poet's voice, leading our feeling, helping us to feel more deeply, more relevantly. Often, too, the voice we hear is generic, distant, imperious, as if God were to speak of his servant Anne. Sometimes, to end this list, the poet speaks for Anne, knowing that, poet as she was in her own need, she often failed to speak for herself, or spoke haltingly, lacking one of the gifts.

So to the dream songs of an imaginary Jew. The hint is given in Song 48, where we read of

> a Greek idea,
> troublesome to imaginary Jews,
> like bitter Henry, full of the death of love.

Or again in Song 310:

> Henry, monstrous bug, laid himself down
> on the machine in the penal colony
> without a single regret.

Monstrous bug; that is, Gregor Samsa in Kafka's *Metamorphosis.* Laid himself down; that is, the officer in Kafka's *In the Penal Colony.* At this stage Henry has only to name a victim, and he becomes that victim. The corresponding gesture in the poet has the effect of sacrificing a single voice, John Berryman's voice, for the sake of other voices. The poet gives up his egotistical sublimity, accepting the modest role of medium. He becomes a shell, through which the sea speaks. In Song 38 the poet Robert Frost is invoked as "the quirky medium of so many truths." A comic version of the poet as medium is given in Song 143, the poet as vaudeville man: "Honour the burnt cork." Hazlitt said of Shakespeare that "he was nothing in himself; but he was all that others were"; an ideal state, endless humility, toward which the inventor of Henry strives, in principle. In principle, in theory, and in the practice of the *77 Dream Songs,* where the grace of humility receives many poetic favours. In these poems the content may be drawn, for all I know, from Mr. Berryman's own experience. He may indeed have seen a woman, "complexion Latin," filling her compact and delicious body with chicken paprika; he may have seen Paul Muni in *The Prisoner of Shark Island;* his mother may have said to him, "Ever to confess you're bored means you have no Inner Resources." It may be so. But in these well-tempered songs the poet has imposed upon these experiences a particular test; he has not merely transcribed them as remembered. Rather, he has tested them, sending them away to reside in another character, Henry, and receiving them back only when they have survived the journey. That is to say: even if these are his own experiences, he has tested them as if they were newly invented. Actual experience has always one advantage; it does not need to be invented. But to transcribe the experience is one thing; and it may not be enough. There is another way; to begin by depriving the experience of its advantage, and then to insist that it must earn any merit to be assigned. The merit is earned by subjecting the experience to new trials, different from those mysterious trials which it survived by coming into time and history. We say that these new trials are aesthetic, but that is only another way of saying that, for poetic purposes, history is not enough. There is also art.

This is why we attend to virtues and vices in poetry only to the extent that they are now, at last, verbal; they have survived their own element and now they have established themselves in a new element, words, grammar, syntax, rhetoric. Often when we attend to a phrase, a line, a stanza in a poem, we delight in its finesse, its propriety; knowing that this perfection is the second and later grace, the first being perhaps a moral perception, the adjudication of acts and sufferings in the world before these have become verbal. Mature art is the process of a double establishment, the result of a double test. I think of Mr. Berryman's Song 16, beginning "Henry's pelt was put on sundry walls." The poem is apparently indebted to an aphorism by (I think) Gottfried Benn: "we are using our skins for wallpaper, and we cannot win." The sentiment is congenial, however rueful, because it endorses Berryman's notion of the poet as society's scapegoat, its chosen victim. The poem is concerned with the cost of public victory in private defeat. Cocktail bars are gorgeously furnished, clothed with the richest wallpaper, because a poet's skin is ready. In Sealdah Station "some possessionless / children survive to die," and therefore "the Chinese communes hum." The song ends:

>   Two daiquiris
> withdrew into a corner of the gorgeous room
> and one told the other a lie.

Perhaps it is enough to receive this in the witty terms in which it is given. But even if the experience is recalled rather than invented, it is not merely transcribed. Indeed, it would be useful to ponder the relation between the experience and its final establishment in the words. I have no information on its first establishment, apart from the liberty of an amateur guess. My guess is that the experience was either actual or virtual; such incidents are common. Perhaps the first stage began and ended there, as a minor incident. The second stage began, I continue to guess, when the poet introduced the incident into a poetic rhythm already partly rehearsed, a rhythm of the public and the private worlds, set off one against the other. In another cadence, this might set the pretentious public world against the even deadlier facts of the case. For this purpose it would be necessary to reduce the participants; as by calling two people two daiquiris. It would then be proper to give the public setting in terms grand and false: the two daiquiris "withdrew into a corner of the gorgeous room." And then the bare private truth: "and one told the other a lie." The second establishment, then, is an act of the imagination, conspiring with certain possibilities in diction, syntax, and rhythm. History and fact are not enough.

The procedure is strict, the aesthetic abstemious. I shall argue on the evidence of the later Songs that Mr. Berryman found the rules too hard, and sought an easier course, at some cost to the poems. The long dream began with Henry already ill, at a loss, defeated; the game is up. In Song 28 he

says, "If I had to do the whole thing over again / I wouldn't." Song 29 has
all the bells saying, "too late." So Henry's letter to the world, reasonably
enough, is a rejection slip, a curse. The bad gangs thrive. Nature is good,
but man is not: "Pleased, at the worst, except with man, he shook / the
brightest winter sun." There is still time for another song, a fine gesture:
"But the snows and summers grieve & dream." For the rest, Henry's life is
a crash programme, a holding operation so long as the operation holds. There
is a plot of sorts: Henry down to the grave and, briefly, back again. But increasingly, as the night darkens, the singer wearies of the rigour, the discipline
of the dramatic imagination. If Wordsworth got away with the egotistical
sublime, why not Henry, why not Mr. Berryman? The change comes, as a
matter of aesthetic insistence, in Song 141:

> Duly he does his needful little then
> with a chest of ice, a head tipping with pain.
> That perhaps is his programme,
> cause: Henry for Henry in the main:
> he'll push it: down with anything Bostonian:
> even god howled "I am."

Anything Bostonian is genteel, proper, Jamesian (Henry). In *Notes of a Son
and Brother* James said that Boston seemed "more expressive than I had supposed an American city could be of a seated and rooted social order, an order
not complex but sensibly fixed." To Henry, no tolerable order is sensibly
fixed; the self, responsible to nothing in Boston, howls, "I am." Song 133 says,
"It seems to be solely a matter of continuing Henry / voicing & obsessed."
The data, Henry decides in Song 148, "were abundantly his / or if not, never."
Increasingly, as the voicing continues, everything becomes not itself but a
function of Henry's obsession. In Song 219 he rebukes Wallace Stevens for
lifting the metaphysics so high that the physics is lost. For himself, in Song
370, he claims empirical innocence, "not a symbol in the place." But in fact
the self is the only centre, and the circumference is derived from that centre.
Whitman, "the great Walt," is properly invoked. The structure of the poem
is glossed in Song 293, "not cliffhangers or old serials / but according to his
nature." I take this to mean: down with any structure Bostonian, objective,
independent. The structure comes from within, or it does not come at all.
There is no classic order among the materials; order is to be imposed rather
than discovered. In Song 305 the aesthetic procedure is given as attention
to the means rather than the end; presumably because a projected end implies
a classic order waiting to be unfolded. The means; what else but to work
according to one's nature. That is to say: anything goes, if it comes from
within. Another version turns up in Song 311:

Hunger was constitutional with him,
women, cigarettes, liquor, need need need
until he went to pieces.
The pieces sat up & wrote. They did not heed
their piecedom but kept very quietly on
among the chaos.

This is ingenious. A poet, living in various degrees of chaos, dissociates himself; allowing to each fragment its corresponding voice. The fragments scream; that is, sing. The whole man, undissociated, is to be found as the sum of his parts; as the *Dream Songs* is the sum of 385 separate songs. The pieces are sanctioned by a nature which is their sum; the more diverse the pieces, the greater the nature. This is not Whitman's way. Whitman's aesthetic implies that the self is the sum of its experiences, not the sum of its dissociated fragments. In Whitman the self is not dissociated, the self is deemed to be whole at any and every moment. The experiences are diverse; as one experience follows upon another, the receiving self is enlarged. But the self is never understood as a fraction; it is always a whole number. The history of the self is the history of its possessions; what it possesses is an ever increasing body of experience. As the experiences accrue, the self expands. So the self corresponds with the world by sharing its procedures; accumulation, addition, arithmetic, possession. In Mr. Berryman's poems the self is heard in fragments. The poet's hope is that as the poems proceed, page by page, the fragments will be so various, so compelling, that only a unified sensibility could emerge, at the last.

Perhaps this goes part way to account for Mr. Berryman's characteristic syntax. He does not run to Whitman's long line, the loose line of feeling. Whitman's syntax is the mark of his confidence: he knows, trusting himself, that he can go along with his experience in any direction; his confidence is expansive because the world is promise. But the world is a threat, to Mr. Berryman; it has made no promise. Everywhere in the *Dream Songs* the world is an obstacle, a troublemaker; it takes away more than it gives. Landscape is often charming, but man's deeds are vindictive. Men walk the earth, it appears, to thwart Henry, finally to break him in pieces. So Mr. Berryman's typical syntax, especially in the later Songs, is intensive rather than expansive; he favours the short line, the isolated perception, as a form of defence or reprisal. Normally the sentence features the bare report, with an air of finality; doom accomplished. Only the voice, constitutionally in need, breaks silence and keeps the show going. After such knowledge, the long dream proposes, there is very little to say; but that little is better than nothing. So: say it. Repeat it, if it helps to fend off the void:

> In sleep, of a heart attack, let Henry go.
> The end of tennis. The beginning of the dark.
> The beginning of the wagon.
> It is the onward coming terrifies.
> Now at last the effort to make him kill himself
> has failed.
>
> Take down the thing then to which he was nailed.
> I am a boat was moored on the wrong shelf.
> Love has wings and flies.

This is more like Roethke's syntax than like anything in Whitman; and for good reason. In Roethke as in Mr. Berryman the only hope is to shore a few fragments against one's ruin. The life of a modern poet is representative; that is, vestigial. The only distinction that is relevant is the distinction between those few fragments and the other thing; nothing, Nil. A corresponding syntax is likely to be aggressive, defensive; it captures one thing here and another there, and it holds on to its possessions. The poet lives by his nature, that is, by his constitutional needs.

We come back to Henry, upon whose needs Mr. Berryman insists. I have argued that in the middle and later Songs it has become increasingly difficult to take Henry seriously as a character distinct from his maker. It is not a question of the materials; though it is easy to demonstrate that, for the most part, Henry's experience in fiction coincides with Mr. Berryman's experience in fact. Often, the occasion of a poem is the arrival of the postman with a letter or this week's issue of the *Times Literary Supplement*. In Song 293 the poet refers to the "hotspur materials" of his book 7, but most of them are, at least in Hamlet's sense, common. The following is a short list of motifs: fear, lust, irritation, "ensamples violent", travel, Death, Death, Death, poetry, rest, marriage, divorce, sex, daughters, butterflies, lectures, money, prizes, fame. More specifically: there are poems about Mr. Berryman's friends and colleagues, Randall Jarrell, Delmore Schwartz, Roethke, Robert Frost, R. P. Blackmur, William Carlos Williams, Yvor Winters; poems about Eisenhower's presidency, an MLA meeting in Chicago or New York, a BBC TV show in which the star was the poet John Berryman, the co-star his daughter, a year lived in Dublin, the misery of Vietnam, Sylvia Plath's suicide, John F. Kennedy, Hemingway, Jonathan Swift, W. B. Yeats; even Christine Keeler. Song 23 interpolated "O Adlai mine." Much of one's life is what the postman brings. No, it is not a question of the materials. But Mr. Berryman claims to give these materials to his man, Henry, and that this makes a difference. There is an established aesthetic tradition to support the claim: its most distinctive modern adepts are W. B. Yeats and Ezra Pound. Yeats says in *Estrangement* that "there is a relation between discipline and the theatrical sense." "If we cannot imagine ourselves as different from what we are and assume that second self, we cannot impose a discipline upon ourselves, though we may accept one from others. Active virtue as distinguished from the passive acceptance of a current code is therefore theatrical, consciously dramatic, the wearing of a mask." This is the text we need: it is the application of the theatrical metaphor to the common idea of a creative imagination. In such cases the imagination is creative because it imagines forms of life different from its own, and assumes those forms. The process is continuously dramatic, interrogative. The relation between discipline and the theatrical sense is based upon the fact that, given the theatrical sense as described, the self may ignore itself, may ignore its own nature. Whitman extends his nature by adding to its experiences. Yeats extends his nature the other way, from within; not by adding to the materials, but by conceiving different ways of receiving them. The multiplicity is active within, not without. The discipline is active within, not without. Pound's theory of the *persona* is more or less the same as Yeats's, so far as it is a genuine theory at all. In practice, Pound's imagination is not remarkable in a theatrical way; it does not naturally operate by conceiving several different selves. It is too authoritarian for that. The result is that when Pound proposes a *persona,* distinct from himself, the distinction is highly doubtful; as in *Hugh Selwyn Mauberley.* Mauberley is like Mr. Berryman's Henry in the later stages of the *Dream Songs;* he is not, in Yeats's sense, a mask, he is merely a disguise. There is a difference. A figure disguises himself for his protection, not for self-discipline. Behind the disguise he is the same as ever, and he is determined to remain so. The last thing he wants is to change. He does not propose to extend his nature; he proposes to defend it. This applies even more to Henry than to Mauberley. In *Mauberley* Pound tries to detect the meretricious elements in his man, and fails largely because he is not gifted in self-detection. But in the later Songs the gap between Henry and his maker is closed: Mr. Berryman's effort to maintain a distance is perfunctory. The hotspur materials are the same materials, and there is no sense of a receiving self different from his own.

Mr. Berryman has proposed to himself the discipline of dramatic character, but he has not, in the later Songs, accepted its obligations. The first result is that discipline is intermittent and haphazard. Yeats's method, if fully endorsed in practice, would ensure discipline at every moment. Mr. Berryman's discipline is not ensured. Sometimes it is provided by a sense of poetic achievements different from his own, and the pressure of a literary tradition. Song 171 accepts the relevance of Waller's poem "Go, Lovely Rose"; so Waller's feeling is a witness, a presence which must not be disgraced. In Song 285 the discipline comes, for the moment, from within; its sign, the ironic use of an elaborately learned idiom:

> Much petted Henry like a petal throve,
> his narthex let the girls & pupils in,
> aptotic he remained
> Henry's own man, when he squirmed not in love,
> fifty pressures herded one discipline:
> the sun shot up, it rained,
> weathering Henry kept on his own side,
> whatever in the name of God that side was.
> And he struggled, pal.
> Apricate never: too he took in his stride
> more than most monsters can.

And so on, for another stanza. Let us say that Henry, on a transatlantic liner, has avoided shipboard romance and is pleased, with reservations natural in the circumstances. Narthex: several meanings, including a tall plant, a perfume case, but especially that part of an early Christian church which was reserved for monks or for women. So: he lets women in, but only under controlled and innocent conditions. Aptotic: referring to a noun that has no distinction of cases; or to languages that have no grammatical inflections; transferred now to a poet, a language-man resistant, unyielding, retaining his virtue. Apricate never: never exposed to the sun, never basking in the sun with the stripped-down girls. The stanza is not momentous, but it has something of that wit which Eliot described in his essay on Marvell: "a tough reasonableness beneath the slight lyric grace." The note of wit is here the mark of discipline. In other moments Mr. Berryman has accepted discipline from other sources. In the *Homage to Mistress Bradstreet* two of the finest occasions accept other voices. In stanza 13, "I found my heart more carnal and sitting loose from God" is taken from Anne's *My Dear Children*. In stanza 33 a wonderful phrase, "Wan dolls in indigo on gold" is taken from Baron Corvo's *The Desire and Pursuit of the Whole*.

It is my impression that in the later Songs attention to other voices has receded. Increasingly, there is one voice, doctrinaire, edgy, magisterial. The question is: what does the change denote? It may be innocent; meaning merely that Mr. Berryman found the pretence a bit of a bore, Henry a nuisance, after a while. Or it may mean that, as the poems proceeded, Mr. Berryman found that the sole indelible interest was his own emotion. Hotspur materials,

hotspur emotions. Santayana, writing of Whitman and Browning as bar-
barians, said that the barbarian is one "who regards his passions as their
own excuse for being." Is it not true that, in the later poems, Mr. Berryman
came to feel thus tenderly for his own passions, so that nothing beyond their
constitutional need seemed real or potent? Keats spoke of the egotistical
sublime as Wordsworthian; it was Wardsworth's way of colouring every
natural form with his own sensibility. At one extreme, such an artist comes
to feel that the natural event is nothing, his own sensibility everything.

So the later Berryman is Wordsworthian, at least in his new character.
But it is necessary to distinguish further, since this way of poetry includes
the best as well as the worst in Mr. Berryman. The relation between passion
and perception is never easy to specify. There are occasions on which the
passion takes the form of energy surrounding the perception; perception is
the centre, passion the circumference. There are other occasions on which
the perception is merely ostensible, and the real centre is the passion; where
the perception is entertained for the sake of the passion. In Song 321, for
instance, Mr. Berryman composes a loud invocation to Ireland, with much
talk of Connolly, Pearse, Joyce, Yeats, Swift, Synge, O'Casey, Kavanagh,
and Clarke. The poem is crude by any reckoning; it is a bad poem. But in
fact it is not a poem about Ireland at all, despite the heroic names; it is about
John Berryman and his high horse. The natural forms, the historical
references, are merely occasional; they are hired to serve the poet, to let him
mount the horse. Obviously it makes no difference to the poem, and no
improvement, if we agree to call the horseman Henry rather than Mr. Berryman. In Song 385, on the other hand, while the mode is still Wordsworthian, the direction of feeling is something other (I give the poem entire):

> My daughter's heavier. Light leaves are flying.
> Everywhere in enormous numbers turkeys will be dying
> and other birds, all their wings.
> They never greatly flew. Did they wish to?
> I should know. Off away somewhere once I knew
> such things.
>
> Or good Ralph Hodgson back then did, or does.
> The man is dead whom Eliot praised. My praise
> follows and flows too late.
> Fall is grievy, brisk. Tears behind the eyes
> almost fall. Fall comes to us as a prize
> to rouse us toward our fate.

My house is made of wood and it's made well,
unlike us. My house is older than Henry;
that's fairly old.
If there were a middle ground between things and the soul
or if the sky resembled more the sea,
I wouldn't have to scold

                                    my heavy daughter.

The reference to Henry is perfunctory; the play is not a *Henriad*. Rather,
our poet is speaking *in propria persona*, husband and father, poet, too,
representative man. The first stanza is all reverie, the mind moving easily,
picking its way by association, one sound calling to another: heavy daughter,
light leaves; flying, dying. "They never greatly flew"; in context, after 384
poems in which success and failure were pondered, the sentence is more
evocative than it would be elsewhere. Recall in *Ulysses:* "They flew. Where
to? Paris and back. Newhaven—Dieppe" (I speak from memory). For the
moment, the words stand for all forms of loss, including the irreversible loss
from which the whole enterprise began. From loss to genial success: Ralph
Hodgson is hardly a heavyweight success, no Shakespeare, no Dante. But
for that very reason he is invoked here, to mark the easy happiness available
to those good people who accept what they are given by the gods. Hodgson
is memorialized in Eliot's *Five-Finger Exercises* as the delightful owner of
a Baskerville hound, unnumbered finches and fairies, and 999 canaries. It
is proper, in reverie, to let the name come as it will, mediated through Eliot's
little poem. It is not a time for heavy guns. The key word in this stanza is
Fall, the poet intones it thrice, noun, verb, noun; surrounding it with a cor-
respondent rhyme, "too late," "our fate." Eliot persists in the background,
mainly through the recollection of "Gerontion" enforced by the first lines
of the last stanza here: in Eliot's poem, "My house is a decayed house." In Mr.
Berryman's poem the house is firm, we are the decay. In the last lines the
intimations of loss and fall are translated into immediately domestic terms:
the tone is not apocalyptic, though it might be so if the same losses and falls
were violently sensed. Mr. Berryman's "sense of an ending" is gentle, the
lines—it is proper to say—are beautiful. In the reading, according to the print,
we are to hover between "middle" and "ground"; or rather, we are to feel
the gap while stretching across it. The stretching is desire, the fact is the gap.
The poet longs for a mediating ground, first, between things and the soul;
and then he longs for a structure of correspondence and analogy, one thing
linked to another. The old continuity of things is lost. There are gaps
everywhere; as now between loving father and heavy daughter. Surely this

poem is not the work of a barbarian: the poem is all perception, surrounded by feeling. The feeling is not on show, on parade; it comes into the lines only because it attends upon perceptions which could not appear without that favour. The end is good.

ERNEST C. STEFANIK

A Cursing Glory:
John Berryman's Love & Fame

Several critics have dealt severely with John Berryman's *Love & Fame* primarily because the poems do not conform to what they believe poetry ought to be in form or content. Judging on formulated standards, however, is not the only way of obscuring what is actually in the poems, for the critic, like Keats's poet of negative capability, might discard his own nature and assume that of the poet. Both positions are extreme in perspective, and the reader of poetry, aware of the intentional fallacy, ought to find an objective sympathy, the point at which critical expectation and poetical intention converge, before undertaking an examination of the poetry. The underlying assumption of this reading is that *Love & Fame* is not simply a collection of lyrics assembled under a common title, as several reviewers have supposed, but a narrative that presents a self-portrait of the poet beginning his religious quest, his encounter with God and, concommitantly, with self. Berryman's experience may be ineffable and his topical references inaccessible, but he makes the poetry familiar through stanzaic form, associations, and rhythms. Through his suffering and courage both as a ragged hero and as a foolish victim, he elicits and enlists the reader's sympathies as he reconstructs his past, confronts the unknowable in a meaningless world, and finally adopts a posture of Christian acceptance. The self-revelations are made by steady, harrowing degrees, and the movement of the sequence is towards a learning to live in the present moment by overcoming an obsessive concern for the past and for the future. But in order to perceive this narrative line, the reader

From *Renascence* 25, no. 3 (Spring 1973). © 1973 by the Catholic Renascence Society, Inc.

must first understand how the poems are brought into relation with one another and how, in turn, the final effect is to be realized.

In a 1959 review-article John Berryman makes an arresting statement on the nature and purpose of poetry. He allows that the motive for writing poetry may be "complex beyond analysis," but that is all he allows. "Poetry is a terminal activity, taking place out near the end of things, where the poet's soul addresses one other soul only, never mind when. And it aims—never mind *either* communication or expression—at the reformation of the poet, as prayer does." Chief among the implicit assertions and denials is that poetry is essentially subjective in nature and intent, demanding an intimacy of poet and reader that Eliotic voices or Yeatsian masks preclude. Both poetry and prayer are a response to some crisis in the poet's personality or the contemplation of some problem crucial to him. Reformation is the resolution, involving a conscious disintegration and reintegration of personality. The animating power of the poem, then, by its subjective nature and purpose, is a drive towards the rediscovery of the self that "enables the poet gradually, again and again, to become almost another man." In other words, the individual's response to crisis results in alterations of character and beliefs.

That the drive is so deeply embedded in the poet's personality places, certainly, heavy demands upon the reader. And nowhere in the poetry of John Berryman are these demands more poignantly felt than in *Love & Fame*. In *Homage to Mistress Bradstreet* and *The Dream Songs* the reader is afforded some aesthetic distance as the poet modulates his voice and personal suffering through, in the one case, a reconstructed character and, in the other case, an imaginary character. But in *Love & Fame* the poems are so intensely autobiographical and intimate that the reader is invariably aware that at the center of the narrative is a sentient man at odds with himself, the world, and his God. The poet does not create a world inhabited by fictive personages but represents his real world of the past and present. It is a sequence that chronicles the poet's spiritual progress from misunderstanding and unbelief to the agony of self-realization and acceptance of his lot. The primary difficulty for the reader is affective, for this is not a poem recollected in tranquillity, but one written apparently in the immediacy of crisis—confusion, torment, and anguish; guilt, purgation, and epiphany.

In "Message" Berryman offers a negative statement of intention:

> I am not writing an autobiography-in-verse, my friends.

> Impressions, structures, tales, from Columbia in the Thirties
> & the Michaelmas terms at Cambridge in '36,
> followed by some later. It's not my life
> That's occluded & lost.

The statement is both deceptive and illuminating. Berryman is elsewhere too careful an artist for the reader to blindly accept that the structure is no more carefully conceived than a chaotic stringing of "impressions, structures, tales." With the double disavowal of autobiography, the reader, aware that Berryman's personal life and public career are the ostensible subject of the narrative, must look further for a unifying principle. The search begins and ends with a consideration of the title, *Love & Fame*. It is surprising that no reviewer-critic has yet suggested that the title might derive from Keats's first Shakespearean sonnet, "When I Have Fears." Keats's speaker fears that he may not be able to complete the poetry he sees written "upon the night's starr'd face, / Huge cloudy symbols of a high romance"; he fears that he will not be able to "relish in the faery power / Of unreflecting love!" When he feels these fears of imminent failure in art and life, "then on the shore / Of the wide world I stand alone, and think / Till Love and Fame to nothingness do sink." Neither love nor fame, the dominant concerns of this world, can provide the poet with his identity or lend a satisfying meaning to his life. For Berryman, the insight of Keats's final couplet operates as a variant of the *ubi sunt* motif. It is the realization, repeatedly suggested, that enables the poet to advance spiritually, to live in the present moment instead of lapsing into a futile longing for bygone times or fearing an uncertain future.

The dedication of *Love & Fame* to Tristan Corbière gives a clearer indication of how Berryman intends the book to be read:

> SLEEP! IN YOUR BOAT BROUGHT INTO THE LIVING-ROOM
> SUPREME ADMIRER OF THE ANCIENT SEA
>
> YOUR MOCKERY OF THE PRETENTIOUS GREAT
> YOUR SELF-REVELATIONS
> CONSTITUTE STILL IN THE SUNSET SKY
> A CURSING GLORY.

Corbière, as the dedicatory poem recalls, spent most of his life at Roscoff sailing his boat in a deliberate protest against his sickly constitution. In his only volume of verse, *Les amours jaunes,* he ridiculed the sentimentality and pomposity of the Romantics; but he also treated his own sentiments with humor and sarcasm, such as in the final stanza of his "Sur un portrait de Corbière": "Je voudrais être alors chien de fille publique, / Lécher un peu d'amour qui ne soit pas payé; / Ou déesse à tou crins sur la côte d'Afrique, / Ou fou, mais réussi; fou, mais pas à moitié." Berryman recognizes the Breton poet as a more accomplished practitioner of self-disclosure in a telling, yet softly spoken, desire: "(*I wished I versed with his bite*)." And, it will become evident, Berryman does not write about himself with a tough seriousness; rather his sardonic honesty often takes the form of ludicrous distortion. He is intent upon unearthing his buried self, but the expense of self-revelation is self-mockery. The poet, in a protest against his own sick spirit, writes the book that will restore his lost faith and affirm his being.

Love and Fame is divided into four parts, and the poems are arranged in approximate chronological order, with occasional shifts for thematic reasons. The first two parts concern the poet's student days at Columbia College in New York and at Clare College in Cambridge during the 1930s; the third centers on his immediate present as he confronts his isolation, fears, and incipient madness; and the fourth part marks his entrance into a new life following his awareness of moral and spiritual bankruptcy. It is worth noting that Berryman largely ignores the period of his life between the publication of his first book, *Twenty Poems,* in 1940 and the appearance of the collected version of *The Dream Songs* in 1969. It is as though he wishes to remind the reader that the spiritual crisis and the attempts at resolution, now brought to the foreground, have been an ongoing concern in a poetry that has from the outset been essentially subjective in nature and intent, aiming at the reformation of the poet.

The biographical events that delineate the surface structure of the first two parts of *Love & Fame* need not be recounted here. The incidents and anecdotes present a discontinuous history of the poet's student days; he is a young man preparing for a literary career, plunging into all manner of intellectual and sensual excesses. The image that issues from such a reading is the poet in caricature, an artist misusing his gifts to make trivial comments on a misspent life. The outer world, offering the context of time and space, can have significance only in relation to the inner world of the poet if the work is to rise above the level of gossip. The poet of the interior narrative is a man in spiritual crisis, a man possessed by doubts and fears and needs; he is a man searching for self-understanding through self-recollection. There is a striking contrast between the two worlds inhabited by the poet; the outer one is filled with triumphs and trophies, whereas the inner world is shattered and desolate.

"Her & It," the first poem in the sequence, is the poet's self-congratulation for having found fulfillment in a life of love and fame. The poet, in this seeming world of memory and illusions, is a braggart strutting about and boasting of his sexual and literary accomplishments:

> I fell in love with a girl.
> O and a gash.
> I'll bet she now has seven lousy children.
> (I've three myself, one being off the record.)

. . . .
Time magazine yesterday slavered Saul's ass,
they pecked at mine last year. We're going strong!
Photographs all over!

But the poem concludes with an inexpressible self-doubt: "She muttered something in my ear I've forgotten as we danced." In its syntactical ambiguity the utterance has some significance intuitively recognized but not understood by the poet. This ending of a poem that throughout is concerned with certainties seems misplaced, but it provides the initiative force in the poet's quest for self-understanding and faith in God. The self-congratulatory tone points back to Keats's couplet and serves to disclose some underlying importance, an insight achieved not within the scope of a single lyric but only after an exhaustive examination of the inner world of the poet. Later, in "Monkhood," the seeming arrogance of the poet melts into greater doubts that do find expression:

Will I ever write properly with passion & exactness,
of the damned strange demeanours of my flagrant heart?
& be by anyone anywhere undertaken?
One *more* unanswerable question.

The progress of the poet is an increased awareness of the mutability of love and fame, and the unanswerable questions in the long poem finally overshadow the shows of bravado. In "Freshman Blues" the poet tells of a friend's feared sexual inadequacy and of his own prowess. The central stanza, however, concerns the influence of his father's death:

Thought much I then on perforated daddy,
daddy boxed in & let down with strong straps,
when I my friends' homes visited, with fathers
universal & intact.

The placement of this reflection suggests that the poet's confusion of love with lust and fame with need for affirmation may have its source in this irrecoverable loss. The formative influence of having witnessed his father's suicide has also engendered thoughts of his own death. "Drunks," the recollection of a New Year's Eve party, is a celebration of a new beginning that is marred by a black comment on the past:

I wondered every day about suicide.
Once at South Kent—maybe in the Third Form?—
I lay down on the tracks before a train
& had to be hauled off, the Headmaster was furious.

But new beginnings are not yet possible, for spiritual isolation (whatever its cause) has made the poet a victim of his past, rendering him incapable of living in the present moment, depriving him of faith.

The first part of the narrative ends with the sense of isolation and imprisonment dissipating as the poet prepares to sail for England:

> I wasn't unhappy, I wasn't anything,
> until I pulled myself reluctantly together at last
>
> & bowed goodbye to my lame ducks
> & headed for Pier 42—where my nervous system
> as I teetered across the gang-plank
> sprang back into expectation.

Such a departure presents the possibility of a new beginning for the poet, as though distance can diminish the influence of the past. But Cambridge, he discovers, is "a still more foreign scene" than New York. The first poem of part 2, "Away," continues the expectations of things to come: "I'm on my way to Bumpus' and the Cam, / haunts of the old masters where I may improve" and the retrospective mockery of "Yeats, Yeats, I'm coming! it's me. Faber & Faber, / you'll have to publish me some day with éclat / I haven't quite got the hang of the stuff yet / but I swamp with possibility." The excitement of the voyage and the possibility of a life without reminders of a wretched past cause the poet to ignore rather than confront his past: "I have felt happy / before but not in the flying wind like this" and "I hardly slept across the North Atlantic. / We talked. His panoramas, / plus my anticipations, made me new." The happiness is shortlived, for at Clare the old ghosts of isolation, fear, and doubt appear to haunt the young poet, and he longs to return to the familiar surroundings to escape his present suffering: "I don't do a damned thing but read & write. / I wish I were back in New York! / I feel old, yet I don't understand." The journey to England has thrown the poet back upon himself and has intensified his sense of isolation rather than freeing him as supposed. Improvement, as the poet learns, must be spiritual as well as intellectual. Understanding remains elusive as the final poem in part 2 sounds the same note on which the sequence had begun. "Her & It" and "To B——— E———" express Berryman's shallow belief that reformation can be achieved by recovering lost relationships: "I wish she'd read my book & write to me" and "if you dropped your hand to me / I'd take the next plane to London." But reformation, like salvation, can come about only through a confrontation with the self, in subjective truth, a surrender of the self in the object of love.

Immediately following the abortive attempt to escape memory in order to affirm his being through love and fame of this world, Berryman enters obviously into the religious quest. "The Search" opens part 3 and is the pivotal poem of the sequence. Instead of ending in doubt as did so many poems before, this one finds its beginnings in uncertainty: "I wondered ever too what my fate would be, / women & after-fame become *quite* unavailable, / or at best unimportant." The poet, standing on the edge of understanding, catalogues the studies to which he is indebted in his efforts to find, or rather renew, his faith in God: Guignebert, Goguel, McNeile, Bultmann, Archbishop Carrington, Karl Heim, Wellisch, Luther, Kierkegaard, Bishop Andrewes, and Bishop Wescott. "And other systems, high & primitive, / ancient & surviving, did I not neglect, / sky-gods & trickster-gods, gods impotent, / the malice & force of the dead." But Kierkegaard asserts that the transition from unfaith to faith is not a weighing of possibilities: "Christianity is the precise opposite of speculation . . . the miraculous, the absurd, a challenge to the individual to exist in it, and not to waste his time by trying to understand it speculatively." It is a suffering, something that happens to the individual. Suffering at first causes an absorption in the self, but it also teaches the individual that he is nothing. The poet must realize religion, his love for God, by a decisive leap from objective thinking to subjective faith, driven by the awareness of sin. "The Search" is the first step forward in Berryman's pilgrimage, a spiritual journey that marks his departure from an animal existence and his entrance into a Christian life.

The theme of the religious quest disappears throughout part 3, but the poet is clearly a changed man. He is no longer the seeming braggart; he is derided and humbled. The self-parading of the first two parts is transformed into meditation: "We will die, & the evidence / is: Nothing after that. / Honey, we don't rejoin. / The thing meanwhile, I suppose, is to be courageous & kind." In a further existential attempt to resolve the crisis of spirit, the poet attends to his situation in the present: his isolation ("I feel congruity, feel colleagueship / with even few of my fine contemporaries"); death and absurdity ("*Losses!* as Randall observed / who walked into a speeding car / under a culvert at night in Carolina / having just called his wife to make plans for the children"); the nightmare of history in "The Soviet Union," "The Minnesota 8 and the Letter-Writers," "Regents' Professor Berryman's Crack on Race," "Have a Genuine American Horror-&-Mist on the Rocks," and "To a Woman"; need ("I seldom go out now. She's out of town. / After all has been said, and all *has* been said, / Man is a huddle of need"); despair ("I am busy tired mad lonely & old"); and suicide ("Reflexions on suicide, & on my father, possess me. / I drink too much. My wife threatens separation"). The echoes of parts 1 and 2 become explicitly the voices the poet must answer in order to end his suffering.

The poet has reconstructed his past in an effort to more clearly see his present condition, and to escape the bonds of memory. Berryman exposes the past with the objectivity and candor of a disinterested observer, without granting it some romantic grandeur or heroic glory. Instead, the insistent prate about concupiscence and renown create the image of the poet as a foolish victim. Frankness and self-mockery provide the impetus for the poet to advance into another life rather than retreating into the past, for there is neither solace nor honor in hollow achievements. There is a note of Freudianism that can be discerned in Berryman's self-realizations, urging him toward other-worldly concerns. The aim of psychoanalysis is to effect disillusionment and to dispel delusions. It offers health, but not necessarily happiness. It offers no consolation; it offers no promises. In "Views of Myself" Berryman longs to utter the public confession that will expiate his sins and offer forgiveness:

> I did not censor anything I said
>
>
> & what I said I said with force & wit
> which crushed some no doubt decent & by me now would be spared
> human personalities with shoes on.
> I stand ashamed of myself;
> yes, but I stand.
> . . . .
> When I was fiddling with every wife
> on the Eastern seaboard
> I longed to climb into the pulpit & confess.
> Tear me to pieces!

Freudian candor offers knowledge, but it does not necessarily satisfy feelings. To be happy a man requires faith in his own existence, not merely being rid of shame and guilt. Like psychoanalysis, confession in the Church is the acknowledgement of sins committed; unlike psychoanalysis, confession (in its three-fold aspects of repentance, penance, and absolution) offers a consolation, a forgiveness that weakens the torment of memory and affirms the worth of the individual.

Just as Berryman is aware of the evil in the world as "the 20th century flies insanely on" during the third part, he becomes no less conscious of the evil within himself. Shifted from the mad macrocosm, the poet enters the microcosm of a mental hospital. The insights discovered in this isolated community are in themselves unsatisfying, and the poet realizes that he must return to the religious community for consolation. In "The Hell Poem," the first poem in this cycle, the poet voices his double-edged fear: "Protractions of return / to the now desired but frightful outer world." Hell is isolation, an absence of inner harmony, the state of the unforgiven and the damned: "Will day glow again to these tossers, and to me? / I am staying days." It is possible to avoid the grip of hell's vice through faith. "Purgatory" is the waiting for the end of isolation, a state of remorse and a promise of salvation: "The days are over. I leave after breakfast / with fifteen hundred things to do at home." "Heaven" is acceptance into the paradisal community through a deliberate choice: "Free! while in the cathedral at Seville / a Cardinal is singing. I bowed my face / & licked the monument. Aged women / waited behind me. Free! to lick & believe." The love of God is an act of will, a loss of self in the object of love. Reformation and salvation for Berryman are a movement from the world of the damned to the world of the living, where divine light casts the images of memory into darkness. In the Christian sense, it is a rescue from the kingdom of spiritual death by living in the present moment through faith and grace; it is a return to God and an acceptance of His will.

"The Home Ballad" signals the poet's return from the hell to which he had condemned himself and concludes the cycle within the third part as the poet prepares to advance spiritually. But first the poet comes home to his wife and daughter:

> It's home to my daughter I am come
> with verses and stories true,
> which I would also share with you,
> my dear, my dear,
> only you are not my daughter.

The poet has arrived home at last, having found the firm footing needed to move forward, even though his step wobbles "with one cracked toe": "O I left that wart on my right foot / lurching on my left toe. / It hurt like hell, but never mind—I hobbled on to free." Berryman not only returns to the security of his family, but just as significantly he has emerged from the world of madness as a whole person. The doubt, longing, and despair of the poet in "Her & It" and "To B—— E——" as he gropes for self-understanding in the past become certainty and fulfillment through hope and faith in the present. Having an integrated personality for the first time and having thus gained a vantage point, the poet's acceptance of self makes the acceptance of God's will and love possible. He arrives home swinging his "typescript book like a bee / with honey back to the comb." The concepts of love and fame he carries home at the end of part 3 are radically different from those expressed in the first two parts; through the agency of Keats's insight, love and fame bear different meanings as he presents the manuscript, the product of his "honey almost hopeless angry art," to his wife, "honey Kate":

> It's *Love & Fame* called, honey Kate,
> you read it from the start
> and sometimes I reel when you praise my art
> my honey almost hopeless angry art,
> which was both our Fate—

Rising from the dark world of the self in which he learned the futility of seeking affirmation or identity in shallow concepts of love and fame, the poet enters into a life of hope and faith through resignation of his will. The flight from memory halted and the inner conflicts confronted, Berryman is prepared to make the climactic statement of the sequence, to take Kierkegaard's leap of faith, in "Eleven Addresses to the Lord."

Berryman's poetry of the self becomes now a lay canticle, a poetry of thanksgiving and reverence.

> Master of beauty, craftsman of the snowflake,
> inimitable contriver,
> endower of the Earth so gorgeous & different from the
>   boring Moon,
> thank you for such as it is my gift.
>
> I have made up a morning prayer to you
> containing with precision everything that most matters.
> 'According to Thy will' the thing begins.
> It took me off & on two days. It does not aim at eloquence.

Foregoing eloquence, the prayer aims at sincerity and exactness. The poet, however, for the time being, is not prepared to recite the prayer acknowledging his resignation to the will of God and the abnegation of self: "how can I 'love' you? / I only as far as gratitude & awe / confidently & absolutely go." Still, he is a man capable of accepting Mystery: "I believe as fixedly in the Resurrection-appearances to Peter & to Paul / as I believe I sit in this blue chair." But the belief is a product of reason rather than of faith. In "The Search" he states that "Bishop Andrewes' account of the Resurrection-appearances / in 1609 seemed to me, seems to me, it." With similar assurance he cannot proclaim his unquestioning love for God:

> Holy, as I suppose I dare to call you
> without pretending to know anything about you
> but infinite capacity everywhere & always
> & in particular certain goodness to me.

Uncertainty resides not in the poet's inability to understand God's nature but in his own "double nature," wishing to believe but unable to make a subjective choice, the commitment of faith, that transcends reason. For now the rational choice is between Christ's mercy and "the gloomy wisdom of godless Freud." Christ is the Savior of mankind, offering forgiveness and compassion; but to Freud belong "the lost souls in ill-attended wards, / those agonised thro' the world."

> I say "Thy kingdom come," it means nothing to me.
> Hast Thou prepared astonishments for man?
> One sudden Coming? Many so believe.
> So not, without knowing anything, do I.

In the third Address, the troubled poet offers a petitionary prayer to the Lord to grant him those attributes which will unite his divided self and secure the *visio dei:* strength in repentance ("guard me / against my flicker of impulse lust"); perseverance ("Sustain / my grand endeavours: husbandship and crafting"); serenity ("Forsake me not when my wild hours come"); patience ("achieve in me patience till the thing is done"); solace ("Make me from time to time the gift of the soft shoulder"); love ("Empty my heart toward Thee"); courage ("Let me pace without fear the common path of death"); and forgiveness ("Cross I am sometimes with my little daughter: / fill her eyes with tears. Forgive me, Lord"). The poet concludes his prayer with a summary plea: "Unite my various soul." In petition the poet is attempting to find a meaning in his life and the hope to avoid guilt that threatens to destroy faith.

In order to discover the dimensions of holiness, Berryman recognizes that the rationalist spirit must be abandoned:

> Across the ages certain blessings swarm,
> horrors accumulate, the best men fail:
> Socrates, Lincoln, Christ mysterious.
> Who can search Thee out?
>
> except Isaiah & Pascal, who saw.
> I dare not ask that vision, though a piece of it

> at last in crisis was vouchsafèd me.
> I altered then for good, to become yours.

The poet announces this change in the sixth Address: "Under new management, Your Majesty: / Thine. I have solo'd mine since childhood, since / my father's suicide when I was twelve / blew out my most bright candle faith, and look at me." His faith in his "poor father frantic" shattered, the poet also turned away from his spiritual Father.

>   Confusions & afflictions
> followed my days. Wives left me.
> Bankrupt I closed my doors. You pierced the roof
> twice & again. Finally you opened my eyes.
>
> My double nature fused in that point of time
> three weeks ago day before yesterday.
> Now, brooding thro' a history of the early Church,
> I identify with everybody, even the heresiarchs.

Whether this is the catharsis of Aristotle, Joyce's epiphany, or what the depth psychologists call "insight experience" is unimportant. What matters is Berryman's readiness to accept the will of God rather than obeying only self-will. The poet praises God for his goodness and greatness, but he never blames the evils in his own life or in the world on Him. In this respect the poet resembles Job: "Naked came I out of my mother's womb, and naked shall I return thither: the Lord gave, and the Lord hath taken away; blessed be the name of the Lord" (1:21). Berryman is now able to accept the mutability of the world and the inevitability of God's will; and the final effect of the sequence inalterably moves towards an affirmation of the poet's being and a reversal of failure, concluding with a gesture of surrender to God's will:

> Make me too acceptable at the end of time
> in my degree, which then Thou wilt award.
> Cancer, senility, mania
> I pray I may be ready with my witness.

The final section of *Love & Fame* brings into focus the relation of poet and auditor that Berryman's earlier definition implied. In several lectures, T. S. Eliot referred to the three voices of poetry: the first voice is the poet talking to himself; the second is the voice of the poet addressing an audience; and the third is the voice of the poet speaking through a *persona*. While these voices enable the poet to make statements at once personal and objective and afford him a dimension of personality, they cannot adequately explain poetry as prayer. Berryman's definition, it will be recalled, is that "the poet's soul addresses one other soul only, never mind when." Prayer is not a dialogue with the self, for someone is being addressed; the one being addressed is not like an audience inasmuch as there can be no direct response; and one cannot speak to God through the agency of an assumed role, for God cannot be deceived. The reader does not even overhear these prayers, rather he attends to them as one might meditate on the lives of the saints or consider their prayers—to deepen religious insight—since no critical judgment is possible.

The first three sections of *Love & Fame* constitute the poet's confession. The poet need not declare his sins before the reader, for the reader can offer neither consolation nor forgiveness; the poet need not declare his sins before God, for God is already aware of them. By confessing, however, the poet admits that he does not understand himself, and the confession of his inadequacies and excesses permits him to reach an understanding. Sins may offend God, but they certainly cannot harm Him. Confession to another man cannot restore a lost relationship since that relationship has been permanently affected, that is, things cannot be as they once were in exactly the same way. But since God's love is constant, confessing to Him fully restores the religious relationship. Through faith, a love for God offers forgiveness, and this pardon gives the poet the courage to forgive himself.

Love & Fame is a long poem of confusion and torment, of consolation and salvation. The narrative describes a movement from a life of excesses and uncertainties to one of meditation and waiting. It proceeds from exuberance of language and scurrilous details to elegance of style and homage to the Lord. The poet is a reformed man: doubt becomes Christian acceptance ("I do not understand, but I believe"); self-praise becomes humility ("I am afraid, / I never until now confessed"); absorption in self becomes concern for others ("Ease in their passing my beloved friends, . . . anyone anywhere indeed"); and desolation becomes fulfillment ("I fell back in love with you, Father"). In other words, the religious quest is inexorably tied to the search for identity. Berryman's cry is not for human assistance; reformation comes about through his belief in his reliance on God. Despair, isolation, and fear, though negative states, lead the way to greater consciousness through suffering. And to end the suffering and the search, the poet has only to utter, "According to Thy will." Acceptance gives him the courage to carry on and to be. John Berryman's pilgrimage is from unconsciousness to heightened awareness, from objective thinking to subjective faith, from fear of failure in art and in life to the willingness to risk failure:

Oil all my turbulences as at Thy dictation
I sweat out my wayward works.
Father Hopkins said the only true literary critic is Christ.
Let me lie down exhausted, content with that.

DAVID KALSTONE

Recovery: *The Struggle between Prose and Life*

Recovery, posthumously published, is John Berryman's unfinished and only novel. It is also, in every willed page, a turn away from the dangers and enrichments of his poetry. It was probably being written at the same time as *Delusions, etc.,* verse published after his suicide last year, and the two books should be read as parallel last acts. The word he chose as title for his final poems drums through the novel as well: "delusion" is no longer a bitter, half-affectionate way of designating his writing, but rather the deadly enemy that keeps him from facing down an alcoholism that will destroy him. In an odd way, *Delusions, etc.* and *Recovery* might make up one book— could even be printed in alternating verse and prose, like a dark parody of Dante's *Vita nuova,* Berryman's struggle leading nowhere, certainly not into a lyric Paradise:

> I don't think I will sing
>
> any more just now;
> or ever. I must start
> to sit with a blind brow
> above an empty heart.

Recovery is, then, not a novel in the ordinary sense, but more like fiction struggling to become truth. The hero, Alan Severance, M.D., Litt. D., a former professor of Immunology and Molecular Biology, a winner of the Pulitzer Prize, "twice-invited guest on the Dick Cavett Show (stoned once,

From *The New York Times Book Review* (May 27, 1973). © 1973 by The New York Times Co.

49

and a riot)" becomes very quickly, like Berryman himself, a writer worrying about alcoholism, about writing, and about telling the truth. Not much trouble has been taken to disguise the facts, and that becomes the point. The most novelistic moment is the opening one when Severance, two policemen beside him, a lost week behind him, stands blinking in the light of the house to which he is being returned:

> Wife facing him, cold eyes, her arm outstretched with a short glass —a little smaller than he liked—in her hand. . . . His main Dean and wife off somewhere right, beyond the couch; no doubt others. His baby (qualm sick—he hadn't thought of the baby in six days while they were looking for him as far away as Zurich and Paris) must be asleep upstairs. It must be nine o'clock, it was Sunday night, no doubt about it. The girl had gone. He was looking into his wife's eyes and he was hearing her say: "This is the last drink you will ever take." Even as somewhere up in his feathery mind he said "Screw that," somewhere he also had an unnerving and apocalyptic feeling that this might be true.

A whiff of Berryman's *Dream Songs*—*qualm sick, his feathery mind* —and of the charming evasions of its hero, Henry Pussy-cat, are before our eyes in this overexposed confrontation with his wife and that "last" drink, "a little smaller than he liked." But endearments and evasions are precisely what Severance tries to leave behind. The prose grays and toughens in the hospital scenes that make up the rest of the book: Severance in group encounters (not ordinary A.A. meetings, but special therapy sessions for hospitalized patients); or being hard on himself in his journals; or struggling with the steps of the Alcoholics Anonymous Code, and especially with the first, the one he cannot face ("We admitted that we were powerless over alcohol—that our lives had become unmanageable").

He comes to one group session armed with a written account, "the drama of his spectacular dream." Don't read it, *tell* it, the group leader urges. But Severance, half an eye cocked to his effect, keeps to the manuscript. In the dream, having failed to accept the first half of Step One in the A.A. Code, he wanders out of the hospital on a pass, ends up in a theater on the university campus. A few people are waiting for a German film to be shown, and a pretty, one-eyed girl leads him to his darkened office. They start to make love, but a little boy is awake in another bed nearby. Severance reaches for the girl and wakes up.

The dream account finished, Severance looks up expectantly ("His cards were on the table. . . . He felt ready for the Antarctic") only to find the leader and group lazily unimpressed. The therapist tells him to pretend to *be* the amphitheater, something he does with ease, extending his arms to imitate the shape. In that role, he is asked if he can see Alan Severance. He can.

> "How does he look?"
> "Not so good," Severance considered. "He's tall, very thin. He's badly dressed, I can't see why he came. Inappropriate. He looks like hell."
> "How does that make you feel, Amphitheatre?"
> "I don't give a *damn* about it," he exploded.

The leader then asks Severance to think about the ease with which he did the impersonation and about the changes he'd make in the dream. Perhaps (in the role of theater) he should feel guilty about "poor Alan." "In fact I *won't:* screw him. *I give shows,* all day and even late in the evening (no?), of all *kinds.* Let him solve his own problems—I'll schedule him if I'm free."

Several troubled days pass, and Severance begins to see the dream in a new light; what he had presented proudly as a picture of his "true" life, he suddenly sees as the image of his illness and delusions, his own unblinking, perpetual theatricality, while the ragged "real" Alan stumbles around, unrecognized, untended. As for the girl? Thrown into the account as a pathetic attempt to show one of the female members of the group that his sex life was important here. And the child?

Severance's dream is at the heart of the novel, both because of its content and because he insisted on writing it out for the group. His pleasure in being articulate, his theatricality, keep getting him into trouble, and there is a sense in which this book is nothing more than a series of chastening revisions, refusals of style. A statement written Thursday is re-examined Friday:

> *Comment:* if this statement has literary merit, that I think is not a con, only the product of the fact that a lifelong effort to put things shortly and forcibly is unbreakable, and harmless, except insofar as it may persuade others to share the patient's delusion and so support his illness (any writer's, or even scientist's permanent message perhaps is really just this: *come and share my delusion,* and we will be happy or miserable *together.*)

"Literary merit . . . not a con": "con" not "pro?" or con game? The literary ball is, even here, in play when Severance is trying hard to retire it. And those fears that fame may only support the writer's delusions are the very real ones voiced in Berryman's own penultimate book, *Love & Fame.*

He is clearly in these last books in search of some new and humbling style. *Recovery* doesn't make *Delusions, etc.* a better book, but it helps us see the impulse behind it. The prayers that crowd both of Berryman's last volumes of poetry, designed to chastise the ego, in fact have their own stylistic ease and rhetorical traps. In *Recovery* it is easier for Severance, with his memories of a Catholic boyhood, to accept A.A.'s Second Step ("Came to believe that a Power greater than ourselves could restore us to sanity") than the devastating admissions of the first, that his life was unmanageable.

But the truer narrowing of manner, the truer exercise, comes in the vigilance, the continual revisions of his journals, the fear that "he seemed to have nothing in common with these sensible and aspiring people," members of his "group" so much drabber, so much more conveniently deluded than himself. He submits with charity, clarity and respect to their stories.

For Berryman the new and harrowing departure must have been the almost impossible demand that exposure, truth about the self, might even be divorced from "literary merit." That had been, after all, the secret strength of Henry Pussy-cat in the *Dream Songs,* the resourcefulness with which vulnerability leapt to power, flirted with danger, kept its skeleton, Mr. Bones, charmingly by its side. That very resourcefulness is the enemy of *Recovery,* just as the copious dark renewals of almost 400 dream songs would be a threat to the merciless candor of the Twelve Steps.

Recovery, the new discipline of prose, brought Berryman quite literally to a parting of the ways acknowledged in his leading character's name. For a moment he allows Severance to try seeing it conscientiously another way:

> The even deeper delusion that my science and art *depended* on my drinking, or at least *were* connected with it, could not be attacked directly. Too far down. The cover had to be exploded off, then the undermadness simply withered away.

But *Recovery* remains in fact and necessarily unfinished. The Twelve Steps of Alcoholics Anonymous stand alone at the end of the book like the army of unalterable law.

EDWARD MENDELSON

How to Read Berryman's Dream Songs

Anyone who writes about *The Dream Songs* puts himself in a dangerous position. The poem's landscape resembles in some places a minefield where an explanatory footstep triggers explosions of warning and invective, bursting in the face not only of critics but of all readers. Berryman's mildest warning to his expositors is both a simple renunciation and a complex, tragic claim:

> These Songs are not meant to be understood, you understand.
> They are only meant to terrify & comfort.

Henry (Henry Pussy-cat, Henry House, Mr Bones, Berryman's verbal stand-in, the poem's agonist) maintains that the "ultimate structure" of the Songs is inaccessible to critical analysis, that the songs lack the regular articulated structure that informs "cliffhangers and old serials," that his "large work . . . will appear, / and baffle everybody." One response to bafflement seems to have little chance of success, considering its source:

> When the mind dies it exudes rich critical prose,
> especially about Henry.

Henry knows the etiology of lit. crit., so "back on down boys; don't express yourself," he warns. "His foes are like footnotes" ("comic relief,—absurd"). The structure of the Songs does not articulate deep inside the poem where criticism could rout it out, but is "according to his [Henry's] nature": the skeleton of the poems is "Mr Bones" himself.

From *American Poetry since 1960*, edited by Robert B. Shaw. © 1973 by Edward Mendelson. Carcanet Press, 1973.

Berryman's ludditisms (there are dozens of them) against the critical act amount to an elliptical statement about the poem's organization, its way of being. Unlike most of the recent verse that gets filed away in one's memory under the heading "confessional," Berryman's poem invents a form and language assertively its own, an achievement possible only because Berryman wrestled successfully the master voices of Hopkins, Auden, Cummings and Pound. He also has a strategy of his own, one which looks at first like the familiar confessional self-justification ("Miserable wicked me, / How interesting I am," Auden parodied in another context) but is in fact far more complicated. The title *The Dream Songs* asserts the subjectivity of the poem's occasions: dreams are events absolutely inaccessible to shared or common experience. But neither are they events subject to the organizing power of the dreamer himself. The poem claims to derive from mental activity at a place so deep in the poet's self that the self is no longer in control. Berryman makes an explicit disclaimer of responsibility in a forenote to the completed work: "Many opinions and errors in the Songs are to be referred not to the character Henry, still less to the author, but to the title of the work." That is to say, the songs are not what they appear to be, a transparently autobiographical series of dramatic monologues (trespassed by other voices now and then), but a verbal corporation whose members are uncontrolled responses to—and translations from—the world of experience, and whose rules are flexible and mostly hidden.

Yet the poems are not only dreams but "Songs," and they are always patterned and often musical. Berryman suggested the solution to the paradox of the title *The Dream Songs* in an interview: "Henry? He is a very good friend of mine. I feel entirely sympathetic to him. He doesn't enjoy my advantages of supervision; he just has vision." *Entirely sympathetic:* Berryman is too shrewd not to mean this in its fullest sense, that Berryman's feelings and Henry's are precisely the same. My *advantages of supervision:* though the statements in the poem are in Henry's voice, the Apollonian will to pattern and outline is the poet's own. The portion of the songs which is the most regular in form and meter, most grave in language, is the Opus Posthumous series, written after Henry's "death" (in the center of the poem) when he is most subject to supervision by the living. And an arithmetical precision surrounds the songs, though Henry keeps mum about it: seventy-seven songs in the first volume, *77 Dream Songs* (1964); 77 × 5 in the completed 385 Songs; fourteen (7 + 7) in the Op. Posth. series that opens the second volume, *His Toy, His Dream, His Rest* (1968); seven epigraphs; seven books in all. And the title of the second volume comes from a source no less formal and playfully sedate than the Fitzwilliam Virginal Book, where three songs may be found in sequence with the titles "A Toy," "Giles Farnaby's Dreame," and "His Rest". (The connection was noted by Professor Edith Borroff of Eastern Michigan University; to whom my thanks.)

The songs have a formal frame, and, despite dozens of variations, each Song is built upon a regular pattern of three six-line stanzas, rhymed variously, with the number of feet in each line varying around 5–5–3–5–5–3. Berryman said that the Songs are not individual poems but "parts" of a single poem. As for the structure of that single poem, Berryman allowed in another interview that there is a "plot" to the work, but "its plot is the personality of Henry as he moves on in the world." After sixty years of *The Cantos,* readers are more or less accustomed to poems organized in the autobiographic-picaresque mode, but Berryman's Songs, unlike the Cantos, have a recognizable beginning, middle, and end. A poem may be autobiographical, and Henry's public experiences are the same as Berryman's, but before personal experience can fit into a literary form it must endure a cataclysmic transformation. Berryman wrote that one problem involved in a long poem is "the construction of a world, rather than the reliance upon one existent which is available to a small poem"—and this is an invitation to a phenomenological rather than structural reading of the Songs.

This issue deserves further definition. Everything in a poem that makes its world different from that of life is derived ultimately from the *closure* of art, its beginning and middle and end. In life no one has any clear sense of one's beginning, nor, after the fact, can one have any sense at all of one's end. (In a late Canto Pound put it simply: "No man can see his own end.") One can close one's life, as Berryman did, but one cannot look up at the clock afterwards and begin something new. In an age that worships process and fragmentation, tentativeness and aporia, even the most deliberately fragmented works of literature, even the last shavings of *The Cantos,* still imply the existence of larger closed structures which they are fragments *of.* Though Henry "moves on in the world," and, at the end of the first volume of the Songs, is explicitly "making ready to move on," the whole poem is finished and sealed. (There are, to be sure, miscellaneous Songs outside the main work, but these have the role that Wordsworth hoped to assign his minor poems in relation to his projected masterwork *The Recluse:* "little cells, oratories, and sepulchral recesses" attendant on the central edifice.) The world of *The Dream Songs,* the world that is "according to [Henry's] nature," depends *from* the kind of events that happen there, the verbal events that translate the dream.

Don Quixote met a prisoner who had written his own story, "La vida de Ginés de Pasamonte." "Is it finished yet?" asked Don Quixote. "How can it be finished," answered Ginés, "when my life isn't." Berryman's special kind of transformation of extended personal experience into finished forms is probably his most important achievement, a model of method, if not a model of what to do with a method. At a time when most "confessional" verse tends to the dreary anecdote told in formless chat, Berryman's enterprise towards an idiosyncratically appropriate language, in an appropriate form, is courageous and rare. He said that "we need a poetry that gives up everything —all kinds of traditional forms—and yet remains rich." To make such poetry involves a long and risky effort, and Berryman certainly did not develop his style all at once. His earliest work, written in what he dismissed as "several fumbling years," was written "in what it's convenient to call 'period style', the Anglo-American style of the 1930s, with no voice of my own, learning from middle and later Yeats and from . . . W. H. Auden." But although Berryman managed it well, the voice of the "period style" was insufficient for his purposes. In one early poem, for example, he begins by out-Audening Auden:

> The statue, tolerant through years of weather,
> Spares the untidy Sunday throng its look,
> Spares shopgirls knowledge of the fatal pallor
> Under their evening colour,
> Spares homosexuals, the crippled, the alone,
> Extravagant perception of their failure;
> Looks only, cynical, across them all
> To the delightful Avenue and its lights.

The voice is Auden's but the heart is absent. Yet Berryman does not want to maintain this clinically hard detachment, and he reaches at the end of the poem a tone quite different, a tone which is the poem's real object:

> the dark apartment where one summer
> Night an insignificant dreamer,
> Defeated occupant, will close his eyes
> Mercifully on the expensive drama
> Wherein he wasted so much skill, such faith,
> And salvaged less than the intolerable statue.

Insignificant dreamer . . . wasted so much skill, such faith. The ironic depreciation hides the twin giants, self-aggrandizement and self-pity. Berryman wants to fit himself into the poem, but the voice won't let him do it until the last lines, and even then only with a strained tone and forced bitterness. The early poems are always assured and learned, always excellently sleek examples of their kind, but they never quite land successfully in the fields of egocentricity over which they so longingly hover.

Berryman devised various strategies for making his personal statements, but during the 1940s, at least, most of these strategies were limited to dramatic indirection. Some of the best poems in his second book, *The Dispossessed* (1948, including most of his first book, 1942, titled *Poems*—of course), are the "Nervous Songs," spoken by "the demented priest," "a professor," "the captain," "the young Hawaiian," "the tortured girl," "the man forsaken and obsessed," and so forth. Each poem is a complete dramatic lyric in itself, but together they coalesce into the different aspects of a single "personality," one dissociated and tense, but still ultimately complete and whole. This unification is of course never stated, only implied: each "Nervous Song" speaks for a different kind of "nerve." In *Berryman's Sonnets,* written apparently in 1946 and published when they came of age twenty-one years later, a love affair provides the occasion for a sonnet sequence in which aggressively modern clotted syntax and eclectic diction depend heavily upon Petrarchan form and convention: through Sidney by Hopkins. Here, as in the later poems of *The Dispossessed,* Berryman began to twist received syntax in his first experiments towards the language of *The Dream Songs,* but his essentially traditional forms (for some short poems he even borrowed terza rima) still restricted the force of the idiovocal statements he was trying to learn to make.

With *Homage to Mistress Bradstreet* (1956) Berryman first successfully fused his by now perfected syntax into a thoroughly personal form and subject. This remarkable poem, probably the most consistently successful that Berryman ever wrote, has a narrative "plot" which may be described briefly. The poet imagines the body of Anne Bradstreet, and "summons" her from the centuries; she speaks her history, which, through one of Berryman's best imaginative leaps, turns out to be a grimly witty narrative of modern, almost suburban isolation and detachment, set in Puritan New England; Berryman and Anne, each to the other a ghostly presence, speak a dialogue, and each *almost* takes the other for a lover. But Anne escapes the (to her) temptation offered by the twentieth-century voice, and asserts her seventeenth-century independence. Berryman's voice returns to the poem only after Anne's death. The structural device through which Berryman first creates Anne Bradstreet, then is thrown off by his own creation, might appear to be a conventionally modernist sleight-of-hand, a familiar form of play with the status of appearances, but Berryman summons a vast emotional universe of personal loss and assertion to the device, and succeeds in rendering it as deeply moving as it is artificial. The tortured syntax, here as earlier borrowed from Hopkins but rendered insistently secular, finally enjoys a wide enough range of situations to render into its language. Berryman moves easily from the grave to the comic, as in the arrangements for Anne's marriage, her resigned loss of sensual "bliss" to religious severity:

vanity & the follies of youth took hold of me;
then the pox blasted, when the Lord returned.
That year for my sorry face
so-much-older Simon burned,
so Father smiled, with love. Their will be done.
He to me ill lingeringly, learning to shun
a bliss, a lightning blood
vouchsafed, what did seem life. I kissed his Mystery.

Or the astonishingly persuasive rendering of her first childbirth:

No. No. Yes! everything down
hardens I press with horrible joy down
my back cracks like a wrist
shame I am voiding oh behind it is too late

hide me forever I work thrust I must free
now I all muscles & bone concentrate
what is living from dying?
Simon I must leave you so untidy
Monster you are killing me Be sure
I'll have you later Women do endure
I can *can* no longer
and it passes the wretched trap whelming and I am me

drencht & powerful, I did it with my body!
One proud tug greens Heaven. Marvellous,
unforbidding Majesty.
Swell, imperious bells. I fly.

(There is little that is quite as intense and various as this in all of English poetry.) And finally, Berryman's meditation after Anne's funeral:

Headstones stagger under great draughts of time
after heads pass out, and their world must reel
speechless, blind in the end
about its chilling star, thrift tuft,
whin-cushion—nothing. Already with the wounded flying
dark air fills, I am a closet of secrets dying

. . . .

> O all your ages at the mercy of my loves
> together lie at once, forever or
> so long as I happen.
> In the rain of pain & departure, still
> Love has no body and presides the sun,
> and elfs from silence melody. I run.
> Hover, utter still,
> a sourcing   whom my lost candle like the firefly loves.

(The phrase "Love . . . presides the sun" recalls the final line of the *Paradiso*, "L'amor che muove il sole e il altre stelle," and suddenly deepens Berryman's conversation with the dead.)

The lost and isolated voice of the poem gains force through its reduplication in the seventeenth and twentieth centuries, but Berryman was not satisfied. *The Dream Songs* resume his quest for a single voice, but the quest is not completed or resolved until the middle of the work. In *77 Dream Songs* Henry "has a friend, never named, who addresses him as Mr Bones and variants thereof," and usually engages Henry in the midst of one of his bursts of blackface or burnt-cork monologue—another distancing pose which Berryman managed to give up before too long.

> You may be right Friend Bones.
> Indeed you is. Dey flyin ober de world,
> de pilots, ober ofays. Bit by bit
> our immemorial moans
>
> brown down to all dere moans. I flees that, sah.

What is characteristically Berryman's in this sort of passage is not the distancing dialect so much as the sudden shift to a vaguely "high" style in "our immemorial moans," which, in addition to the effect of the dialect, distances the Song doubly. Berryman is always ready to walk along the dangerous cliffs of self-indulgence ("O ho alas alas / When will indifference come, I moan & rave"), but only by taking risks can he achieve the mutual conciliation of the colloquial and the formal which the Songs propose, bend to the breaking point again and again, and finally ratify and consummate.

The risks of Berryman's style are great (rhymes on "O" or "pal" have little merit, unless some lies in their nose-thumbing insouciance towards The Tradition), but the risks of his subject are greater. Although there is no lyric or narrative stance available in literature that is more tedious than the Wild Old Wicked Man, Berryman persists in delighting in it. Leaving aside for a moment the "plot" of the poem, one can approach it usefully according to Berryman's own suggestions. In the interview where he denied the presence of an "ulterior structure," he indicated that what is most important in the poem's organization is the *kind of event* that happens in any of its various territories: "Some of the Songs are in alphabetical order [117–122, for example, allowing an obvious inversion of the first two phrases of 118; and so much for narrative pattern]; but, mostly, they just belong to areas of hope and fear that Henry is going through at a given time." The primary event in the Songs is of course the dream, yet what ordinary language knows as dreams are imitated rarely. Abrupt endings, sudden shifts in referent and style (recalling to its source the technique named by MacNeice the "dream parataxis"), fantasies of sexual power and weakness, all refer obliquely to dreams, but Berryman uses the word "dream" in a wider sense. Disputing Freud, he writes in a late Song that "a dream is a panorama / of the whole mental life." This statement is a revision of the romantic conception of the dream—a conception elevated by Freud from poetic assertion to scientific dogma—which is premised on the belief that dreams are messages from the psychic interior. When Berryman elevates his domestic miseries and petty wrongs into the material of secondary epic—without, apparently, it ever occurring to him that the subject might not deserve so much paper and type— he adopts a standard romantic convention, but does so partly in order to invert it. Berryman's most characteristic literary *manner* is that of a Wordsworth *in extremis* ("Wordsworth, thou form almost divine, cried Henry"), aware of the real pain in the world: his poems intimations of mortality, tranquillity (at best) recollected in emotion; his great work not a preparation for future effort, but a record of loss, a Postlude, or the decay of the poet's world. But instead of listening, resolving, communing, Henry acts, and his most characteristic *action* is scrambling or stumbling up to proceed again, after one more defeat, the death of one more friend, one more hollow and temporary pleasure. Henry's dreams give no comfort. Freud suggested that dreams are the guardians of sleep. Not Henry's dreams:

> I can't go into the meaning of the dream
> except to say a sense of total LOSS
> afflicted me thereof:
> an absolute disappearance of continuity & love
> and children away at school, the weight of the cross,
> and everything is what it seems.

Everything is what it seems: the loss is real; no romance or celebration can remedy it. Berryman's stance refuses the private luxuries of the romantic vision, a privacy he finds in its most limiting form in Wallace Stevens. The song "So Long? Stevens" brilliantly demolishes this extreme version of romantic self-consciousness:

> He lifted up, among the actuaries,
> a grandee crow. Ah ha & he crowed good
> . . . .
> What was it missing, then, at the man's heart
> so that he does not wound? It is our kind
> to wound, as well as utter
>
> a fact of happy world. That metaphysics
> he hefted up until we could not breathe
> the physics.

Berryman's dreams, for all their irresponsibility, are responsive, openly conscious as well as self-conscious, or so Berryman claims. Again from an interview: "What is wrong with poetry now is that poets won't take on observation, dealing with what is sent into individuals from the universe. It would seem to be that the job of the poet, if I may speak of such a ridiculous thing, is to handle the signs, to field them as in baseball."

So much does Berryman claim for his art. But do the events in the dreams or in their Songs stand up to the claim? Berryman's notion of "what is sent into individuals from the universe" is necessarily determined by his idea of the "universe" itself. *Homage to Mistress Bradstreet* is among other things an historical narrative, yet its central statements are "about" isolation and love. Anne Bradstreet seems at times an historical convenience. She is not a Yeatsian "mask" but a *projection*. In *The Dream Songs* the poem's universe is that of a man at the extremes of noisy passion and unhappiness, but also, alas, when considered outside his world of private eros and thanatos, *l'homme moyen social*. Berryman and Lowell admire each other enthusiastically in print, but their phenomenal worlds are vastly different: where Lowell takes everything in the *polis* for his subject, Berryman's social commentary—except where the subject is at least marginally "literary," as in the trials of Soviet poets—is nearly as crazy as the later Yeats, and much less sonorous. "I'd like to write political poems, but aside from *Formal Elegy* [which hovers somewhere near John Kennedy], I've never been moved to do so." (Actually this is not quite true: *Poems* and *The Dispossessed* include some political verses reading like watered Auden. And Berryman once described the early "Winter Landscape" as a poem which indicates "what is necessary to be said—but which the poet refuses to say—about a violent world." This borders on the sophistic, but Berryman's refusal to talk about that which he cannot talk about is finally an honorable one. Graves's subject matter is no wider than Berryman's, but Graves decorously writes lyrics while Berryman raises problems for himself by exploding his discontents into epic.)

What is sent into Henry from the universe falls mostly under the vivid scarlet rubrics of death, survival, love, and fame. To the right and left of him fall so many poets; so many deaths seek him out:

> I'm cross with god who has wrecked this generation.
> First he seized Ted, then Richard, Randall, and now Delmore.
> In between he gorged on Sylvia Plath.

Roethke, Blackmur, Jarrell, Schwartz, Plath—Berryman's staying power seems so much more strained, his survival so difficult, compared with the losses that surround him. Not that he is himself exempt. The very first Song in the whole work marvels at Henry's persistence after a "departure" from felicity and coherence, a departure that the line following relates elliptically to the Fall:

> All the world like a woolen lover
> once did seem on Henry's side.
> Then came a departure.
> Thereafter nothing fell out as it might or ought.
> I don't see how Henry, pried
> open for all the world to see, survived.

And throughout the first volume Henry refuses to wake, or is mutilated, blinded, or stalled:

> They sandpapered his plumpest home. (So capsize.)
> They took away his crotch.

And

> —What happen then, Mr Bones?
> —I had a most   marvellous piece of luck. I died.

(This ends book 1.) And

> I am obliged to perform in complete darkness
> operations of great delicacy
> on my self.
> —Mr Bones, you terrifies me.
> No wonder they don't pay you. Will you die?
> —My
>   friend, I succeeded. Later.

And when he isn't dying, Henry spends much of his time in hospital, immobilized.

The second volume of the Songs, *His Toy, His Dream, His Rest,* begins with Henry's "posthumous" works, when "Good nature is over" and he lies in "a *nice* pit":

> I am breaking up
> and Henry now has come to a full stop—
> vanisht his vision, if there was, & fold
> him over himself quietly.

The grave is not without its consolations, however, and when Henry's responsibilities become an issue at law, "this august court will entertain the plea / Not Guilty by reason of death." Though Henry's trial is interrupted by the news that he "may be returning to life / adult & difficult," no one need worry. After he has been dug up, and has "muttered for a double rum / waving the mikes away," two weeks later he returns to the graveyard, desperate to get back underground:

> insomnia-plagued, with a shovel
> digging like mad, Lazarus with a plan
> to get his own back, a plan, a strategem
> no newsman will unravel.

In the next book, the metaphor of Henry's death translates itself, reasonably enough, into a long stay in hospital, and a more or less ordinary narrative resumes. By book 6 it is not Henry who is elegized but Delmore Schwartz who is granted a long series of elegiac Songs before Berryman sets him "free of my love," in the conventional end-of-elegy hope that he may "recover & be whole."

Henry's own elegies also end with consolation. Set against his reiterated, battological dyings are his movings-on ("recoveries" is too strong a word), which are figuratively the "movement" of the poem. The areas of hope and fear in which Henry finds himself have their geographical analogues—from India, where "his migrant heart" hurts at the thought of stability and repeated Spring, to Japan, where in the permanence of a temple he remembers that "Elsewhere occurs . . . loss," and finally, amazingly "in love with life / which has produced this wreck," to Ireland, the site of the seventh and longest book of the Songs. Always Henry is surprised at his own resilience:

> it is a wonder that, with in each hand
> one of his own mad books and all,

> ancient fires for eyes, his head full
> & his heart full, he's making ready to move on.

Moving-on in his epic impetus. With no Ithaca or Penelope (or dozens of them, which means the same thing), no historical destiny or Roman Imperium, no Beatrice or St. Francis to draw him onwards, his straitened private energy must suffice.

Whether or not it *does* suffice for almost four hundred Songs is open to question, and one suspects, as one nears the end of the poem, that energy-scrambling-for-a-system-to-act-in is a theme pathetically at variance with the scale of the whole enterprise. Berryman suspects this also, and Henry's energy does have contexts, although they seem more and more narrow as the poem proceeds. Part way through *His Toy, His Dream, His Rest* the interlocutor and friend who addresses Henry as Mr Bones drops almost entirely from sight, and Henry is left to speak alone. Berryman finally achieves the single voice he worked towards for thirty years, but one might be dismayed by the uses to which he applies it. (Although so assertively single a voice can only, perhaps, be assertively single-minded.) Henry's chief interests, especially in the later songs when the elegiac note has faded, are two, and the poem stutters over them almost incessantly: Henry's delight in, and difficulties with, (1) fame and (2) women. His response to publicity seems rather out of proportion, as if the occasional notice granted a very good minor poet by media that glut themselves on "celebrity" could give that poet the public currency of a Yeats, or even a Churchill. What fame he does have, and the grateful attention of his friends, fully justify a supple and active response like this one:

> he staked his claim upon obscurity:
> a prayer to be left alone
> escaped him sometimes or for a middle zone
> where he could be & become both unknown & known
> listening & not.

("Obscurity" is of course both "difficulty of interpretation" and "lack of recognition.") But a Song that begins by musing, "Fan-mail from foreign countries, is that fame?" and continues through a catalogue of awards and interviews, to end with the throwaway line, "A lone letter from a young man: that is fame"—can only sound hollow and mawkish. (It is just conceivable, though unlikely, that this is self-parody. But Berryman *likes* the subject too much for that.)

Nor does the unedifying spectacle of Henry's relations with women have much to recommend it. Early in the book Berryman manages some fine dramatic absurdity:

> Filling her compact & delicious body
> with chicken páprika, she glanced at me
> twice.
> Fainting with interest, I hungered back
> and only the fact of her husband & four other people
> kept me from springing on her.

And later he sounds disingenuous at finding the situation reversed:

> a Belfast man
> last night made a pass at my wife: Henry, who had passed out,
> was horrified
> to hear this news when he woke.

But usually he is much nastier than this, and seems to realize it fairly well—which does not improve the situation. The women of *The Dream Songs* are divided roughly into two familiar classes: those he went to bed with, and those he did not. The former find themselves dismissed with an epithet ("whereon he lay / the famous daughter"), the latter idealized and transfigured, their names prefixed by "Lady." In neither case does there seem to be much participation ("Women serve my turn"—*Homage to Mistress Bradstreet*). In both the relation is with another human being as object, whether debased or idolized, which is why "He was always in love with the wrong woman," and why, for all his sexual energy and success, he finds sex degrading: "Them lady poets must not marry," and Berryman thinks one of those ladies is even "too noble-O" for sexual experience.

Death is the heaviest burden, drawing the Songs constantly to earth. Survival, moving-on, is the essential form taken by the poem's energy. The objects of that energy become the title of Berryman's next book, *Love & Fame:* and in reference both to that book and to the Songs, the first term in the title seems euphemistic, the second hyperbolic. (Berryman himself may have seen the title in an ironic light, as its possible literary source, Pope's "Eloisa to Abelard", bears a reminder of defeat: "Lost in a convent's solitary gloom . . . There dy'd the best of passions, Love and Fame.") The deepest goal of Henry's energy, its ultimate use, is the familiar lowest common denominator, power. "Love" in Berryman's poetry stands for the exercise of sexual power, or the worship of sexual power in idealized women. His use of fame is best described by Elias Canetti:

> Fame is not fastidious about the lips which spread it. So long as
> there are mouths to reiterate the one name, it does not matter
> whose they are. The fact that to the seeker after fame they are

indistinguishable from each other and are all counted as equal shows that this passion has its origin in the experience of crowd manipulation.

(*Crowds and Power*)

Berryman writes often that he prefers the praise of his friends to the baying of the crowd, but taking into consideration all his references to fame, the use of this passage does not appear unjust.

But Berryman is no naif. His power-plays are not simply subject matter for his poem, but are enacted in the poem itself. Berryman is smart enough to realize that he presents himself in the least prepossessing manner he can imagine: his personal offensiveness is not accidental but entirely deliberate, for what he wants from his readers is their critical approval despite their personal disapproval, their assent despite their awareness of what they are assenting *to*. What Berryman hopes to enjoy is not the power to delight or enchant, but the power to control those who are both conscious and unwilling.

American poets have never been able to consider themselves part of a clerisy or of any comfortably well-defined class, and for that reason have always been far more concerned with power than their European contemporaries. Berryman's generation of poets seems to have been more obsessed with the attainment and use of power than any other in America, and its obsession proved costly. Jarrell, Shapiro, Lowell, Roethke (of whom Berryman said "He was interested in love and money; and if he had found a combination of them in something else, he would have dedicated himself to it instead of poetry"), Berryman himself—all tried or still try to exert more control than words ever made possible over people, politics, the literary pecking-order, and time which no one controls.

Yet no matter how irritating or boring or murky the Songs can be on occasion, they remain the most courageous and interesting poetic experiment of their decade. When they succeed, when they open into something rich and strange, no other poem in their historical neighborhood can equal them. Few who have written on Berryman have been able to avoid quoting one in particular of the early Songs entire, and there is no reason to buck the trend:

> There sat down, once, a thing on Henry's heart
> so heavy, if he had a hundred years
> & more, & weeping, sleepless, in all them time
> Henry could not make good.
> Starts again always in Henry's ears
> the little cough somewhere, an odour, a chime.
>
> And there is another thing he has in mind
> like a grave Sienese face a thousand years

would fail to blur the still profiled reproach of. Ghastly,
with open eyes, he attends, blind.
All the bells say: too late. This is not for tears;
thinking.

But never did Henry, as he thought he did,
end anyone and hacks her body up
and hide the pieces, where they may be found.
He knows: he went over everyone, & nobody's missing.
Often he reckons, in the dawn, them up.
Nobody is ever missing.

This song, number 29, exemplifies in an unusually clear and regular manner
the paratactic method by which almost all the Songs are organized. The first
sestet describes an experience in intensely private terms; the "thing" is on
Henry's heart, the cough "in Henry's ears." In the second sestet he notices
or remembers the world outside, and does so through a metaphor ("a grave
Sienese face") whose vehicle at least is publicly accessible, although the tenor
is only an unspecified guilty "reproach." Rather than locating sound "in
Henry's ears," it is the bells, outside, that speak; and although blind, Henry
at least "attends." Finally, in the last sestet, he acknowledges almost in defeat
the social world of others, all those who persist in surviving despite his dreams
of violence (the cause of the "reproach" is now identified), who remind him
that the thing on his heart is only private. This neat enactment of Husserlian
epistemology (awareness of self, things, others) recurs throughout *The Dream
Songs,* but often in reverse order—with the awareness of others narrowing
down to awareness of self—or in some other variant pattern. And this paratactic method informs the relations between Songs as well as within them. The
two final Songs provide perhaps the best example. In the first Henry stands
over his father's grave, initially with restrained anger, then in stagy fury:

> I spit upon this dreadful banker's grave
> who shot his heart out in a Florida dawn
> O ho alas alas
> When will indifference come, I moan & rave
> I'd like to scrabble till I got right down
> away down under the grass
>
> and ax the casket open ha.

The poem is bloody with death and separations. But the very last Song sub-
sumes the death of one man into the cycle of seasons, where no endings are
final:

My daughter's heavier. Light leaves are flying.
Everywhere in enormous numbers turkeys will be dying
and other birds, and all their wings.
They never greatly flew. Did they wish to?
I should know. Off away somewhere once I knew
such things.

Or good Ralph Hodgson back then did, or does.
The man is dead whom Eliot praised. My praise
follows and flows too late.
Fall is grievy, brisk. Tears behind the eyes
almost fall. Fall comes to us as a prize
to rouse us toward our fate.

The dead father in the previous Song balances the growing, "heavier" daughter
in this one. Henry's rage against his father is transmuted into praise for the
dead poet, his obsession with the past metamorphosed into concern for his
daughter and her (implied) future, his destruction of his father's casket transfigured into his calm respect for the permanence of his house, also wooden:

My house is made of wood and it's made well,
unlike us. My house is older than Henry;
that's fairly old.

And the Songs close heart-rendingly with a meditation and plaint on the incoherence of the world, the dualism that divides soul from flesh and so from
all "things," the discontinuity that makes Henry scold his child, "heavy" and
a "thing," but loved:

If there were a middle   ground between things and the soul
or if the sky resembled more the sea,
I wouldn't have to scold

my heavy daughter.

And at the same moment that it closes, the poem thrusts itself out of its frame
into the undefined future.

Love & Fame (1970), which lies outside the range of this survey, continues Berryman's development of a personal voice. He drops the Henry-
doppelgänger and speaks autobiographically and directly in his own name.
The title of one poem, "Regents' Professor Berryman's Crack on Race," would
have been impossibly direct only a few years earlier, but with directness came
a dangerous facility and self-importance. The book makes pleasant reading,
but the struggles of The Dream Songs have diminished to chat. Berryman's

last book, *Delusions, etc.*, indicates that the mad-lyric mode was Berryman's mainstay to the end, intensely personal, slightly desperate, persistent in its survivals, its paradoxes, and its celebrations.

Finally the survivals gave out. Most of this essay had been written when the news came that the body of John Berryman had been found on the bank of the Mississippi River near the campus of the University of Minnesota. Berryman had walked to the railing of a bridge, waved to a passerby, and stepped off. Whatever the pressures and necessities may have been to which Berryman finally yielded, we probably have no right to know them. But his wave of farewell, so unlikely in those circumstances, was a thoroughly public gesture: Henry's last.

JOHN BAYLEY

John Berryman:
A Question of Imperial Sway

Berryman, like Lowell and perhaps more so, is the poet of the time whose size and whose new kind of stylistic being shrugs off any attempt at enclosure. But one thing about both is obviously true. *Life Studies, Notebook,* and *Dream Songs* show that verses, old-fashioned *numbers,* are still capable of being what Byron wanted—"a form that's large enough to swim in and talk on any subject that I please"—and not only the capable but the imperially inevitable form. Compare their talking verse—dense as lead one moment and light as feathers the next—with the brutal monotony of that dimension of talking prose which Hemingway evolved, and which Miller, Mailer, Burroughs, and others have practiced in their various ways. In the *Dream Songs* and *Love & Fame* Berryman makes that kind of prose appear beside his verse not only doltish and limited but incapable even of straight talking.

Formalistically speaking, curiosity has no place in our reception of the Berryman experience. The medium makes the message all too clear. In spite of all the loose ends of talk, the name-dropping and the facts given, we have no urge to find out with whom, when, why, and what; and this is not a bit like Byron. "I perfect my metres," writes Berryman, "until no mosquito can get through." Let's hope he's right. In every context today we sup full of intimacies. The group therapy of our age is its total explicitness; privacy and reticence have lost all artistic function and status: and so a lack of curiosity is not abnormal in the reader or even unusual. But Berryman seals off curiosity

From *Contemporary Poetry in America,* edited by Robert Boyers. © 1973 by Skidmore College, © 1974 by Schocken Books, Inc.

with a degree of artistic justification against which there is no *ad hominem* appeal.

The implications of these two phenomena—a new verse and a new self in it—seem to me what discussion of Berryman has to be about. There is no point in prosing along with detailed technical discussion of his verse, for its idioms and techniques are all completely self-justifying and self-illuminating.

"Poetry," said Thoreau, "is a piece of very private history, which unostentatiously lets us into the secret of a man's life." The matter would only have been put thus by a North American, at once orphan and contemporary of romanticism. The triumph of Berryman's poetry is that in becoming itself it has learnt how to undermine the apparent relevance to the poetic art of that niggling adverb: by flinging it suddenly on its back he has revealed that utter and shameless ostentation can become the same thing as total form, and virtually the same thing as the impersonality which our knowledge and love of the traditions of poetry condition us to expect. To let us in unostentatiously usually means today to be *confiding*. Elizabeth Bishop makes her Fish her poem, but is at the same time both confiding and self-justifying, as is such a typical poem of Wallace Stevens's final period as "The Planet on the Table." So at the other extreme of length and technique is *Paterson*. These confidences produce the impression that the poet is (to turn Stevens's own words against him) "an obstruction, a man / Too exactly himself." Such confidences cease to be important when they are made by a poet as far back as Wordsworth, but in our own time they are very important because they collapse style, the only thing that enables us to guess at the authority of a modern poet. At the moment they are not "soluble in art" (the phrase from the prologue to *Berryman's Sonnets*) though they may dissolve in time—or the whole poem may.

One thing which that in other respects overrated European author Beckett shares with Berryman and Lowell is the masterly inability to confide. None of them are deadpan: indeed all seem very forthcoming, but what Berryman calls "imperial sway" (Pound was "not fated like his protegé Tom or drunky Jim / or hard-headed Willie for imperial sway") manifests in them as a kind of regal blankness: it is not for them to know or care whether or not their subjects are listening.

Berryman cannot be "exactly himself," for he is so present to us that the thought of the real live Berryman is inconceivable, and scarcely endurable. His poetry creates the poet by a process opposite to that in which a novelist creates a character. We get to know Macbeth, say, or Leopold Bloom, to the point where we enter into him and he becomes a part of us; like Eurydice in Rilke's poem he is *geben aus wie hundertfacher vorrat*—bestowed upon the world as a multitudinous product. Berryman, by contrast, creates himself as an entity so single that we cannot share with or be a part of him. Such an autobiography as his does not make him real in the fictional sense. Everything is there, but so is the poetry, "language / so twisted and posed in a form / that it not only expresses the matter in hand / but adds to the stock of available reality."

That is Blackmur, one of Berryman's heroes: his wisdom put into a lapidary stanza and three quarters, ending with the poet's comment: "I was never altogether the same man after *that*." *That* is after all, though, a conventional formalistic and Mallarmean utterance, and the great apparent size of Berryman and Lowell is that they have achieved a peculiarly American breakthrough: the emancipation of poetry from its European bondage as *chose preservée* and its elevation into a form which can challenge and defeat the authority and easygoingness of prose at every point. As Valéry perceived when he coined the phrase, Europe can never get over its tradition that poetry occupies a special place, and that prose has grown all round it like some rank and indestructibly vital weed, isolating it in an unmistakable enclave. Wallace Stevens concedes the same thing, in his practice, in his Jamesian persona ("John D. Rockefeller drenched in attar of roses" as Mary McCarthy put it) and in his comment that "French and English constitute a single language" (exclusive of American presumably). Looking back in England we see that Wordsworth, the great seeming liberator, was more subjected than he knew; as he grew older the "poetic" engulfed him; Coleridge's attempts to write a "poetry that affects not to be poetry" renounce all tension, and lack even the circumambulatory virtues of *Biographia Literaria*. But whatever the difficulties of emancipation American writers had to overcome, this was not one of them. Whitman showed the way. Pound, as he says, "made a pact" with him, and the *Cantos*, no less than *Leaves of Grass*, never strike us as tacitly admitting that the same kind of thing could be or is being said in prose.

For one thing, the "I" is wholly different. Coleridge's and Wordsworth's "I" is usually themselves, the "man speaking to men," in either verse or prose. Even in such a masterpiece as *Resolution and Independence* "I" is not metamorphosed by the medium, by the poetry. Hence, even there, the poetry is not doing its poetic job to the hilt. A prose Wordsworth is, or would be, perfectly acceptable, but a prose Whitman "I" or a prose "Henry" Berryman would be intolerable. To make a poetic "I" as free and even more free, as naturalistic and even more so, than a prose ego, and yet quite different: that is the secret of the American new poetry which appears to reach its apogee in Lowell and Berryman. By this they show not only that verse can still do more than prose, but that the more closely it is involved in the contingent, the more it can manifest itself as the aesthetically and formalistically absolute.

I must return to this point in a moment, but let us first dispose of Berryman's own comments about the "I" of the *Dream Songs*.

> Many opinions and errors in the songs are to be referred not to the character Henry, still less to the author, but to the title of the work. . . . The poem then, whatever its wide cast of characters, is essentially about an imaginary charactaer, (not the poet, not me) named Henry, a white American in early middleage in blackface, who has suffered irreversible loss and talks about himself sometimes in the first person, sometimes in the third, sometimes even in the second; he has a friend, never named, who addresses him as Mr. Bones and variants thereof.

This of course is rubbish in one sense, but in another it is a perfectly salutary and justified reminder by the author that when he puts himself into a poem he formalizes himself. To labor the point again: Mailer is always Mailer, but Berryman in verse is Berryman in verse. That does not mean that he is exaggerated or altered or dramatized: on the contrary, if he were so the poem would be quite different and much more conventional. Berryman of course deeply admired and was much influenced by Yeats, who helped him to acquire the poet's imperial sway over himself and us, but he is not in the least concerned with Yeats's doctrine of the Masks, and with trying out contrasting dramatic representations of the self; such a cumbrous and courtly device of European poetry does not go with American directness and the new American expansiveness. Why bother to put on masks when you can make the total creature writing all the form that is needed?

Byron and Pushkin also emphasised the formal nature of their poetic device, often in facetious terms and in the poems themselves—making characters meet real friends and themselves, etc.—Berryman's gambit to emphasize a comparable formalism has a long history. None the less his comments are misleading in so far as they imply something like a dramatic relation between characters and ideas in the *Dream Songs*. The hero of Meredith's *Modern Love* would be as impossible in any other art context as Henry, but he is in a dramatic situation, and in that situation we can—indeed we are positively invited to—judge him, as we judge Evgeny Onegin. And to judge here is to become a part of. The heroes of such poems with dramatic insides to them are not taken as seriously as heroes in prose; they are unstable and frenetic, capable of all or nothing, because we do not get accustomed to them: they appear and vanish in each line and rhyme. None the less they are stable enough to be sat in judgment on, and Berryman's Henry is not. Ultimately, the formal triumph of Henry is that because he is not us and never could be, he has—like our own solitary egos—passed beyond judgment.

The paradox is complete, and completely satisfying. Clearly Berryman knew it. "These songs are not meant to be understood you understand / They are only meant to terrify and comfort" (366). But though it is not dramatic the interior of the *Dream Songs* is grippingly exciting, deep, detailed and spacious. Moreover it is not in the least claustrophobic in the sense in which the world of Sylvia Plath involuntarily constricts and imprisons: on the contrary, like the world of early Auden it is boisterously exhilarating and liberating. It has no corpus of exposition, sententiousness, or pet theory, which is why it is far more like *Modern Love* or *Evgeny Onegin* than the *Cantos* or, say, *The Testament of Beauty*. It never expounds. Another thing in common with the Meredith and Pushkin is the nature of the pattern. Each "Number" is finished, as is each of the intricate stanzas of their long poems, but in reading the whole we go on with curiosity unslaked and growing, as if reading a serial. The separate numbers of the *Dream Songs* published in magazines could not of course indicate this serial significance, which is not sequent, but taken as a whole reveals unity.

The Russian formalists have a term *pruzhina*, referring to the "sprung" interior of a successful poetic narration, the bits under tension which keep the parts apart and the dimensions open and inviting. Thus, in *Evgeny Onegin*, Tatiana is a heroine, a story-book heroine, and a parody of such a heroine; while Evgeny is, conversely, a "romantic" hero for her, a parody of such a hero, and a hero. The spring keeps each separable in the formal art of the poem, and the pair of them in isolation from each other. I am inclined to think that Berryman's quite consciously contrived *pruzhina* in the *Dream Songs* is a very simple and very radical one: to hold in opposed tension and full view the poet at his desk at the moment he was putting down the words, and the words themselves in their arrangement on the page as poetry. When one comes to think of it, it is surprising that no one has thought of exploiting this basic and intimate confrontation before. (The weary old stream of consciousness is something quite other, being composed like any other literature in the author's head, irrespective of where he was and what he was being at the time.) The extreme analogy of such a confrontation would be Shakespeare weaving into the words of "To be or not to be," or "Tomorrow and tomorrow and tomorrow" such instant reactions and reflections as "Shall I go for a piss now or hold it till I've done a few more lines"—or—"I wonder what size her clitoris is"—or—"We must be out of olive oil." Of course there is no effect of interpretation in Berryman; but the spring does hold apart,

and constantly, a terrifying and comforting image of the poet as *there*—
wrestling in his flesh and in his huddle of needs—while at the same time poetry
is engraving itself permanently on the page. It is this that keeps our awed
and round-eyed attention more than anything else: our simultaneous sense
of the pain of being such a poet, and of the pleasure of being able to read
his poetry.

It is also instrumental in our not judging. The poet is not asking us to
pity his racked state, or to understand and sympathize with the wild bad
obsessed exhibitionist behavior it goes with. These things are simply there,
as formal achievement, and Henry James, that great Whitman fan, would
oddly enough, I am sure, have understood and been gratified by it. He
suggests it in the advice he gave to the sculptor Andersen about how to convey
the tension and the isolation in an embracing sculptured couple.

> Make the creatures palpitate, and their flesh tingle and flush, and
> their internal economy proceed and their bellies ache and their
> bladders fill—all in the mystery of your art.

"Hard-headed Willie" in his magisterial way, and with his "blood, imagination, intellect running together," might also have given a clue; but when he
says "I walk through a long school-room questioning" or—

> I count those feathered balls of soot
> The moorhen guides upon the stream
> To silence the envy in my thought.

it is well understood that he is doing no such thing. This is the rhetoric of
the moment, not its apparent actuality; the thought he is silencing and the
questions he asks have all been cooked up in the study afterward. His air
of immediate imperiousness, with himself and us, is a bit of a fraud, and
this seasons our admiration with an affectionate touch of decision. Yeats is
the boss whose little tricks we can see through and like him the more for:
all the same, we do judge.

And with Berryman we don't; the spring device forbids it. How judge
someone who while talking and tormenting himself is also writing a poem
about the talk and torment? Except that we know, deeper down, that this
effect *is* a formalistic device and that Berryman's control of it is total. And
this knowledge makes us watch the taut spring vibrating with even rapter
attention. There is a parallel with the formalism so brilliantly pulled off by
Lowell in *Life Studies,* where the poetry seemed itself the act of alienation
and cancellation, as if poet and subject had died the instant the words hit
the paper. The formal device or emblem above the door framing the two

collections might be, in Lowell's case, a speech cut off by the moment of death: in Berryman's, a Word condemned to scratch itself eternally, in its chair and at its desk.

Lowell forsook that frame, and in *Notebook* approaches the idiom of the *Dream Songs* (I waive any inquiry, surely bound to be inconclusive, into questions of mutual sympathetic influencing). But in achieving the note of continuing casualness, in contriving to stay alive as it were, *Notebook* remains individual pieces, fascinating in themselves, but lacking the tension that makes *Dream Songs* a clear and quivering serial. The comparison may be unfair, because *Notebook* may not be intended to be a narrative poem, but it shows how much and how successfully *Dream Songs* is one, and *Love & Fame*.

If I am right in thinking that Berryman's aim is to hold in opposed tension and full view the poet and his words, I may also be right in supposing that *Homage to Mistress Bradstreet* was inspired, in the form it took, by the same preoccupation. What seems to have been the donnée for Berryman there was the contrast between the woman as she presumably was, and the poems that she wrote. Berryman's ways of suggesting this are on the whole crude—I do not see they could be anything else; but the idea obviously fascinates him. Why couldn't her poems be *her,* as he wills his to be him?—the poem celebrates a gulf and a contrast.

> When by me in the dusk my child sits down
> I am myself. Simon, if it's that loose,
> Let me wiggle it out.
> You'll get a bigger one there, & bite.
> How they loft, how their sizes delight and grate.
> The proportioned, spiritless poems accumulate.
> And they publish them
> away in brutish London, for a hollow crown.

Homage to Mistress Bradstreet is far from being a masterpiece; it is a very provisional kind of poem. Its virtues grow on one, but so does a sense of the effort Berryman was making to push through a feat of recreation for which a clarified version of the style of Dylan Thomas was—hopefully—appropriate. Had Thomas, instead of lapsing into "Fern Hill," been able to write a long coherent poem on a real subject—the kind of subject touched on in "The Tombstone Told When She Died"—it might have been something like this. But Thomas never got so far. We know from *Love & Fame* that Berryman felt the impact of Thomas early—in Cambridge, England, before the war— found him better than anyone writing in America, and made great use of him, the kind of use a formidably developing poet can make of an arrested

one. The superiority of *Mistress Bradstreet* over the poems that are
unemancipated from Auden—"World-Telegram," "1 September 1939,"
"Desire Is a World by Night," etc.—strikingly show how Auden was far too
intellectually in shape to be successfully digested by Berryman as Thomas
had been.

The feeling imagination, the verbal love, in fact, of *Mistress Bradstreet,*
is most moving; and the image of her reading Quarles and Sylvester ("her
favorite poets; unfortunately") is, I am convinced, a counter-projection of
the image later willed on us by the grand, fully "voiced" Berryman of his
own self at his own desk. Finding his own voice is for Berryman a
consummation in which his own self and his poetry become one. Nor would
it be fanciful to see this as the climax of a historical as well as of a personal
process. Poetry, in its old European sense, *was* very largely a matter of getting
out of your own perishable tatty self into a timeless metaphysical world of
order and beauty. We have only to think of Spenser scribbling in Kilcomman
Castle, transforming the horrors of the Irish reality into the beauties of *The
Faerie Queene;* while Donne—often taken as "modern"—is no less a
transformer of the casual and the promiscuous into metaphysical fantasy and
form.

From Bradstreet to "Henry," who is no mask but a nickname in the
formal spousals of poet to reader, is therefore a journey of almost symbolic
dimensions, and one which only Lowell and Berryman could have successfully
accomplished. Whatever their technical interest and merits, all their early
poems were strangely clangorous and muffled, as if a new god were trying
to climb out from inside the machinery: they needed the machinery to establish
but not to *be* themselves. *Berryman's Sonnets* are brilliantly donnish in the
way they cavort around the traditions and idioms of the genre, and it is indeed
part of that idiom that there is no inside to them, no personal, nondramatic
reality.

> Keep your eyes open when you kiss: do: when
> You kiss. All silly time else, close them to.

In combination with such admirable and witty pastiche the gins and limes
and so on of the *Sonnets* strike one as mere modern properties, and quite
singularly not about what Berryman is. His use of Donne here is more
generous than Lowell's grabbings out of the past; yet if Lowell wears his
versions more ruthlessly he does it also more comprehensively.

Their absolute need of at last finding, and then being, themselves, could
be seen in the light of Auden's comment: "when I read a poem I look first
at the contraption and then at the guy inside it." To both Auden and Yeats

it would make no sense to be in search of their own voices. They remain what they were from the beginning. When Yeats says—"It is myself that I remake"—he is subsuming guy and contraption under a single flourish, but in fact the continuity between Yeats young and old is unbroken, and so with Auden. There is never any doubt what guy is in the contraption and that he is the same one. I would say, therefore, that there is a radical and important difference, *in this respect,* between the poetry of Auden and Yeats and that of Lowell and Berryman; and, interesting as it is, I would not agree with the conclusion that M. L. Rosenthal comes to in "The Poetry of Confession." He feels that the Americans "are carrying on where Yeats left off" when he proposed that the time had come to make the literal Self poetry's central redeeming symbol:

> I must lie down where all the ladders start,
> In the foul rag-and-bone shop of the heart.

But that is surely Yeats striking out a new line, apparently turning a somersault but really remaining the same old aesthete and tower-builder who chided the contingencies of this world for "wronging your image that blossoms a rose in the deeps of my heart." Yeats had always affirmed the self: he took it for granted, he did not have to find it: and in "Sailing to Byzantium" he exaggerates almost to the verge of parody the traditional view that seems to start Berryman off in *Mistress Bradstreet:* that "once out of nature" and in the world of art the perishable and tatty self enters a new dimension of being, becomes a poet. What is fascinating about Berryman's enterprise is that starting from "the proportioned spiritless poems" he tries to reconstitute, so to speak, the perishable being who so improbably produced them. That seems to me the significant American poetic journey—to discover the living ego as it has to be ("I renounce not even ragged glances, small teeth, nothing")—and it is the exact reverse of Yeats's pilgrimage. In finding themselves Lowell and Berryman must indeed renounce nothing, not a hair of their heads, "forever or/so long as I happen." Such an achievement is a triumph quite new to poetry and confers on it a new and unsuspected authority. Thomas Wolfe said something like: "I believe we are lost in America but I believe we shall be found." Lowell and Berryman could have nothing to do with the lush fervor of the sentiment. None the less, in terms of poetry they embody such a faith and justify it.

II

This is indeed glorious but not necessarily satisfactory. Let us try to see what has been lost as well as gained. My contention would be that the two poets reverse completely one canon of the European aesthetic tradition, as represented by Yeats, and those other European Magi Rilke and Valéry, but in another way they are willy-nilly bound to it. Their spectacular breakthrough into contingency is only possible because of the other Magi article of belief that things have no existence except in the poet's mind. So that in the iron selfhood the two poets have created, the most apparently feeble, hasty, or obviously untrue comment, sloughed off from day to day, acquires an imperishable existence when it is unsubstantiated on the page. The poems in *Love & Fame*, where even the nickname "Henry" has been dropped between us (as nicknames come to be dropped between old married couples), are apparently bar-room comments on Berryman's past, nothing more, and the people, events, feuds and boastings in them are as commonplace as the lunch-hour. The lines are like a late Picasso drawing, the realized personality of genius implicit in every flick of the pencil. (One wonders whether Edmund Wilson, who maintained in "Is Verse a Dying Technique?" that modern poetry is the prose of Flaubert, Joyce and Lawrence, had a chance to read them.)

And yet something is missing, the something that might join all these things to life itself. Such a poetry is not "earthed"—cannot be—for it has nothing of the *accidental* and inadvertent in it, no trace of genuine impurity. Art is all trickery, but it is trickery which can join up with our own lives and dreams, events and responses, our own self-trickery maybe. And can it be that in so meticulously creating the contingent self Lowell and Berryman have had to cut it off from the outside world? That is what I meant by saying that the poet is created here by a process opposite to that in which the novelist creates his characters. The novelist arrives at the reality of the world because his art is not and cannot be fully under his control. He cannot make everything himself: his readers must supply it; and the people and things he writes of will become real not only because his readers are doing a lot of the work themselves but because what he invents will become true by repetition and by being taken for granted; the man he shapes for us on page 2 will have become his own man by page 200. And this is as true of Joyce as of Trollope; it is equally true of much poetry in which "things" and a "world" are created—*Evgeny Onegin* or "The Eve of St. Agnes." But is not true of Lowell and Berryman, however much they may seem to be putting things and a world before us.

Some time ago, in a book called *The Romantic Survival,* I made a point about the world of Auden's poetry which I still think important, though the rest of the book no longer seems very relevant to me. It is that Auden, following Yeats, had carried the personal and legendary domain of that "Last

Romantic" one stage further, creating his characteristically and ominously centripetal world of stylized meaningfulness—derelict factories, semi-detached houses, "the silent comb/Where dogs have worried or a bird was shot." What gave this world its instant authority was its appearance of stern political and social finger-pointing with its actual invitation to conspiracy and relish in the landscape of the evil fairy, the Death Wish. "Auden has followed Yeats," I wrote, "in showing how the intense private world of symbolism can be brought right out into the open, eclectized, and pegged down to every point of interest in contemporary life." And yet Auden constantly reminded us— his wittiest spokesman was Caliban in "The Sea and The Mirror"—that the realities of such poetry are necessarily mirror realities.

> All the phenomena of an empirically ordered world are given. Extended objects appear to which events happen—old men catch dreadful coughs, little girls get their arms twisted. . . . All the voluntary movements are possible—crawling through flues and old sewers, sauntering past shopfronts, tiptoeing through quick-sands and mined areas . . . all the modes of transport are available, but any sense of direction, any knowledge of when on earth one has come from or where on earth one is going to, is completely absent.

The *bien pensants* of contemporary culture have made so much of the desolating, but also heartening and "compassionate" sense of the pressures of life, of the sheer difficulty of being oneself, which Lowell and Berryman have conveyed in their poetry, that a qualification along these lines may be in order. Auden finds the trick to let out Yeats into a new world of legend: Lowell and Berryman—on a scale and with a virtuosity of which today only American poets are capable—let him out in his turn, into a place where "*all the phenomena of an empirically ordered world are given,*" and "*all the voluntary movements are possible.*" Its very completeness precludes any attachment to mundane eventfulness—"From a *poet?* Words / to menace action. O I don't think so." Berryman's remark echoes what Auden constantly reiterates. Theirs is a breath-taking achievement, with results not at all like Auden, but I doubt it could have been done without him. As Berryman so engagingly puts it in that superlative *Love & Fame* poem "Two Organs":

> I didn't want my next poem to be *exactly* like Yeats
> or exactly like Auden
> since in that case where the hell was *I?*
> but what instead *did* I want it to sound like?

Temperamentally, one infers, Berryman could hardly be more different from either Yeats or Auden. He was "up against it" in a sense (I take it) unknown to their basically sane and self-centering personalities, but he adapts the mirror world of their invention to sound like what he wants to be. Success is shown by the failure of the alternatives taken by poets in a comparable situation (not of course of Berryman's stature, but that begs the question): the "confidences" of Anne Sexton and the "blown top" meaninglessness of Kenneth Fearing, for example. Berryman takes from Auden not only the mirror world but the wry unswerving knowledge of its use, which adds—as it does in Auden—a further dimension to the meaning of the poem. An instance would be 97 in the *Dream Poems,* which deliberately lapses delicately into gibberish and concludes:

> Front back and backside go bare!
> Cat's blackness, booze, blows, grunts, grand groans.
> Yo-bad yom i-oowaled bo v'ha'l lail awmer h're gawber!
> —Now, now, poor Bones.

This is not like Lear's fool, clowning to hide desolation and fear, though something like his voice can be heard at times in the *Dream Songs.* It is a humorous, rather than a witty, exploitation of the formal idiom; its camp "blackface" touch not unlike Auden's handling of Jewish Rosetta in *The Age of Anxiety.* Both poets know that they can only move us by means of a sort of carnival exploitation of the mirror world: Caliban, with his virtuoso eloquence, and Rosetta with her day dreams, would be equally at home among the exuberance and desperation of the *Dream Songs.* "A man speaking to men" does not say, as Henry does, "He stared at ruin. Ruin stared straight back." The humor of Groucho Marx, even if corny, also belongs to the mirror world.

And so does the straight talk. We can have no objection to sentiments like

> Working & children & pals are the point of the thing for the grand
> sea awaits us which will then us toss & endlessly us undo.

or

> We will die, & the evidence
> is: nothing after that.
> Honey, we don't rejoin.
> The thing meanwhile, I suppose, is to be courageous and kind.

because they are less earnest than sparkles from the wheel, and have been so wholly cauterized by contrivance. We can have "a human relation," for what that's worth, with poets far less good than Berryman. We can enter into such and share their feelings in a way impossible with him, for all the openness and Olympianly inclusive naturalness of his method. It is strangely unsatisfactory that in his poetry the poet cannot put a foot wrong. He can go off the air (Auden can too) but that is a different thing. If any technological habit has unconsciously influenced this kind of poetry it may be the record player with its click on and off, its hairline acoustics and relentless sensitivity. Both Lowell's and Berryman's poems have the flat finality of something perfectly recorded, and just the right length for perfect transmission. I notice writing down quotations that they do not sound very good, even when I had admired them as part of the poem: for the proper rigorous effect every word of the poem must be there.

This again excludes the accidental. The tone does not change or modulate, does not sag accidentally or rise with deliberate effort; the "supernatural crafter" is too much in charge, as he gives us an inkling in "The Heroes."

> I had, from my beginning, to adore heroes
> & I elected that they witness to,
> show forth, transfigure: life-suffering and pure heart
> & hardly definable but central-weaknesses
>
> for which they were to be enthroned and forgiven by me.
> They had to come on like revolutionaries,
> enemies throughout to accident and chance,
> relentless travellers, long used to failure
>
> in tasks that but for them would sit like hanging judges
> on faithless and by no means up to it Man.
> Humility and complex pride their badges,
> every "third thought" their grave.

Compare and contrast with that the young Stephen Spender's hopefully confiding and altogether by no means up to it poem "I think continually of them that were truly great." Spender gives it away by the touching solemnity of knowing he is writing a poem, a poem about heroes, the truly great. An all too human poem, as human as the embarrassment with and for the author that flushes us as we read it, but at least we know from it what we do *not* feel about those who "left the vivid air signed with their honour," etc. By patronizing it we engage with it: by disliking its sentiment we adjust our own. And we respond to it; it is not a null poem, even though it combines the inadvertent and the contrived in an unstable state.

Great as well as small poets are, or have been, rich with this inadvertence. Keats, writing in halcyon good faith,

> Let the mad poets say whate'er they please
> Of the sweets of peris, fairies, goddesses;
> There is no such a treat among them all,
> Haunters of cavern, lake, and waterfall,
> As a real woman.

seems not to know how it was going to look, or what the reader was going to think, and certainly not how revealing of his genius the lines are. Byron always seems to know, with his posturing and easy anecdotage, and the wholly controlled and calculated swagger of the jotting on the back of *Don Juan.*

> O would to God that I were so much clay
> As I am blood, bone, marrow, passion, feeling,
> Having got drunk exceedingly today
> So that I seem to stand upon the ceiling.

These lines mime a loss of control and a hungover truculence, and yet every so often he forgets himself genuinely in a way there is no mistaking, as in the lines written when he heard his wife was ill. The chagrined pity of its opening seems to try, and fail to be, all self-pity, until a kind of hangdog solicitude turns to and takes refuge in the relieved virulence of satiric declamation. There is even an unexpectedly startled and self-disconcerted note in the famous lines: "How little know we what we are, how less / What we may be." Hardy is in this kind of way the most vulnerable of all great poets, as witness the end of "After a Journey," where the poet revisits the sea-haunts where he had first fallen in love with a wife long estranged and now dead.

> Trust me, I mind not, though Life lours,
> The bringing me here; nay, bring me here again!
> I am just the same as when
> Our days were a joy and our paths through flowers.

"I am just the same as when": the reassurance he gives and needs to give has all the eager clumsiness of life: we can hear the relief of saying it, a relief all the greater because it can't be true.

I labor this incongruous mixed bag of examples because they all seem to me to contain something naive and direct that has vanished or is vanishing from the performance of good poetry. In them we seem to meet the poet when he doesn't expect it; like Sartre's voyeur he is looking at something else so intently that he is unaware of the reader behind him. And can it be that Berryman's preoccupation—for it appears to be that—with establishing the poet's existence in all its hopeless contingency ("I renounce not even ragged glances, small teeth, nothing,") is both an attempt at what earlier poets—and bad poets today—do without meaning to, and a recognition that only a formalization of such directness is possible to him? We can see it in the cunning control of that same poem, "The Heroes," which slides casually into the subject *a propos* of Pound, a "feline" figure ("zeroing in on feelings, / hovering up to them, putting his tongue in their ear"); then goes on to distinguish this from the "imperial sway" exercised by Eliot, Joyce and Yeats; rises to the celebration of heroism already quoted; and in the last verse shows us where the first six came from.

> These gathering reflexions, against young women,
> against seven courses in my final term,
> I couldn't sculpt into my helpless verse yet.
> I wrote mostly about death.

The ideas are referred to a pre-poetic stage in the poet, when they were tumbling in the dark together with feelings about girls and resentment against classes. That self could not have written the poem, but it had the ideas, and is coincident with the self that is now sculpting the poetry effectively—perhaps more than coincident, because its topic was the inclusive and unsculpturable one of death. Imperial sway can only be exercised over the words that make up the self.

The last line does not nudge us; it simply looms up—a perspective on the dark contingency of the self that heroes don't have, for they can be sculptured into verse. The self that can't remains pervasively present, disembodied above the poem like a Cheshire cat. There is no question of making or remaking that self in Yeatsian style, nor of making legendary figures out of the poet's *entourage,* as both Yeats and Lowell in their different ways have done. Professor Neff, who gave Berryman a C out of malice at Columbia, in the next poem "Crisis," is paid the subtle compliment of a rapid, unimpartial write-off; there is no attempt to enshrine him in some immortal rogues' gallery, and Mark Van Doren in the poem is also and simply a real person, as in conversation. The poet's mother and father appear in an equally unspectacular way (contrast again with Lowell), figures briefly revealed by night, unless the night, or pre-dawn, time of most pieces, like the seeming traces of drink or drugs, is another convention for conveying the continuity and actuality of the self.

The self can appear in that dark past as in grand guignol, surrounded by ghosts indistinguishable from itself (129: "riots for Henry the unstructured dead") or it can be transposed into a hauntingly meticulous *doppelgänger*, as in 242.

> About that "me." After a lecture once
> came up a lady asking to see me. "Of course.
> When would you like to?"
> Well, *now,* she said.

After a precise, casual, brittle account of the quotidian campus scene—the poet with lunch date, the lady looking distraught—comes the pay-off.

> So I rose from the desk & closed it and turning back
> found her in tears—apologising—"No,
> go right ahead", I assur-
> ed her, here's a handkerchief. Cry". She did. I did.
>   When she got control, I said "What's the matter—if you
>   want to talk?"
> "Nothing. Nothing's the matter." So.
> I am her.

Naturally: she could be nobody else. Only through Berryman can the poem move us, but it does move. The hopelessness, the stasis, is completely authentic. Not so, I think, those poems in *Love & Fame* about the others in the mental hospital, Jill and Eddie Jane and Tyson and Jo. For all their "understanding" "The Hell Poem" and "*I* know" have something insecure about them, as if threatened by the presence of other people. The poet was not threatened of course—we feel his openness, his interest—but the poem is caught between its equation with contingency and the fact that, as form, its contingency can only be "me."

The Berryman *pruzhina,* or spring, snaps as the real presence of these others pulls it too far apart. For the young Berryman, as he tells us in "Two Organs," the longing was to write "big fat fresh original & characteristic poems."

> My longing, yes, was a woman's
> She can't know can she *what kind* of a baby
> she's going with all the will in the world to produce?
> I suffered trouble over this.

"I couldn't sleep at night, I attribute my life-long insomnia / to my uterine struggles." Nothing is more graphic in Berryman than the sickness and struggle of finding oneself about to become a poet, lumbered with an unknown fetus that when it arrives will be oneself. We may note that this is the exact opposite, in this mirror world, of true childbirth, which produces *another person*. Still, the pains are real enough, and so is the comedy. Indeed the black comedy of Beckett again comes to mind, a theater of one. "By virtue of the aesthetic form," generalizes Marcuse, the "play" creates its own atmosphere of "seriousness" which is *not* that of the given reality, but rather its "negation." The kind of portentousness is here in a way, and the theory of the "living theater" has certain affinities with Berryman's drive—if I am right about it—to coincide poet as man with poem as thing.

Berryman's fascination with becoming himself as a poet has—given his genius—an almost equal fascination for us, but it has a drawback too. We can contemplate it but not share it—it is not really a part of the universally identifiable human experience, the experience in Byron or in Gray's "Elegy," to which, as Dru Johnson observed, every bosom returns an echo. What we have instead is extreme singularity, the Berrymanness of Berryman, which we and the poet stare at together: that he absorbs us as much as he absorbs himself is no mean feat. We want indeed to know "of what heroic stuff was warlock Henry made"—the American hero whose tale can be only of himself and who is (unlike Wordsworth) bored by it.

> Life, friends, is boring. We must not say so.
> After all, the sky flashes, the great sea yearns,
> we ourselves flash and yearn,
> and moreover my mother told me as a boy
> (repeatingly) "Ever to confess you're bored
> means you have no
>
> Inner Resources." I conclude now I have no
> inner resources, because I am heavy bored.
> Peoples bore me,
> literature bores me, especially great literature,
> Henry bores me.

Delightful! Our bosoms return an echo to *that,* as to the celebration of the same mother in 100, and her "two and seventy years of chipped indignities," but what principally gets to us is the performance of birth, the pleasure of finding the fetus so triumphantly expelled. *"Le chair est triste, hélas, et j'ai lu tous les livres"*—that sensation, too, for Mallarmé, existed to end up in a book, and so it is with the perpetual endgame of Berryman—"after all has been said, and all *has* been said."

We do miss a *developing* world. Having found himself on the page the poet has found hell, or God—it is much the same, for in either case there is nothing further there. Compare with the world of Hardy, say, who was not bored but went on throughout a long calvary continuing to *notice* things outside himself, able to bring the outside world into his poetry while leaving it in its natural place. (Marianne Moore and Elizabeth Bishop have done the same.) And among Hardy's preoccupations "the paralysed fear lest one's not one"—a poet that is—did not, as far as we can see, figure. But it is the detriment and dynamic of Berryman's book. Hardy had things easier, for he did not in the least mind writing bad relaxed poems, and this itself helps to keep him in the outer world, the world of *true* contingency. His is the natural contrast to the place discovered and developed by our two in some ways equally Anglo-Saxon giants.

> I say the paralysed fear that one's not one
> is back with us forever.

So it may be. The struggle to become a great poet, to exercise imperial sway, may indeed be increasingly and ruinously hard, obsessing the poet's whole outlook. But they have shown it can be done.

The novelists of our time have not succeeded in creating a new fictional form as they have created a new poetic one—and that seems to me to have real significance. The bonds that enclosed the novelist and compelled him into his form have up till lately been social as well as aesthetic ones. There was much that he could not say "in so many words," and which therefore had to be said by other means—a style had to be found for creating what society could not tolerate the open expression of: such a style as is created, for example, in the opening lines of *Tristram Shandy*. But in a wholly permissive age the formal bonds of poetry remain drawn taut because they depend on sculping a voice, graving a shape and pattern. The bonds of fiction slacken into unrecognizability because the pressures of society itself, not of mere craft, which used to enforce them, have withdrawn. The novel form today has no inevitable response to make to its unchartered freedom; it can only concoct unnecessary ones, resurrected devices like those of Barth, Burroughs, Vonnegut and others, which do not impress us with self-evident authority but act as an encumbrance, get in the way. Like the novelist the poet can say anything now, but he must exercise imperial sway as he does so. If he can, poetry has the edge again, and Lowell and Berryman have honed it to a razor sharpness. Despairing art critics, we learn, have been asking not what art is possible today but *is* art possible. As regards poetry, we have our answer. It is still adding to the stock of available reality while expressing the matter in hand.

JOEL CONARROE

After Mr. Bones:
John Berryman's Last Poems

There are writers—Pound, Pynchon, Roth, Ashbery, for example—who tend to evoke extreme responses, one reader's energetic disgust countered by another's passionate advocacy. John Berryman is such an artist, a man damned and praised in equally unambiguous terms, so that anyone approaching him by way of his critics rather than though his work must be very confused indeed. Louis Simpson, reviewing *Recovery* (a posthumous novel), announces that "drunks are boring—there is no exception to this rule—and *Recovery* is about a drunk." He goes on to reveal that the generation of Lowell, Schwartz, and Berryman was motivated solely by "a desperate, insatiable desire for fame. So they destroyed themselves, for you can never be famous enough if you are the kind of person who wants to be famous." So much for them! On the other hand (and I like to think it is the upper hand), Donald Davie, writing about *The Freedom of the Poet* (a collection of critical essays, also posthumous), expresses his opinion that "the man behind this book was not only one of the most gifted and intelligent Americans of his time, but also one of the most honorable and responsible."

These mutually exclusive reviews are not atypical, nor, given the amount of material in manuscript and the fact that Berryman's enlightened publishers continue to bring forth volumes, are they the last of their sort we will see. In the years since his suicide in January 1972, Farrar, Straus & Giroux has brought out three books, and another is announced for fall 1977. *Delusions, etc.*, the final collection of poems, already in proof when the poet jumped

From *The Hollins Critic* 13, no. 4 (October 1976). © 1976 by Hollins College, Virginia.

to his death, appeared in 1972. (It was nominated that year for a National Book Award.) *Recovery,* left unfinished, was published (with a touching foreword by Saul Bellow) along with work drafts and notes indicating how it was to be resolved, in 1973. *The Freedom of the Poet,* treating subjects as diverse as Nashe, Monk Lewis, Shakespeare, Henry James, Dreiser, Anne Frank, and Dylan Thomas, appeared (this time with an affecting foreward by Robert Giroux) in 1976. The forthcoming book, *Henry's Fate & Other Poems,* edited by John Haffenden (who is writing the authorized biography), will contain, among other things, the late dream songs that have been appearing so regularly over the past two years in *The New Yorker, American Poetry Review, Atlantic, The Times Literary Supplement,* and elsewhere; it is certain to be a publishing event of major importance. There may be, in addition, still more volumes, since in his final years Berryman was immersed in a number of projects, including a children's life of Christ, a study tentatively titled "Shakespeare's Reality," and an anthology of poems he admired. Though he has been dead nearly five years now his spirit, never so thoroughly present, will remain with us.

My purpose in this essay is to examine the last two poetry collections Berryman actually saw through proof—*Love & Fame* and *Delusions, etc.,*— in order to assess both their place in the overall oeuvre and their significance, recognizing of course that it is still too early to make any really definitive evaluations. Since it is helpful to see these works in context, I want to comment briefly on the books that preceded them. I start at the beginning: Berryman began writing as a very young man. Emerging from the adolescent fog that characterized his four years at the South Kent School in Connecticut, he encountered, at Columbia, Mark Van Doren, who became both his literary mentor and his surrogate father—Berryman's own father had killed himself when the boy was eleven. Throughout his Columbia and Cambridge University years (1932–38) and into the middle 1940s the young poet wrote the lyrics that were later collected in *Short Poems* (1967). With a few notable exceptions this work has no voice, or, rather, it has too many voices, with Van Doren, Yeats, Auden, and Ransom as the most audible echoes—Yeats saved Berryman from the then-crushing domination of Eliot and Pound. Ominous, flat, social, indistinctly allusive, and exhausted, most of these poems, invariably organized in prudent stanzas with carefully plotted rhyme schemes, seem to have been written by a well-programmed computer with Weltschmerz. There are references to heartbreak, fear, sorrow, and hatred, but it is clear that the poet, keeping his most intimate feelings in harness, was far more conscious of civic woe than of his own. It is hard to believe that the public voice of this work would modulate into that of Mr. Bones, of *The Dream Songs,* a man to whom nothing in the world is more important, or, in an odd way, universal, than his own private sorrows. The poetry of *The Dispossessed* (1948) shows a slight movement in the direction of the later work, particularly in a marvelous sequence of "Nervous Songs" that anticipate, both in form and content, the dream songs. For the most part, however, the apprentice work is very much a product of its time.

The two sequences written during his thirties show Berryman escaping the domination of Auden and company to invent a language peculiarly his own. His *Sonnets,* written in 1948 (but not published until 1967), are the record of a knock-down-and-drag-out adulterous love affair. Couched in the most conventional of forms, they nevertheless bristle with the pain, euphoria, jealousy, and wrenching despair that are so clearly missing in the impersonal earlier lyrics. Only a theme that appealed to his deepest needs could have brought this poet to the necessity of "crumpling a syntax," could have transformed an empty monk of the Yeatsian order into love's "utraquist," one who speaks or writes two languages, such as Latin and the vernacular. It is primarily the experiments with colloquial language, slangy, often inelegant, hot off the heart, that give this book of conventional structures its unconventional power and importance.

If the love recorded in these sonnets dared not speak its name, at least publicly, for some twenty years, the duet with Berryman's spiritual mistress of the period, Anne Bradstreet, appeared, following five years of research and strenuous crafting, in 1953, as soon as it was completed. It was this poem that dramatically moved its creator, then thirty-nine, into the front rank of living poets. The *TLS* referred to *Homage to Mistress Bradstreet* as a path-breaking masterpiece, Robert Fitzgerald called it "the poem of his generation," and Edmund Wilson labelled it "the most distinguished long poem by an American since *The Waste Land.*" Its fifty-seven stanzas (the model is Yeats's "In Memory of Major Robert Gregory") are characterized by a soaring lyricism, by intensely compressed discords, jagged, Hopkinsesque rhythms, unexpected allusions, puns, repeated harmonies, scrupulously crafted image patterns, haunting cadences. There is nothing like the language of this sequence in Berryman's earlier work, and certainly nothing quite like the poem in American literature. Had he written nothing else Berryman's position as a significant poet would be assured.

He went on, however, to create his "Song of Myself," his *Cantos,* his *Paterson.* The 385 Dream Songs, composed over a period of more than ten years, record the life in progress of an imaginary character, named, among other things, Henry House, who bears a striking resemblance to the poet himself. Again adopting a fairly rigid form (eighteen lines made up of three six-line stanzas), the songs reveal, in a fashion alternately disturbing and hilarious, Henry's griefs, lusts, joys, terrors, and hopes, his preoccupation with his dead father, and his quest for his lost Father. The sequence represents Berryman's attempts to get his guilt and fear out in the open as a means of exorcizing them. The vitality, grave comedy, and outright buffoonery of much of the work vitiate against an uncritical acceptance of the nightmares the songs contain, the wit and high spirits warding off much of the horror. It is, however, because the nightmares are recounted, the terrors revealed, the guilt expressed, that the poet can go on dreaming and muddling through. Henry, as he says at one point, is "obliged to perform in complete darkness / operations of great delicacy." These operations are on himself, and somehow, God knows how, he manages to endure. Some of the songs are baffling and others are remarkably self-indulgent. On the whole, however, the sequence is an eccentric masterpiece, a triumph of technical virtuosity, invention, and imagination. Berryman created for this work a luxuriant language, one made up of archaic and Latinate constructions, crumpled syntax, odd diction, idiomatic conversation, blues and nursery rhyme rhythms, minstrel show dialect, and a number of other things as well. It is a language that has been praised, damned, imitated, explicated, annotated, and thoroughly misunderstood. The songs, though, as Henry says, "are not meant to be understood, you understand. / They are only meant to terrify & comfort." This they do superbly.

When Berryman completed this massive sequence he thought of himself as an epic poet and had no expectation of writing any more short poems. One day, however, he composed a line, "I fell in love with a girl," and, liking its factuality, continued in the same vein. The subject was entirely new, he felt, "solely and simply myself . . . the subject on which I am a real authority, so I wiped out all the disguises and went to work." Writing feverishly for five or six weeks, he produced a completed manuscript, which he sent to various friends (Richard Wilbur, Mark Van Doren, Edmund Wilson) for suggestions, most of which were followed. In 1970 *Love & Fame,* containing something to offend nearly everyone, was published, and in 1972 a revised version, with some of the more tasteless poems deleted, came out.

In this book Berryman leaves behind both his persona, Henry, and the baroque intricacies of the songs—the poems are written in a direct, unadorned style often resembling prose. The work, which appears at first glance to be a series of uncensored personal revelations, some fairly startling, took a drubbing from many reviewers. The unprecedented exhibitionism of the first two sections in particular caused unsympathetic critics to overlook the later poems, which quietly undercut the hubris of the earlier parts. In the 7000 lines of the *Songs* Berryman is able to say the most intimate and outrageous things. Since he is speaking through Henry, however, a reader, even if he makes little distinction between poet and speaker, can attribute any especially shocking excesses to the "imaginary" character. It is one thing for Henry Pussy-cat to lust after every young woman he sees, quite another for John Berryman, sans mask, to announce, in the first stanza of a book, that he fell in love with a "gash" and that he has fathered a bastard. And isn't it, after all, *regressive* for a distinguished poet and chair-holding professor to carry on about adolescent fondlings, student council elections, penis lengths, college grades, and the number of women (79) he bedded as a young man?

If these things were all the book contained it would, indeed, be appropriate to dismiss *Love & Fame* as a tasteless mistake. The work, however, is more complex and more serious than the bawdiness of the opening sections might suggest. In a foreward to the second edition, Berryman, after characteristically attacking those who misread the book, suggests that each of the four movements (he means, I think, each of the last three) criticizes backward the preceding one. My own sense is that the book can most helpfully be analyzed in terms of its two halves, the second representing a total repudiation of the values inherent in the two sections that make up the first. The title helps explain this movement. At the end of Keats's sonnet "When I Have Fears That I May Cease To Be" the speaker announces, "then on the shore / Of the wide world I stand alone and think / Till Love and Fame to nothingness do sink." In the second half of Berryman's book this notion of declining to nothingness is fully examined: love and fame, postulated in the first parts as lust and Public Relations, yield to "Husbandship and crafting." The book, thus, takes a dramatic turn at the beginning of section three, progressing from the poet's randy and confident young manhood into his depressed present, from ribald skirt-chasing and self-promotion to a humble series of prayers to God, who judges a man's merit not by his verses but by his virtue. We move from "*Time* magazine yesterday slavered Saul's ass, / they pecked at mine last year. We're going strong!" in section one, to these representative lines from the book's second half:

> It seems to be DARK all the time.
> I have difficulty walking.
> I can remember what to say to my seminar
> but I don't know what I want to.

> I said in a Song once: I am unusually tired.
> I repeat that & increase it.

I'm vomiting.
I broke down today in the slow movement of K.365.

This passage is from part 3, in which, leaving behind all the youthful euphoria and pretensions, the enthusiasm and awkwardness, the hope and energy, the poet experiences a dark night of the soul that is followed by a gradual recovery, or, to use the word that figures importantly in two of the later poems, by survival. The final section is made up of "Eleven Addresses to the Lord," and these, continuing the quest for faith documented in *The Dream Songs,* and looking forward to the more troubling prayers of *Delusions, Etc.,* suggest that the Berryman of the last books is, more than anything else, a religious poet, a man seeking desperately to recover the faith of his childhood, a son engaged in a struggle with a Father who is simultaneously his antagonist and the only possible source of hope. "I believe," he seems to say throughout these prayers, "help thou my unbelief."

Composed in the four line stanza (borrowed from Emily Dickinson) that makes up the whole of the book, the prayers, though at times tediously predictable ("Master of beauty, craftsman of the snowflake"), are moving petitions from a self-effacing suppliant, "severely damaged, but functioning." They resolve the themes introduced in the earlier sections: "I fell in love with a girl" gives way to "I fell in love with you, Father," and the preoccupation with the sort of fame associated with *Time* is replaced by the assertion that "the only true literary critic is Christ." (Hopkins to Bridges: "Fame in itself is nothing. The only thing that matters is virtue.") The book's final line reveals how far the poet has travelled from his obsession with public approbation: "I pray I may be ready with my witness."

The fact that *Love & Fame* has been almost universally disliked (there are a few notable exceptions to this response) can be explained, I think, in two ways. It is not, first of all, a good seminar text. A generation of teachers and critics responsive to the labyrinthian complexities of Nabokov, Robbe-Grillet, Lowell, Beckett, and others (including Berryman himself) find little here to uncover, nothing to illuminate. There are so few mysteries, metaphysical or stylistic (the most interesting questions are structural) that the most one can do by way of explication in many cases is simply to read a poem out loud. What is one to demonstrate, after all, about lines, however crafty, that sound so much like prose? Left with practically nothing to say, critics have assumed that it is the poems themselves that have little to say.

The book has also been consistently misread, or worse, not read at all, by those who damn it most vigorously. If one believes, with Louis Simpson, that Berryman was moved only by an insatiable desire for publicity, then a book called *Love & Fame,* replete with name-dropping, preening, and references to media triumphs, is clearly going to serve as a red flag. And if a reader is so annoyed by the poet's supposed vanity that he fails to notice that love and fame finally sink to nothingness, then the capacity for misinterpretation is virtually unlimited. An example (unfortunately not isolated) of inattentiveness to the text that borders on the bizarre is found in a book called *The Confessional Poets* by Robert Phillips. Berryman, Phillips writes, came to equate fame with money and love with lust: "It is this self-aggrandizement and lack of compassion which make Berryman's late confessions a series of false notes. . . . Rather than displaying moral courage, these poems display instead immoral callowness." Apparently agitated by the alleged offenses of the book's first parts, this critic clearly did not bother to read the crucial third section.

Obviously those whose evaluations are based on prejudice rather than on perception will find much to despise in this unconventional book. Fortunately, however, Berryman, like Joyce, Pound, and others who have been subjected to misinterpretations, is too powerful a writer to be harmed, ultimately, by this sort of sniping. In saying this, I do not mean to imply that *Love & Fame* represents one of the poet's major achievements. It is neither so brilliant nor so interestingly eccentric as either *Mistress Bradstreet* or the *Songs.* There is, nevertheless, after the complexities of these sequences, much that can be said for a work that strives for direct, unambiguous communication, and that more often than not achieves its goal. The Berryman canon, missing this vulnerable book, would be noticeably slighter.

Delusions, etc., though it contains a handful of poems that are superior to anything in *Love & Fame,* stands, by contrast, as an honorable failure. Why is this so? Largely, I think, because the work, lacking the internal development of the earlier book, is a miscellaneous collection of often incoherent utterances from a soul in a state of intense agitation, a state that precludes, more often than not, the kind of control required if desperate emotion is to be translated into formal art. The first and final sections reveal the poet's anguished quest for faith, the opening poems organized around canonical hours ("Lauds," "Matins," etc.), the closing poems around a series of prayers ("Somber Prayer," "The Prayer of the Middle-Aged Man," etc.) that resemble canonical hours without a sequential pattern. These "holy" poems, unlike those in *Love & Fame,* tend to be disputatious, as if the poet, protesting too much, were now trying to convince himself and his God of his faith. He is actually attempting, as A. Alvarez has suggested, to defend himself against his own depression: "Berryman's poems to God are his least convincing performances; nervous, insubstantial, mannered to a degree and intensely argumentative." Helen Vendler is even less sympathetic, calling the book as a whole "dead" and the religious poems "no good": "When he became the redeemed child of God, his shamefaced vocabulary dropped useless."

The three parts that stand between the opening and closing prayers have their own inner logic, but taken together they comprise an altogether odd miscellany. The second (possibly modelled on section three of *Life Studies*, in which Lowell describes a cluster of alienated artists—Ford, Crane, Schwartz—with whom he identifies) pays tribute to five "makers" whose lives form an almost unbroken chronological chain: Washington (1732–1799), Beethoven (1770–1827), Emily Dickinson (1830–1886), George Trakl (1887–1914), and Dylan Thomas (1914–1953). The thirteen poems of part 3 are generally undistinguished, though this section does contain "He Resigns," in its eloquent understatement as moving as anything Berryman wrote, e.g.,

> I don't want anything
> or person, familiar or strange.
> I don't think I will sing
>
> any more just now:
> or ever, I must start
> to sit with a blind brow
> above an empty heart.

Part 4 consists of five poems, three so weak as to be virtually unreadable, the others dream songs, the haunting beauty of which reminds us of just how much Berryman lost when he gave up Henry:

> it occurred to me
> that *one* night, instead of warm pajamas,
> I'd take off all my clothes
> & cross the damp cold lawn & down the bluff
> into the terrible water & walk forever
> under it out toward the island.

In contrast to these luminous lines, much of the work seems to have been written out of habit rather than from any strong emotional necessity, and much of the language is clotted and obscure:

> and mine O shrinks a micro-micro-minor
> post-ministry, and of Thine own to Thee I have given,
> and there is none abiding but woe or Heaven,
> teste the pundits. Me I'm grounded for peace.

There are, occasionally, lucid phrases that float to the surface of this generally murky language, and these provide some affecting moments: "I'm not a good man," "I've got to get as little as possible wrong," "I have not done well." Moreover, as I suggest earlier, though the book as a whole is inferior to *Love & Fame* it does contain several poems that are finer than anything in that work, and I include here "He Resigns," the two dream songs, and "Beethoven Triumphant." Berryman's friend William Meredith has said of the latter that it has "the force and complexity of a late quartet." I want to close my generally unenthusiastic commentary on the book by touching on this singularly impressive poem.

Made up of twenty-seven stanzas ranging from four to eleven lines each, "Beethoven Triumphant" reveals Berryman as historian, as music critic, and as eulogist. The poem bears a striking resemblance to *Homage to Mistress Bradstreet,* borrowing from that work a mode of intense compression ("tensing your vision into an alarm / of gravid measures, sequent to demure"), inclusion of little-known biographical facts ("When brother Johann signed 'Real Estate Owner,' you: 'Brain Owner' "), movement from objective narrative to direct address ("Koussevitzky will make it, Master; lie back down"), emphasis on physical decay ("your body-filth flowed to the middle of the floor"), and introduction of contemporary detail ("I called our chief prose-writer / at home a thousand miles off"). As in his earlier poem Berryman conjures up the spirit of a long dead artist, analyzes, lovingly if somewhat pedantically, the basic qualities of this artist's nature, and provides a valedictory coda. Where the Bradstreet sequence closes on a note of quiet affection, however, the Beethoven tribute ends with a powerful crescendo: "You march and chant around here! I hear your thighs." The final phrase, which sounds so odd out of context, actually works, resolving an image introduced in the opening stanza.

Berryman clearly empathizes with the composer, whom he shows to be misunderstood, physically disabled, a troubled sleeper, eccentric, churlish, absentminded, vain. In lines that echo the "Ode on a Grecian Urn" (and that suggest his own desire for oblivion) he rejoices that the man died during his prime, thus spared the burdens of old age: "Ah but the indignities you flew free from, / your self-abasements even would increase." And he attempts to approximate, through his language, the glories of "the B Flat major," "the Diabelli varia," and "the 4th Piano Concerto" as a way of documenting this sense of identification. His poem, with its irregular stanzas, is not meant to suggest a concerto, or a sonata, or a symphony, but its richly musical individual lines clearly do attempt to suggest Beethoven's powerful rhythms and ecstatic tonalities. Nowhere in Berryman is the language purer. The

opening lines, for example, melodious, even cello-like, are representative:
"Dooms menace from tumults. Who's immune / among our mightier of
headed men?" In addition to the obvious assonance of Doom-tumults-who-
immune, there are secondary harmonies provided by from-along-of, and by
menace-headed-men. The slant rhyme and the numerous "m" sounds add
to the consonance, as does the insistent percussive beat. "One chord thrusts,
as it must / find allies, foes, resolve, in subdued crescendo," the poet writes
later, the sound, once again, underscoring the sense of the words.

It is somehow fitting that his final book should find its noblest moments
in a tribute to Beethoven since Berryman took seriously the idea of "the
mysterious late excellence which is the crown / of our trials & our last bride"
(*Dream Song* 324), an excellence that he admired in Yeats, Williams, and
Goya, as well as in Beethoven. That his own last books are not among his
most impressive is, of course, distressing, and we are left with the inevitable
speculations about where his art would have taken him had he chosen to
live—he was, after all, only fifty-seven when he died. Whether he would have
gained "the crown of our trials" is impossible to say, though *Delusions, etc.*,
which seems to be the product of a mind at the end of its tether, suggests
that this is unlikely. The only thing we can be certain of, however, is that
he would have surprised us with an altogether unexpected mode—he never
repeated himself, each of his books being as different from the one that
precedes it as that book, in turn, is from its immediate predecessor. Who
would have predicted that *Delusions, etc.*, would follow *Love & Fame*, that
Love & Fame would emerge from the *Songs,* that the songs themselves would
be the next step after *Mistress Bradstreet?* Anyone willing to speculate on
the sort of work Berryman might have written in his sixties (or seventies!)
is either clairvoyant or reckless.

What we do know, of course, is that his final books, whatever their
virtues (and these, particularly in the case of *Love & Fame,* are considerable),
represent a falling off from his strongest work. We should not regret their
existence, however, disappointed as we may be that they are not more
consistently fine. Nor should we, in our haste to evaluate Berryman's overall
achievement, attach undue importance to these rather desperate works. To
do so would be to lose sight of the fact that this man, whatever his personal
and aesthetic crises, gave us the *Sonnets* and *Homage to Mistress Bradstreet.*
And, God bless him, he gave us Henry:

> My friends,—he has been known to mourn,—I'll die;
> live you, in the most wild, kindly green
> partly forgiving wood,

sort of forever and all those human sings
close not your better ears to, while good Spring
returns with a dance and a sigh.

DIANE ACKERMAN

Near the Top a Bad Turn Dared

In a natural way, John Berryman is oblique, private, elliptical. We seem to overhear him. Locked in a verbal spasm, he has trouble, often enough, in getting out or across, and an essential part of his performance is a rheumatism of the sensibility, in which the grammar is so knotted up that his poems evince the difficulty of getting them written at all. Beginning, he seems not quite to know what is nagging at him; finished, he has allowed into the poem various accidents, concomitants, and ricochets. As A. Alvarez observes, "you either love or loathe" his jagged, high-strung outbursts. One of the most ego-ridden poets, he makes authoritative rhetoric out of the nervous tic, and an original voice as well. It is almost out of the question to confuse lines by Berryman with those of any other poet, though like a celebrant magpie he echoes dozens of poets from Pound and Stevens to Hopkins and Cummings. His "grammaticisms" alone would identify him, I suppose: his wrenchings or mutilations of grammar are not those of others. In fact, nearly everything about him is manneristic and, at times, he seems almost like an involuntary exercise in the manner of poet as idiosyncratic paradigm. A hard nut to crack, he is a poet fully qualified for exegesis and often badly in need of it.

My purpose here is not to look at him in the round, but to consider certain tendencies in *Homage to Mistress Bradstreet* and *Delusions, etc.* There were times when Berryman verged on the metaphysical mind, although never sustainedly; it seems to have haunted him, the possibility of getting into such

From *Parnassus: Poetry in Review* 7, no. 2 (Spring-Summer 1979). © 1980 by Poetry in Review Foundation.

a frame of mind (and reference) flickers in his work like morganatic fire. It shows up in *Dream Songs,* I think, in the persona of intervening Mr. Bones, the death-figure who puts awkward questions at the wrong moments only to answer them himself in a weird combination of black lingo and uncouth blues. Henry, the poet figure whose interior biography the Songs jerkily reveal, owns Mr. Bones and, presumably, goes on owning him until Mr. Bones owns him, which is when the Songs end, as they did in 1972. But I don't think it would be right to regard *Dream Songs* as metaphysical: a big pack of cards having to do with travel, children, politics, liquor, sex, theology, other poets, they impose on us voluptuously, but their drift is social. The wit is, too, and of course the bizarre tone—full of jangling self-interruptions that generate even further useful disturbances—might almost qualify him as an inheritor from Donne and Cowley. But to do so would be merely to make of him a superficial metaphysical, the essence of *Dream Songs,* in my view, being that he cannot break out of his bag of skin. True, he writes, "We are using our skins for wallpaper and we cannot win," which implies that the outside world keeps on coming through or that the self keeps leaking out; but in the end this is more like a problem with the plumbing. The poet is unhappy because he cannot forget himself. Henry is upset because he can't escape the poet who doubles as Mr. Bones. The entire sequence is an almost spastic search for a self, and it's not a self blurred through transcendental overlap with rocks and stars and trees, it's a self blurred by its own chemistry. If Berryman reaches out in these short poems, it's to bring himself back, not to steal a magic from the universe at large. Psychologically of enormous interest, especially for devotees of Berryman *in toto*, they are actually a bit short—in voracious interest, in intuited vastness, in empathetic penetration—compared with certain other works, to which I must now turn.

Homage to Mistress Bradstreet is an imaginary portrait almost in the manner of Walter Pater; indeed, Berryman's real-life alias has more fictional range than does the invented, arbitrary one of Henry. The answer, I think, is that, down the track, there was something precise and vivid to aim at, whereas Henry is too much Berryman himself to have edges. The one poem is a monument, the other a potpourri of broken images. Not that *Homage* isn't a poem of voices; it is, and these include the poet's own, as the first of the appended Notes informs us: "The poem is about the woman, but this exordium is spoken by the poet, his voice modulating in stanza 4, line 8 [4.8] into hers." In fact, vocally, it is a polyphonic *tour de force*, sometimes achieving the uncanny effect of what has been presented serially becoming simultaneous: the voice lingers in one's ear and overshoots the next voice that comes along. Most impressive of all, the rhythm of Anne Bradstreet's

mind comes boldly through, not only from Berryman's study of her own
Meditations and his occasional use of phrases from them (some of which
she had culled from the Scriptures), but also from his almost involuntary
impersonations, which leave her mental gait on the silent white space around
the poem like an oral signature. Adroit, subtle, tight, *Homage*—if it were
nothing more—is an astonishing feat of invasive homage; her mind breathes
again and, courtesy of the later poet, makes new images galore:

> Drydust in God's eye the aquavivid skin
> of Simon snoring lit with fountaining dawn
> when my eyes unlid, sad.
> John Cotton shines on Boston's sin—
> I ám drawn, in pieties that seem
> the weary drizzle of an unremembered dream.
> Women have gone mad
> At twenty-one. Ambition mines, atrocious, in.

To begin with, it is hard to parse, even retrospectively, and the first three
lines in particular. Very well, then, the reader concludes: fall back on
something else—an asyntactical reading, as if the lines were in Chinese, and
all of a sudden "lit" emerges as the verb, not a past participle. The gain, I
think, is the suggestion (which you're not obliged to cancel even after the
verb has revealed itself) that she assimilates phenomena to herself through
constantly expanding appositions: "Drydust" = "skin" = "sad." She might
be concluding that "Drydust" is "sad," as perhaps the encrustations of an
after-weeping are; we are wake up, with 'sleep' in our eyes, as if we have
been weeping all night, and this doesn't have to go by the board when we
reach the second conclusion, via grammar, that Simon's skin is dry. My point
is that, through grammar or "grammaticism," Berryman offers optional
readings which, rather than providing us with alternative insights into Anne
herself, multiply her world instead, attuning us to things she may not be aware
of, but which the intruding poet has supervised. And the motion thus implied,
on our part complied with, not only turns the duo Bradstreet-Berryman into
the Marcus Aurelius of Massachusetts, but also provides the poem with
almost supernatural auspices that enter her occasional use of an acute accent
on a word ("ám" in the above) and turn the whole thing ontological. The
implication is that she might *not* be "drawn" and, if not drawn, might not
even exist. Her death keeps her company throughout, and the intrusive other
poet—both ventriloquist and dummy—uses her as proxy for his own process
of getting used to such a *null* idea.

Four stanzas further on, the ontological clamp makes her scream, and

the blurt-rhythms enact a moment of biology that seems to her very much
between life and death.

> So squeezed, wince you I scream? I love you & hate
> off with you. Ages! *Useless.* Below my waist
> he has me in Hell's vise.
> Stalling. He let go. Come back: brace
> me somewhere. No. No. Yes! everything down
> hardens I press with horrible joy down
> my back cracks like a wrist
> shame I am voiding oh behind it is too late.

This is vivid empathy of course; how many male poets have gone so alertly,
so keenly, to the core of a female experience? Pain, relish, and disgust come
together here to make a shocking, though far from sensationalist whole. The
odd thing, as so often in Berryman, is that the means to this effect feels also
like the means to something bigger that looms just beyond the stanza's edge.
It's not just a woman, a woman poet, it's a human being in fit of being
tweaked by body chemistry, if you like by the matrix of all human life. The
apparatus, the cadences, the sheer drops, the psychodramatic speaking of
the unspoken in response to the unspeakable, all betoken the sense of being
put upon by the universe; only—this qualifier will reappear apropos of
Berryman—he never quite takes it to the limit to say, for example, the stuff
that stars are made of is giving her hell, just as having to *be* was hell for
him. All the physical sensations are there, the dizzying lapse from pain's peak,
but tilted downward, as it were, away from the domain of the mystic to that
of the doctor or midwife. He, too, contracts.

　　Further on the poem's nature (and caliber), as the epitome of a certain
kind of sensation, becomes even clearer when Berryman introduces

> faintings black, rigour, chilling, brown
> parching, back, brain burning, the grey pocks
> itch, a manic stench
> of pustules snapping, pain floods the palm,
> sleepless, or a red shaft with a dreadful start
> rides at the chapel, like a slipping heart.
> My soul strains in one qualm.

This is the iconography of panic, the physical equivalent of a pandemonium
which Berryman excels at conveying without, however, getting quite past
it into an imaginative survey of its sources. Somehow he stays with the
physical end of the stick that is divine or cosmic. And when he has her exclaim

> I see the cruel spread Wings black with saints!

or

> torture me, Father, lest not I be thine!

he himself is on the edge of something he can't altogether manage. I mean faith or vision; he wants something beyond either, and he isn't prepared to deal in either as a means to that end. The result is that he gets next to nothing, although accumulating by the score states of mind of almost terrifying jagged intensity. In the following, for instance, what is clear is his vicarious flailing:

> I'll—I'll—
> I am closed & coming. Somewhere! I defile
> wide as a cloud, in a cloud,
> unfit, desirous, glad—even the singings veil—.

The ardor of the would-be recipient is undeniable, but it ends feeding on itself, masticating its own convoluted texture. If ever a poem sat on the edge of an abyss, *Homage* does: it teeters, wobbles, falls apart, invites some cosmic power to rend it further, rends itself, comes provisionally together again, and comes to a dead stop with "a sourcing whom my lost candle like the firefly loves." It is no accident that he puts a double space between "a sourcing" and "whom": in that gap languishes the ghost of a missed connection which the relative pronoun disguises as "whom" while really implying whatever might have gone into the space. And it is no accident that the note to stanza 35 refers us to "cliffhangers" right after a note, concerning 33, on rapture of the deep *("Délires des grandes profondeurs")*.

I have said enough, I hope, to establish Berryman, in this long poem at least, as the master of the ceremonies of homelessness. Not at home in the universe, he isn't located anywhere else. Unable to sift from cosmic phenomena the one he wants (maybe a personal intervention in his life by a caring God?), he transcribes the froth of wanting. In other words, he uses Anne Bradstreet to delineate the bitter-sweet, thwarted transcendence of a non-believer who asks only: Why should all this emotional ferment lead to nowhere, have no point? He aspires to a metaphysical habit in almost purely emotional terms without the least reaching out into the cosmic evidence. Or, if he does so, he does it allusively with an incurious nod: "The fireflies and the stars our only light." If you scrutinize the early and later poems together with *Homage*, you find a characteristic motion of his mind made plain: into gaps he keeps on finding, he stuffs not answers—or epiphanies, visions, saliences—but big fat badges of ruinous emotion:

                                        Your fears,
Fidelity, and dandelions grown
As big as elephants, your morning lust
Can neither name nor control. No time for shame,
Whippoorwill calling, excrement falling, time
Rushes like a madman forward. Nothing can be known.

Nor measured, says Heisenberg. Nor whistled, says Wittgenstein. But that's
too easy—what can be known, and know it we do, is how he feels being
thus adrift, unhoused, not so much "ill" at ease as *terminally* ill at ease. At
times he expresses it with lucid control:

        What I am looking for *(I am)* may be
        Happening in the gaps of what I know.

That is almost definitive. It will never be untrue of him. Images of ruin
abound, from the voluntary of his Demented Priest who says "Someone
interferes / Everywhere with me" to that of the Young Hawaiian who swims
alone ("Whom Nangganangga smashed to pieces on / The road to Paradise")
and the Professor who envisions meeting his refractory class ("in Upper
Hell / Convulsed, foaming immortal blood"). Numerous personae act out
his uneasiness, his sense of doomed velleity. The bridegroom extends his hand
and places it in the womb, for lack of anything more ambitious to do. The
tortured girl can no longer remember what her torturers want her to say.
Again and again Berryman confronts himself with giving the mind something
really worth doing or "the sick brain estop." His position, if that isn't too
stern a word for it, is that the mind is redundant, existing only to invent
problems it can never solve. In the end we cannot help ourselves, and that
wan line in "Not to Live" takes on the force of an etymological reminder:

        a flux of a free & dying adjutant.

Adjūtāre means to assist or aid, which seems to be the one thing we cannot
do for ourselves, "free" as we might be, even "dying" as we are.
    Small wonder, then, that Berryman becomes the poet of metaphysical
desolation, overloaded with feelings that don't belong anywhere. What
becomes his forte is the desolating image in which fright, jitters, nightmare,
and general ontological vertigo get the reader on the raw and rake the flesh:

        With a bannister he laid a blue bone bare
        A tongue tore hard but one boot in a groin
        Sank like a drift   A double fist of hair
        Like feather members that will not rejoin

> Flat slams below there but I blew my drag
> Against my ash and strained.

Piled-up stresses evince his stress. The violence violates an old decorum of having something to say; all he has "to say" is how he feels, and he feels lousy because he has no idea of what he wants, except it's what he doesn't have. A famous, nerve-numbing, drum-beating line does the work of many:

> Near the top a bad turn some dare. Well,
> The horse swerves and screams, his eyes pop.

Such is his compression of panic, and Berryman never loses the ability to produce (perhaps after Hopkins) lines that embody an almost unidentifiable terror, which is perhaps in the long run all this poet ever had.

Twenty years separate *Delusions, etc.* from *Homage.* The imagery has widened out, especially the cosmic sort, from references to "the Local Group" (of galaxies, that is), the Hale reflector, Wolf-Rayet stars (which are *extremely* hot ones), to God as "Corpuscle-Donor," "pergalactic Intellect," and such novelties as collapsars and the expanding universe:

> Finite & unbounded
> the massive spirals absolutely fly
>
> distinctly apart, by math and *observation,*
> current math, this morning's telescopes
> & inference.

But the references come out of duty, not enthusiasm. Many of the poems in *Delusions, etc.* add up to what he slyly calls "Opus Dei," otherwise to be described as

> (a layman's winter mockup, wherein moreover
> the Offices are not within one day said
> but thro' their hours at intervals
> over many weeks—such being the World)

Agile, suave in the extreme ("my heart skips a beat / *actuellement*"), full of cultural and historical allusions, the poems are monuments to a failed religious attitude. As much dares as entreaties, as much acts of defiance as calls for help, they more or less ask the Creator why the hell He hasn't come yet and gotten John Berryman, whose untidy, cussed, bad-mouth waiting is getting on John's overwrought nerves. In the wake of Auden's clinical and public-school "Sir," Berryman comes up with a miscellany of vocatives, from "Your Benevolence," "Thou hard," "Dear," to "You," "in-negligent Father," "Sway omnicompetent," and others; but, although he works dismally hard at his new-found vocation of convert-disciple-prodigal unbeliever—he only keeps running headlong into the old panic which no flip "Okay" is going to mitigate. Shuddering and quaking, he says:

> High noon has me in pitchblack, so in hope out.

and

> Shift! Shift!
> > Frantic I cast about abroad
> for avenues of out: Who really this this?
> Can all be lost, then?

and

> Dust in my sore mouth, this deafening wind,
> frightful space   down from all sides, I'm pale
> I faint for some soft & solid & sudden way out.

which confirm him as a poet of unsignifying pain, whose yearning is as metaphysical as Herbert's, say, whose images are as dishevelled as those of Cowley and Carew, but whose mind just cannot shed ego and hitch an atomic or molecular or electromagnetic lift along one of the avenues of out. It is a sad spectacle, an even sadder sound, when he recites the physique of *Angst*. That is what he does from his beginning to his end and he has few competitors for his demoralized post. Perhaps no one else has done this narrow, yet inescapable thing quite so vividly, knowing that at the end of the line (end of the life-line) there is only sensuous escapism:

> O PARAKEETS & avocets, O immortelles
> & ibis, scarlet under that stunning sun,
> deliciously & tired I come
> toward you in orbit, Trinidad!

or something unspeakably bleak (and literally so):

> I don't think I will sing
>
> any more just now;
> or ever. I must start
> to sit with a blind brow
> above an empty heart.

Neither putting parakeets in upper case, as if to make them even bigger and more special (a super-species), nor telegraphing "or ever" with a semicolon that slows everything to an almost permanent halt anyway, changes the basic hurt. Berryman may not have cut through to the x for unknown that he craved and coveted with all his being; the increasing scope of his references has more a look of trophy-hunting than that of awed immersion; he never achieved what a *Newsweek* reviewer incredibly gifted him with (an "austere, level voice . . . so quiet it's sometimes hard to hear him"!); but it is impossible not to recognize the gibbering convulsions of his need. I think of him as a naturally metaphysical spirit, but one unable to sense the wonder that accompanies what he thought the *insult,* the *snub,* behind the nomenclature, almost as if the Local Group—never mind its inclusion of the Milky Way system, the Andromeda and Triangulum Spirals, the Magellanic Clouds, the two dwarf systems in Sculptor and Fornax, and maybe even two objects in Perseus called Maffei 1 and 2—were something from which he'd been shut out. That is the least we can say about him, though; the best is that he somehow mustered the courage to face ontological precipices dared by only a few.

JEROME MAZZARO

The Yeatsian Mask: John Berryman

The Dream Songs (1963–69) opens with John Berryman's hero having to say "a long / wonder the world can bear & be," and he continues this "long wonder," warning readers in song 308 not to "seek the strange soul, in rain & mist," but to "recall the pretty cousins they kissed, / and stick with the sweet switch of the body." The advice to seek verification of the songs in the ordinary events of life proposes a mimetic process with which readers might empathize, and it echoes statements like William Carlos Williams's in *Kora in Hell* (1920): "The trick of the dance [the poem] is in following now the words, *allegro*, now the contrary beat of the glossy leg." Williams, moreover, is among the poets whose deaths move Henry in the course of the poem. Yet, as John Bayley in "John Berryman: A Question of Imperial Sway" (1973) persuasively argues, Berryman constructs his hero by a process opposite to Williams's mirroring or the mirroring that novelists do to create character. Rather than allow entrance into the poem by permitting an identification with his speaker, Berryman assembles a voice "so single that [one] cannot share with or be a part of him." In short he creates out of his speaker a new object in nature which is not him but which is not nature either. He repeats—despite his expressed reservations about Williams—Williams's eventual modernist equivalent of the enlargement of nature by imitation. As Williams had phrased it in his *Autobiography* (1951), "It is NOT to hold the mirror up to nature that the artist performs his work. It is to make, out of the imagination, something not at all a copy of nature, a thing advanced

From *Postmodern American Poetry*. © 1980 by the Board of Trustees of the University of Illinois. The University of Illinois Press, 1980.

and apart from it." It is to make, in terms closer to those Berryman might accept, an approximation of W. B. Yeat's mask or antithetical self and to set the result in a world colored, like that of his contemporaries, by W. H. Auden and the views of Darwin, Marx, and Freud.

In this regard Berryman advises his readers in a note to the volume against mistaking Henry House alias Henry Pussy-cat, Henry Hankovitch, and Mr. Bones for the poet. Henry is "an imaginary character (not the poet, not me) . . . a white American in early middle age sometimes in blackface, who has suffered an irreversible loss and talks about himself sometimes in the first person, sometimes in the third, sometimes even in the second." The separation of Henry and Berryman may not be easy for readers predisposed to a close coincidence between life and art, for much as one may grant that Henry is the composite of the age and that the intention of the rhetoric is to divorce him from his creator, one notices that Henry shares with his author degrees from both Columbia and Cambridge, intervals at Harvard, Princeton, and the University of Minnesota, travels in both Asia and Ireland, friendships, illnesses, loves, prejudices, prizes, reputations, and a sentimental attachment to what, in "The Death of Randall Jarrell" (1966), Karl Shapiro calls "Who's First," that game of deciding who holds first place among living American poets. Henry is obviously intended as a double figure for Berryman, and he functions psychologically in that way as Mr. Bones (Henry's death urge) and the blackface interlocutor of Henry form a still further breakdown. Mr. Bones, as Berryman told Richard Kostelanetz (in 1970), is the voice of a Job's comforter telling Henry always that "you suffer, therefore you are guilty." The interlocutor, however, is never named.

Yet, just as the rhetoric of Henry is divorced from the normal language of Berryman or the eschatological view that Henry shares with many poets of the period may not, in fact, by Berryman's own, the relationship between the two figures extends beyond similarity to contrast and contiguity. As Berryman admits of Henry, "he doesn't enjoy my advantages of supervision; he just has vision. He's also simple-minded. He thinks that if something happens to him, it's forever; but I know better." Nor does Henry pay income taxes. Instead he represents "the individual soul under stress," opened to far more opportunities for experience than any of the poet's other personae; and he owes this openness as much to the "I" of Walt Whitman's *Song of Myself* (1855) as to any changes that might have occurred in the poet's life. If pressed, Berryman will confess that "we touch at certain points," but Henry's problems result from systems of chance and causality that are within literature's power to change, whereas those systems of chance and causality to which his creator is subject cannot be altered: they must be lived through. Moreover Henry has for his forebears the whole of western literature, its traditions and ranges, while Berryman has a precise limited ancestry and tradition and a mobility that, by comparison to Henry's, seems restricted. Yet, as the poet told Kostelanetz, he can speak of "Heisenberg's theory of indeterminacy" and "scholarly questions" and "modern painting" while, owing to the range of diction in *The Dream Songs,* Henry cannot.

Berryman's interests in the achievement of such a discrete voice date from the thirties and his admiration for Yeats. Yeats's "mask" had been the method of his ascertaining his opposite "true" self in a philosophical system in which opposites call each other into account. Auden's Darwinism and Marxism had reinterpreted these masks along the lines of biological and social roles. Therefore a concept of aesthetic distancing like Keats's "negative capability" would lead not, as T. S. Eliot in "Tradition and the Individual Talent" (1917) supposes, to a loss of personality but—for both Yeats and Auden—to an antipersonality. In 1936 the young Berryman, full of such notions, had taken high tea with the Irish poet, whom he reports to have said: "I never revise now . . . but in the interests of a more passionate syntax." As early as "A Note on Poetry" (1940) the young poet had converted these "interests" into technical matters, "a delight in craftsmanship . . . versification, rime, stanza-form, trope . . . by which the writer can shape from an experience in itself usually vague, a mere feeling or phrase, something that is coherent, directed, intelligible." This delight in craft, he adds, is "rarely for its own sake, mainly as it seizes and makes visible its subject." Twenty-five years later he would still be attacking Eliot's belief in "impersonality," but "passionate syntax" was now something to shield rather than make visible the subject—a strategy of skills which, "like any craftsman," a poet "who deserves to know them deserves to find them out for himself." He would now boast of knowing "more about the administration of pronouns than any other living poet writing in English or American," of being "less impressed than [he] used to be by the universal notion of a continuity of individual personality," and add that he thought art technical: "I feel myself to be addressing primarily professional writers or will be writers and teachers."

The note which prefaces his own selection for *Five Young American Poets* (1940) is devoted mainly not to these matters of syntax and personality but to an explanation of a poem, "On the London Train" (1939), clearly indebted to Auden in its flat, contemporary, class trappings and to Sir Thomas Wyatt through either Yeats or Berryman's teacher, Mark Van Doren, in its yearning for high style. The subject is a solitary man in a train compartment, whose social protective armor still does not prevent women from looking at him and fancying in their loneliness some idyllic tryst. He, in turn, imagines some virgin whom he would approach in the manner of the lovers in Wyatt's "They Flee from Me," and who subsequently, in the manner of Auden's women, will see that his wounds get proper medical attention. The narrator then intrudes to suggest that if one "could summon a lover from a former time, or summon John Donne from his grave," one would proclaim as had Wyatt that the pursuit of love is unpleasant and that the anguish persists beyond the marriage bed. In a final moralizing stanza Berryman, again in the manner of Auden, aligns the poem's various paradoxes into "shell" and "life." The "sea-shell" puzzling Destiny is also the train and the protective armor of the passenger, while the lives it contains become the train's passengers and the passengers' fantasies. The discrepancy between fixity and motion which results from obstinately remaining out of life's stream becomes in the narrator's words "too little recompense" for those like the passenger "who suffer on the shore."

The syntax of the poem is spare, "elliptical and indistinctly allusive: casual in tone and form, frightening in import," reflecting the Auden climate that Berryman claims set in by 1935. This climate, as Berryman says in "Waiting for the End, Boys" (1948), is indebted to Yeats's later poetry, although Berryman admits that safeguards prevented Auden from being overwhelmed. Jarrell in "Changes of Attitude and Rhetoric in Auden's Poetry" (1941) views the "eccentric syntax" of early Auden as a similar "creative extension" of language; and assuredly the syntax in the early works of both Auden and Berryman does not of itself preclude novelistic ways of creating character. Both remain tied to a traditional use of predicaments—those concrete situations of personality and circumstance that allow readers to identify themselves with what is being depicted: how a man of virtue, for example, might react to a specific attempt at seduction. Over an extended number of circumstances and a variety of personal characteristics, these predicaments set up so closed a system of logic that the reader can swear the character is "real," that, in short, the reader can predict its behavior in circumstances that are not contained in the work. In briefer pieces, one makes the same logical assumptions, but one bases them on premises that are more generalized: all lonely men act this way, or one has known this to happen before. For Auden the individual qualities of personality take on the color of class values which are apparent in the Berryman poem. The ironic moralizing on which he ends the poem assumes some system of normative behavior inspired by Destiny. One's amusement at the passenger's self-satisfaction at "remaining on shore" comes from the sense that man is a social being and, painful as love may be, man cannot remain removed from it. As the poet will later tell Jane Howard (1967), "it's terrible to give half your life over to someone else, . . . but it's worse not to."

Much as "On the London Train" explores one extreme of Berryman's experiments with character and passionate syntax, "At Chinese Checkers" (1939) explores the other. Its flat Audenesque game of chinese checkers is so presented as to warrant response by means not of Auden's ironic detachment but of Yeats's ceremonial involvement. Cast in eight-line stanzas that are a variation of those used by Yeats's "In Memory of Major Robert Gregory" (1918), the work navigates through a reef of echoes. One reads of "passionate activity," "dreadful leniency," the "mountainous dead world" as well as of "a voice that even undisciplined can stir / The country blood." Yet neither the stanza form nor the phrases so redeem the importance of the initial recovery and the speaker's inability to concentrate on the game before him that a subsequent comparison of these activities to Delmore Schwartz's inability to bring his mind to bear on the day's needs gains the significance Berryman wants. The comparison works instead to trivialize Schwartz's efforts, much as failed Yeatsian lines like "Venus on the half-shell was found a dish / To madden a fanatic" and "Marbles are not the marbles that they were" work to trivialize the Yeatsian elegance that elsewhere appears. In an ironic structure such as "On the London Train" the poet might have succeeded with such definition; but here, remaining serious as he does in the final stanza, he is guilty of what Jarrell in reviewing *The Dispossessed* (1948) labels as a slavish adherence to "Yeatsian grandiloquence" that results at times in "monumental bathos."

Thus, at the beginning at least, Berryman could be grouped with other poets of his generation as one who, though he had moved toward passionate syntax, had not yet achieved an individual voice. Like Theodore Roethke and Jarrell before him, Berryman seems more concerned in his first volume with bringing his talent into line with a tradition than in establishing himself as an independent voice albeit, as Daniel Hughes suggests in "The Dream Songs" (1966), the echoes may have resulted from a desire by the poet "to take Eliot and Yeats and Auden on their own grounds, and do it better." Although Dudley Fitts was already finding the grammar of these early poems a "fanfare of ship-wrecked syntax, textbook inversions and alliterations" and "somehow without the excitement that attends the transformation of a craft into a completely realized art," Jarrell was citing the volume's most extreme dislocations of syntax—"The Nervous Songs"—as the direction that the poet should be moving in. His citation of these works and the enigmatic parts of Berryman's other pieces is part of a view Jarrell derived from Auden— namely that poetry represented the Freudian ego, embodying in its realization both id and superego. This psychological part of Auden, which had been pointed out by Schwartz and others, is precisely what Berryman is rejecting in favor of a Yeatsian view of masks.

Yeats's masks are predicated not upon an individual memory of Freud but upon a racial memory akin to Carl Jung's racial unconscious and along with that a psychological typology that goes back to the Greek Stoics. By the end of Yeats's life, these masks had been divided into twenty-eight phases that ranged from a nonhuman first phase to that of the fool and had represented an enlargement of an early belief that masks were what people assumed to bridge the discrepancies between their own and other people's conceptions of themselves. Nowhere does Berryman publicly acknowledge an affinity with Jung, though in song 327 Henry chides Freud for having enlightened—but misled—others. Henry insists, in echo of James Joyce, that "a dream is a panorama / of the whole mental life"; and in the next song, he refers to "his ancient brain," suggesting something like a racial recall. Berryman, however, goes only so far as to acknowledge the possibility of Freud's late work having entered his writing, especially *Civilization and Its Discontents* (1929). The comment follows a condescending description of a woman who sees Henry "corresponding vaguely to Freud's differentiation of the personality into superego or conscience, ego or façade or self, and id or unconscious." Berryman adds that he did not know whether or not she was right, but that he had not begun with so full-fledged a conception. *Recovery* (1973), the poet's unfinished posthumously published novel, describes its autobiographical hero, Alan Severance, as having "been a rigid Freudian for thirty years, with heavy admixture however from Reich's early work"; and one assumes that if the poet understood or sympathized with Jung it was mainly through an interest in Yeats.

"The Nervous Songs," which represent Berryman's clearest approximation of an acceptance of Yeatsian masks in the early poems, are again realized so as to bring the Irish poet in line with the social concerns of Auden. Based as are *The Dream Songs* on Yeats's *Words for Music Perhaps* (1933), the lyrics depict the poet's confrontation with the twenty-eighth phase, when the physical world suggests to the mind "pictures and events that have no relation to [one's] needs or even to [one's] desires; [one's] thoughts are an aimless reverie; [one's] acts are aimless like [one's] thoughts; and it is in this aimlessness that [one] finds [one's] joy." Yeats began to compose his lyrics in the spring of 1929 after a long illness; his mood was one of "uncontrolled energy and daring." He wrote Olivia Shakespear that his "songs" were "songs," "not so much that they may be sung as that I may define their kind of emotion to myself. I want them to be all emotion and all impersonal." Later he added in another letter: "Sexual abstinence fed their fire. . . . They sometimes came out of the greatest mental excitements I am capable of." "The Nervous Songs" use the same six-line stanza basic to Yeats's pieces, but with neither his compulsion to rhyme nor his inclination to add occasional refrains. The sexual appetite of Berryman's girl in "Young Woman's Song" is not the exuberance of Crazy Jane but the result of capitalism which forces one to pay £3.10 for a hat and to turn one's body into a commodity. Similarly the discrepancy between thinking and the world in "The Song of the Tortured Girl" results from Nazi torture rather than from some godly gift. If Berryman's people are to act as mediums through which new truths are made known, it will be less by any Yeatsian accident of identity than by means of an overwhelming social coercion.

At the same time that Berryman was working on the last poems of *The Dispossessed,* he wrote a number of sonnets that he later published as *Berryman's Sonnets* (1967). The poems record an adulterous affair which he undertook during the spring and summer of 1947. The works were not originally intended for public view and carry on in private the experiments with characterization and passionate syntax that are more conservatively displayed in the published volume. By basing the predicaments of the various pieces on literary as well as life circumstances, the poet begins to construct a language and syntax and view of personality whose relations to nature are blurred. Lise (or Chris, as it was probably) is always trying to break through a cloud of literary convention, jargon, textbook inversion, and alcoholic fantasy. She is variously Petrarch's Laura, Sidney's Stella, Shakespeare's young man, Anne Frank, the daughter of a Tulsa oilman, and Ilse Koch—the conventional "cruel mistress" whose function it is to make the lover suffer either requited or unrequited love. The poet, too, seems unable to determine whether he is a character in life or literary history or literature. He embarks on a comparable variety of roles, including eventually that of Don Quixote, who evinces similar self-confusion in Cervantes's novel. Quixote's being a character in fiction leads Berryman finally to present his adultery as if it were fictional as well, and this approach may account for his eventually releasing the lyrics. He adds to the original 111 poems four new sonnets and a Henry-like proem that cites Jacques Maritain to the effect that wickedness is perhaps soluble in art.

Critics have been able to detect in these sonnets prefigurations of the techniques that the poet would later display in *The Dream Songs.* Hayden Carruth in "Declining Occasions" (1968) summarizes these devices as "archaic spelling, fantastically complex diction, tortuous syntax, formalism, a witty and ironic attitude toward prosody generally." But one thing that is not found here is a picaresque hero. Berryman is a serious, romantic, and passionate lover, and his attempts to deflate this image often make him resemble the cross-gartered Malvolio of Shakespeare's *Twelfth Night.* He is in life the passenger that "On the London Train" depicted, caught up in the slim chances of realizing the dream of a literary romance and pursuing that opportunity past the point of reason into regions of self-destruction. Berryman relates through Severance that the affair changed him from a social drinker who occasionally got drunk into an alcoholic: "I'd been faithful to my wife— despite heavy provocation . . . for five years. My mistress drank heavily and I drank along with her, and afterward I just kept on." Elsewhere William Martz in *John Berryman* (1969) records that the romance "brought him to the point of suicide, with thoughts of killing both himself and his mistress because she flatly refused to leave her husband and to marry him. His wife, who was ignorant of the affair, persuaded him to undergo psychoanalysis, and he stayed under analysis from 1947 to 1953." The affair with Chris (Lise) was indeed the *crise* he refers to in sonnet 18, and alcohol hazes figure as often as the hazes of literary allusions in the work's unfolding.

What *Berryman's Sonnets* accomplishes is the temporary elimination of Auden's social consciousness, for without a clear distinction between art and nature, one is unsure what social institutions need reform. One can as easily propose, as had Williams in his late works, that it is the mind that requires change. With this removal of social consciousness, there is consequently less need to reproduce actual speech; one can as well produce artificial language, as the sonnets do, accomplishing the modern equivalent of the rejection implied in Ben Jonson's pronouncement that Edmund Spenser, "in affecting the ancients, writ no language." Berryman in "The Long Way to MacDiarmid" (1956) makes explicit this rejection, stating simply that Jonson was wrong in the matter; and presumably the confused realms that the *Sonnets* reflects demand a corresponding language that embodies previous art as well as nature. But, if one eliminates nature as the basic means of verification for thought, what becomes the new basis for credibility in art? Is it to be, as Quixote suggests, faith in the author? If so, is the author like Henry David Thoreau to write about himself because it is a subject that he knows better than anyone else? Berryman suggests as much in "The Poetry of Ezra Pound" (1949): "Yeats, another Romantic, is . . . the subject of his own poetry, himself-as-himself. Pound is his own subject *qua* modern poet." Yet Berryman will infer of Pound's poetry that the personal is not very personal: there is a "peculiar detachment of interest with which Pound seems to regard himself" as well as an "unfaltering, encyclopedic mastery of tone" that somehow offsets a "comparative weakness of syntax." Berryman designates that other master of artificial language, John Milton, "the supreme English master of syntax" and even imitates him in dream song 20 ("Hurl, God who found / us in this, down / something"). All the same one suspects from Berryman's comments on Pound that the real arbiter for credibility is already the liveliness or energy that entices a reader's empathy.

The inclination not to seek verification of thought in nature seems to have been increased by the reception of *The Dispossessed*. Berryman told Peter Stitt in a *Paris Review* interview (1972): "If a writer gets hot early, then his work ought to become known early. If it doesn't, he is in danger of feeling neglected. We take it that all young writers overestimate their work. . . . I overestimated myself, as it turned out, and felt bitter, bitterly neglected." He then went on to add that "Auden once said that the best situation for a poet is to be taken up early and held for a considerable time and then dropped after he had reached the level of indifference." So far as reviews of the volume go, the reception was favorable, and in 1949 he received the Shelley Memorial Award. What the volume failed to do, however, was to secure the poet a standing comparable to the one Robert Lowell achieved in 1946 with the publication of *Lord Weary's Castle* or to the position that Berryman's longtime friend, Dylan Thomas, held by virtue of poetry readings and his *Selected Writings* (1946). The bitterness allied with the disappointment over the failure of the affair the year before and its suggestion that "the old high way of love" that the poet sought was no longer possible led Berryman first to seek verification in psychoanalytical theory in his biography of Stephen Crane (1950) and then to use history in part in *Homage to Mistress Bradstreet* (1956). William Meredith in "In Loving Memory" (1973) reports that by the end of his life, Berryman's antipathy to today's "conventional manners" prompted his statement that "promiscuous honesty" was "often no more than an evasion of the social predicament." His alternative yearning for Yeatsian "decorum, even for old-fashioned manners," was not so much a return to Audenesque "social behavior" as to a "social ideal." Meredith conjectures that "at heart, Berryman was a courtly man, though usually (like most of us) he could act out only a parody of that. The forms of behavior that attracted him were as traditional as the forms of prosody."

The divorce from nature that both the romance and the "bad" reception effected may well account, too, for a terror that the poet began to feel and which increased his need for alcohol. Berryman told Jane Howard that life "is a terrible place, but we have to exert our wills. I wake up every morning terrified," and she went on to comment, "Hence the whisky—under whose influence the terror seems somewhat to diminish—and hence . . . the ink and what it writes." The divorce certainly accounts for the poet's seeking out other alienated figures as "friends." He told Stitt of A. E. Housman, "Housman is one of my heroes and always has been. He was a detestable and miserable man. Arrogant, unspeakably lonely, cruel, and so on, but an absolutely marvelous minor poet, I think, and a great scholar." Earlier he had described with a degree of wonder the fortitude of Gerard Manley Hopkins and Robert Bridges, forging ahead with their poetries despite the neglect of the reading public. But perhaps most importantly the alienation establishes a justification for Berryman's choosing to adapt a modernist view of imitation to postmodernist ends. If, for instance, psychoanalysis creates a mirror image of the self through recollection for the purposes of understanding, why not, as Yeats proposes, construct a nonself or antithetical image for such purposes? Why not use a Yeatsian mask? The purposes of dramatic monologue in writers like Jarrell and Auden do not prevent the nonself from defining the self. Playing at roles is a time-honored approved method of defining one's limits. Simply because these roles in such poets are kept within the confines of novelistic and Freudian characterization does not necessarily exclude one's developing them along other lines. Why can't the roles be developed along the lines of style or passionate syntax alone, for, as Berryman states in "A Note on Poetry," language "permit[s] one to say things that would not otherwise be said at all; it may be said, even that [language] permit[s] one to feel things that would not otherwise be felt."

Homage to Mistress Bradstreet seems to strike an equilibrium between such theories of characterization. Anne Bradstreet's character is still delineated along novelistic lines. Like the poet she is alienated from the beliefs of her day, finding her gift of poetry ignored by her husband and her sensuality forced into submission. These qualities which are presented in a conventional stream of consciousness technique are enmeshed in an unconventional syntax that John Ciardi in "The Researched Mistress" (1957) describes as "a rhythm so intensely compacted and forward moving as to be a communication in itself." The eight-line stanza the poem assumes is again, by Berryman's own indication, a variation of Yeats's "Major Gregory" stanza; but modifications like breaking the stanza "after the short third line," having the next four-beat line lead into a "balancing heroic couplet," then truncating the stanza again, and finally widening it into an alexandrine, produce a far less stately flow. As he suggests, the stanza is "at once flexible and grave, intense and quiet, able to deal with matters both high and low." His subject, he acknowledges, is Bradstreet as a woman rather than as a poet. "The point of the . . . poem," he told Kostelanetz, "was to take a woman unbelievably conventional and give her every possible trial and possibility of error and so on, and wind her up in a crazy love affair, and then get her out of it." The syntax which strives for comparably extraordinary effects continues by its very rejection of the ordinary the disaffection from Auden's social consciousness that the *Sonnets* commenced.

Berryman had begun the poem in 1948, thinking it might run "about seven or eight stanzas of eight lines each"; but he stuck after the first eleven lines. Not until reading a 900-page typescript of Saul Bellow's *The Adventures of Augie March* (1953) was the poet able to continue. He recognized in Bellow's novel "a breakthrough . . . the wiping out of the negative personality that had created and inhabited his earlier work." Augie was nothing like Bellow; he was really an antithetical rather than an objectified self, and the characterization and scope of the work suggested that a comparable achievement in poetry might be possible. Berryman began to reconceive his poem as "a continuity of individual personality" that developed by shifts of association collecting about three occasions of rebellion, each "succeeded by submission, though even in the moment of the poem's supreme triumph . . . the birth of her first child—rebellion survives." The first of these rebellions at fourteen is ended by smallpox, and it concerns Bradstreet's acceptance of her body; the second involves her submission to the hardships of colonial life; and the last, which prompts her imagined romance with the narrator, concerns her submission to a loveless marriage. Out of the fusion of these rebellions Berryman hoped to construct a poem that might rival *The Waste Land* (1922) by offering what *The Dispossessed* had not—a heroine whose survival is inspiring.

Berryman proposes his response to Eliot in what he likes to insist is an "historical poem," even though he confesses that "the affair in the whole middle part of the poem is not historical but purely imaginary." Granting this whole middle part is a temporary lapse, one may still wonder at what kind of "history" *Homage* is. The work alternately suggests that it is historical in subject and in form, a twentieth-century attempt to reproduce a seventeenth-century dialogue of body and soul; yet the poem seems ever altering facts, and the particularly Donnean intensity of the language runs counter to Bradstreet's own preference for Guillaume du Bartas and Francis Quarles. Berryman admits that his heroine "was unbelievably devoted to her husband"; he also describes hugging himself one night, having decided that her "fierce dogmatic old father was going to die blaspheming, in delirium." Alan Holder in "Anne Bradstreet Resurrected" (1969) cites other discrepancies between the poem and its major source, Helen Campbell's *Anne Bradstreet and Her Time* (1891). Berryman has Bradstreet speak when Campbell indicates that she was silent; he intensifies her desire for children; he makes her a closer friend to Anne Hutchinson than it seems she had been; and he attributes to her the deforming effects of smallpox that Campbell assigns to Lucy Hutchinson. Berryman's only allusion to her poetry is to "The Four Monarchs" (stanza 12); he was willing generally to pronounce it dull and didactic; and, indeed, the neometaphysical language and intensity of his voice work against the neoclassical couplet that the real Bradstreet practiced.

Holder rightly asserts that the poem is "operating on the Yeatsian assumption that the artist's nature and his production are antithetical"— that the interesting figure of Bradstreet is also a dull writer; but what Holder does not consider is that Bradstreet is herself an antithetical self for the poet. The work is, as Berryman proposes, "the construction of a world rather than the reliance upon one existent which is available to a small poem." Its system of verification is one of intrarelational elements. The constructed world does not hold its content for comparison to life so much as parts of its content compare to other internal elements along lines suggested by I. A. Richards in "The Interaction of Words" (1942) and expounded by the New Critics. The work may, as Berryman contends, be the "equivalent of a 500-page psychological novel"; but if it is a psychological novel, it is about Berryman as well as Bradstreet. It is a novel whose action repeats that of the passenger in "On the London Train" and the speaker of *Berryman's Sonnets* by creating and courting an ideal love whose actual verification is doubtful and whose existence, in the case of Bradstreet, is less significant than the "peculiar energy of the language" that Stanley Kunitz in "No Middle Flight" (1957) sees resulting from a galvanization of noun and verb and crystallizing Berryman's separate imaginative world. The "essence" of this energy, Ciardi contends, is "the compression of the language to squeeze out all but the most essential syntax (as well as some of that)" so that "relatively few unaccented syllables" remain "and the resultant clustering of heavy stresses, enforced by a heavy incidence of internal pause (caesura) thrusts the poem forward."

Despite Berryman's endorsements from Robert Fitzgerald, Edmund Wilson, Conrad Aiken, and Lowell, Kunitz proposes that "the poem as a whole lacks inherent imaginative grandeur; whatever effect of magnitude it achieves has been beaten into it"; and Ciardi is at a loss to determine "whether the passion is as truly love as he asserts, or more nearly a thing literary and made." To put it another way, both critics were at a loss to determine whether the delight in craftsmanship lies in the craft that makes the subject visible or obscures it. Other critics tried to determine if Jarrell was right in holding that there may be "some last heat or pressure, concentration and indi-vidualization" that turns "a photograph into a painting, a just observation into a poem." That is the position of Lowell in "The Poetry of John Berryman" (1964). Lowell says of *Homage* that "nothing could be more high-pitched, studied and inflamed. One can read it many times, and still get lost in it; with each renewal it becomes clearer and more haunting." It would also be the position that A. Alvarez in *Under Pressure* (1965) would make typical of American writing: "The movement of the modern arts has been to press deeper and deeper into the subterranean world of psychic isolation, to live out in the arts the personal extremism of breakdown, paranoia, and depression." "The Extremist artist," he went on to say in a 1966 postscript to "Sylvia Plath," "sets out deliberately to explore the roots of his emotions, the obscurest springs of his personality, maybe even the sickness he feels himself to be prey to, 'giving himself over to it . . . for the sake of the range and intensity of his art.' " Hayden Carruth would later see something ominous in the growing remoteness of a poet's moving "from a real woman, to the ghost of a woman three centuries gone, to the phantasmagoric world of 'Henry' and 'Mr. Bones.' "

Ciardi's indecision has been the position of most critics who, anticipating novelist characterization and following the lead of Fitts, have found more and more that Berryman's technique calls attention to itself. James Dickey, for example, would soon be complaining that "Berryman is a poet so preoccupied with poetic effects as to be totally in their thrall. . . . His inversions, his personal and often irritating cute colloquialisms and deliberate misspellings, his odd references, his basing of lines and whole poems on private allusions, create what must surely be the densest verbal thicket since Empson's." Jarrell, who was perhaps most responsible for pointing the direction, fell into public silence, content to praise the "intelligence" of Berryman in his "Fifty Years of American Poetry" (1962) rather than consider what must have been an awareness that there may be dangers in excessive heat or pressure, that the self-consciousness of Berryman's syntax had upset the normal balance of superego and id that Jarrell championed as the goal of postmodern verse. Jarrell too must have been disturbed by Berryman's choosing to stress "eccentricity" over normalcy and by his making the "eccentric" writer the hero of culture. How by excluding himself from normative behavior could the poet resolve his vision into acceptable patterns? Berryman himself recurred to one of Jarrell's favorite writers, Rudyard Kipling, for his justification: "As Kipling used to say of his stories, 'I hold them up and let the wind blow through them, and if anything's left, I publish it.' "

Berryman took to heart, however, Kunitz's statement that *Homage* lacked "inherent imaginative grandeur"; and in accepting the National Book Award twelve years later, he wondered how he "dared ever lift [his] head and trouble the public again." Yet he did, and his "survival" provides the guiding image for his hero—a survivor too. Lowell accurately observed of the situation that "it's something to create a sensation when you're over fifty." Most poets retire at the age when Berryman was issuing the first installment of *Dream Songs*. Nonetheless, like Henry and the American Negro whose voice he often assumes, he had stuck it out; he had proved as expert as the Black in survival. As one critic observed of the Negro, "he is familiar with death and yet somehow continually picks himself off the very floor, clambers out of the very basement of modern civilization. Supremely a victim, he escapes self-pity through joy in survival. Like the cat, he has nine lives. Henry's search is to learn to be a cat, simply to continue, as coolly as possible, to play it by ear." Berryman himself adds: "Well, he's very brave, Henry, in that he keeps on living after other people have dropped dead." In "Henry Tasting All the Secret Parts oᶠ Life" (1965) Meredith associates this "survival instinct" generally "with every sort of person and situation," pointing out that it includes even the madmen: three of the songs (52–54) deal directly with insanity and a number of others touch on it with familiarity, making Henry in one way a latter-day, different antithetical self than had been Yeats's Crazy Jane and Tom the Lunatic.

Berryman also moves to a different structure than the basically narrative method of *Homage*. He chooses one closer to that of the *Sonnets,* again basing its stanza on Yeats's *Words for Music Perhaps.* The "original design," as he reveals in song 379, for any would-be "assistant professors become associates / by working on his works" was blurred by "strange & new outlines." He told one interviewer (in 1969) that "some of the Songs are in alphabetical order; but, mostly, they just belong to areas of hope and fear that Henry is going through at a given time." "Its plot," he went on to explain, "is the personality of Henry as he moves on in the world. Henry gains ten years. At one time his age is given as forty-one, . . . and at a later point he's fifty-one." In song 112 he announces: "My framework is broken, I am coming to an end," and in song 348 he suggests that opposed to "the definite hole / in a definite universe . . . Henry & his surviving friends now truly confront" oblongs "when a whore can almost overthrow a government." These "oblongs" appear to have dimensions based in some way on 7, 11, and 5, the product of the first two being the number of songs in *77 Dream Songs,* and the product of the three (385), the total number of songs in the final collection. In "Cagey John" (1968) William Wasserstrom proposes that a numerical relation exists between the epigraph from Lamentations (3:63) and the structure of the first three parts. The parts break down into groups of 26, 25, and 26 songs respectively; and, with seven exceptions, the poems are "arranged in three verse paragraphs each six lines long"; but more significant Wasserstrom restores the first half-verse to Berryman's quotation and finds that its admonition—"behold their sitting down, and their rising up"—contains the germ of the minstrel show and death-and-resurrection motifs on which the poem is principally based.

The total work's division into seven parts—an initial trivium followed by an enlarged quadrivium whose final poems, 384 and 385, echo poems 76 and 77 in the first collection—enforces the overall importance of this number in the work's organization. The number may exist as a totality; or, since the groupings can be seen as two blocks of three separated by the "posthumous" dream songs, one can argue for a breakdown of seven into a 3–1–3 principle. Seven is important in the churches, trumpets, seals, angels, stars, etc. of the book of Revelation to which on at least four occasions (songs 10, 46, 56, and 347) Henry alludes, aside from his making Christine Keeler (in song 348) into a pale reminder of the Whore of Babylon. One would not be too far afield in viewing the combined work, as certainly Henry views it, as the chaos of the Fourth Kingdom awaiting the Second Coming of Christ. Nonetheless Berryman rightly insists that the effect of the organization is not an Apollonian structure but a process of expunging fear that the conclusion of the book's opening epigraph from Lamentations (3:57) anticipates. Later the quotations from Sir Francis Chichester and Major General Charles George Gordon will confirm Berryman's fear underlying the work, which, one gathers, is like the abyss of which Pascal speaks: one is constantly putting obstacles at the edge of it so as not to fall in. The condition is that of "the doomed young envy[ing] the old, the doomed old envy[ing] the young" (song 190); and the unique rhetoric is meant to become a way of escape by separating its hero from its enemy, the fallen masses of mankind.

The "irreversible loss" which prompts the poem's action and which Henry suffers is presented to readers in song 1 as a falling out with a "they" who were "trying to put something over" on him. Henry thus feels the same sort of alienation that Berryman describes for himself, and this alienation is suggested in the sequence by a series of criminal/outsider references. The "unappeasable" huffiness that Henry is made to feel at this falling out echoes dimly the wrath of Achilles on which the *Iliad* begins; it indicates as well a shift, in the terminology of David Riesman's *The Lonely Crowd* (1950), to inner-directedness. The falling out constitutes the discovery of the other or consciousness, often through opposition: one has limits; one extends only so far and at that point something else takes over. Henry recalls that at one time he lacked this sense: "All the world like a woolen lover / once did seem on Henry's side." The differentiation which is implicit in this separation generates a process of empirical self-definition along what William James categorizes as spiritual, social, and material lines. The differentiation allows as well the device of Yeatsian masks by which Berryman had earlier defined self. Anthropologists like Claude Lévi-Strauss theorize that the separation forces a simultaneous need for language, society, and the prohibition of incest; and in *The Dream Songs* Berryman suggests the division has resulted in the work's "original crime: art, rime" (song 26).

On a spiritual plane the separation has a counterpart in Adam's fall from Grace or Lucifer's fall from Heaven, and as the sequence opens, Henry is either hiding all day, as Adam hid after eating the forbidden fruit, or he is hidden from others by the day, as Lucifer in *Paradise Lost* is hidden after his fall. The separation has a psychological oedipal counterpart in man's fall from the womb (Eden) into the world, and Henry seems in the sequence to be greatly preoccupied with his mother (songs 11, 14, 100, 117, 129, 147, 166, 208, 317, and 322) and with birth. Imaged in terms of a lost bed-partner, the separation takes on social echoes from Plato's *Symposium* and Aristophanes' parable. There, as punishment for repeated assaults on Heaven, Zeus halved the essentially primeval man, so that man since, to achieve a feeling of his original fulness, has had to seek his complement. The material separations can be seen in Henry's various attempts to become the things he admires. But the intent of such a separation is ever to find a method for dissolving back into an original unity; and, in song 380, Henry recognizes that, as the content of his outcries does not constitute recognition of a dimension outside the self but an investment of objects with self, the autobiographical mode of Wordsworth's *Prelude* (1850) is the way:

> Wordsworth, thou form almost divine, cried Henry,
> "the egotistical sublime" said Keats,
> oh ho, you lovely man!

As Yeats had indicated, one merges with his work by relating his own subjectivity to a second subjectivity rather than by the method of science which obscures personality by depersonalizing it.

The complexity of this integration of personalities as it deals with subjectively treated literary sources and with life processes completes the work's connection with the epigraph from Olive Schreiner. Her preface to *The Story of an African Farm* (1894) outlines two methods of painting life: the first, objective or stage method, by which characters are marshalled and ticketed along conventional plot lines; and the second, subjective or life method, in which "nothing can be prophesied. . . . Men appear, act and react upon each other, and pass away. . . . When the curtain falls, no one is ready." Berryman claims the second method and its underlying subjectivity for *The Dream Songs*. The method allows him to invest his hero with an admittedly prejudiced awareness of isolation—of his being "at odds wif de world & its god" (song 5)—as well as with a recognition that one method of unification lodges not in love, as it should, but in a threatening rhetoric of conformity:

> It is in the administration of rhetoric,
> on these occasions, that—not the fathomless heart—
> the thinky death consists
>
> (song 10)

It permits him also to give Henry a sense of guilt, which Henry then measures repeatedly against crimes like murder which he judges are greater than his:

> But never did Henry, as he thought he did,
> end anyone and hacks her body up
> and hide the pieces, where they may be found.
>
> (song 29)

Such investments of subjectivity demand, in turn, that readers adjust their normal expectations and view the various and often repetitive roles of Henry and Berryman as single impersonations controlled and colored by discrete shifting intelligences. Neither impersonally realized places and situations nor Yeats's fixed and clearly defined antithetical selves occur. Divorced from Henry and Berryman, such places and situations might be showplaces for presenting a single subjectivity, and the outrageous biases of both voices exist as a block to such presentations. The world one enters is relational rather than material, and, unlike the meditative practices of Donne, Hopkins, and others, the observations that one encounters are meant to be irreducible and unverifiable. The relational emphasis of this world gains credence, moreover, by a suppression of subjective devices like motivation, rationalization, and recall that might otherwise cement verifiable continuity in the characters of Henry and his creator. Henry's sense of isolation, for instance, resists union by a rhetoric of conformity based on will (language) for a "blind" discovery which is preverbal and which, like the ending of *The Waste Land*, "passeth understanding." Songs 155 and 242 present prefigurations of this preverbal world in Henry's silent communications with Delmore Schwartz and a student, and song 366 reemphasizes that "these Songs are not meant to be understood, you understand. / They are meant only to terrify & comfort." The resolution with Berryman when it occurs is based on an implicit but unexpressed continuity that suggests apparent discontinuity while simultaneously embodying love.

Berryman accomplishes the sense of apparent discontinuity which such a relational vision requires by returning again to two methods of mimesis.

He will at times seem to be creating an imaginary world which is self-sufficient
and independent of nature. At other times, as in the elegies of "The Lay of
Ike," he will make pointed reference to a real outside world. In addition to
this general discontinuity, he will use a rhetoric which confuses expectation
by self-consciously altering normal syntax in a number of ways. He will, for
example, invert normal sentence order so that subject-verb-complement
becomes complement-verb-subject ("Hard on the land wears the strong
sea / and empty grows every bed"); or he will use an emphatic verb when
the reader might normally expect a simple tense ("All the world like a woolen
lover / once did seem on Henry's side"); or he will shift from a simple to
an emphatic mood ("never did Henry . . . end anyone and hacks her body
up"); or he will leave out part of a progressive verb ("He wishing he could
squirm again"); or he will violate the normal expectations of subject-verb
agreement ("he don't feel so"). Likewise he will shift the usage levels of his
language from standard to colloquial to vulgate, in the process resurrecting
archaic words like "makar" for poet, infantilisms like "thinky" for
"thoughtful," and slang. He will also shift his pronoun referents from first
to second to third person and from singular to plural and, as in the opening
song, dissolve his own "I" into Henry's "I." Henry will also convert adjectives
into nouns ("said a screwed-up lovely 23"), adverbs into adjectives ("made
Henry wicked & away"), use synecdoche ("Two daiquiris / withdrew into
a corner of the gorgeous room / and one told the other a lie"), and displace
modifiers so that ambiguity results ("Once in a sycamore I was glad / all
at the top, and I sang." Does "all at the top" describe Henry's position on
the tree or does it describe his state of mind?). Still, in the case of these
breaches of expectation, if the discontinuity were real, fragmentation would
occur; yet it does not.

The continuity which allows this apparent discontinuity while at the same
time furthering the work's sense of a "long poem" is shaped by principles
of recurrence. Blocking six lines into stanzas with regular rhymes suggests
an initial mechanical unity that blocking three stanzas into separate songs
conveys to the whole work. The blocking creates an "imaginary score" to
contain the disjunctions, much as music in actual song by its recurrence
contains disjunctive verses or as any mechanical procedure tends by its
approach to unify results. These "imaginary scores" are reinforced by
recurrent words, images, and attitudes as well as by the central figure of
Henry. Henry, who represents Berryman's most original variation on the
Yeatsian mask, tends repeatedly, as had the speaker of the *Sonnets,* to
historicize his plights by comparing them to other famous events in history,
or to dramatize them by imagining himself in movie roles, or to fictionalize

them by relating them to previous literary situations. These multiple attitudinizings and taking of roles have been compared by critics to the transformations about a single psychological type that occur in *Finnegans Wake* (1939); but, perhaps owing to the absence of motivation and rationalization, they come to resemble more nearly what Stephen Leacock in "A, B, and C" (1910) calls "the human element of mathematics." Just as these famous characters of arithmetic problems become tokens to illustrate situations that devolve into mathematics, Henry becomes a token whose situations often relate immediately to a mathematics of syntax and on occasion more remotely to life. The perpetual editorializing that prevents one from viewing Henry independently, and thus forces one to accept or reject his authority, provides no room for deep understanding.

In constructing this new rhetoric which is also to define Henry's and his interlocutor's natures, Berryman makes abundant use of Freud's theories in *The Interpretation of Dreams* (1900) and *Wit and Its Relation to the Unconscious* (1905) on the way that thought functions both in dream work and in wit work. Both dream and wit have in common that they are reactions to censorship in conscious thought, working in dreams through condensation, displacement, and transformation of the optative into the indicative ("it is" for "would it were") and in wit through condensation, displacement, and indirect expression. In dreams censorship is overcome "regularly through displacements and through the choice of ideas which are remote enough from those objectionable to secure passage through." In wit, which neither compromises with nor evades inhibition, the censorship is overcome by letting the unaltered or nonsensical ambiguity of words and multiplicity of thought relations appear to the consciousness at the same time admissible as jest or rational as wit. Thus the dream songs function to allow Henry access into experience which would normally be censored. He feels that he needs this access because he is now "unmistakably a Big One" (song 7) and does not feel like one (song 184). In fact, as the songs unfold, he fears that he will not go out in a blaze of glory like Yeats, Williams, Goya, and Beethoven, that his fate should be for various reasons of worthlessness that of Delmore Schwartz, who might "remember the more beautiful & fresh poems / of early manhood" (song 150).

If Freud provides the method of constructing rhetoric, the particular bidirectional stress that Berryman places on language derives its existence from the writings of Pound and R. P. Blackmur as well as the practices of writers like Cummings, Roethke, and Joyce. Pound in this regard enunciates "the feeling back," and he does so along what Ernest Fenollosa called "the ancient line of advance." As early as *How to Read* (1929) Pound had connected the poet's role to the preservation of language and culture: "The individual cannot think and communicate his thought, the governor and legislator cannot act effectively or frame his laws, without words, and the solidity and validity of these words is in the care of the damned and despised *litterati*. When their work goes rotten . . . i.e. becomes flushing and inexact, or excessive or bloated, the whole machinery of social and individual thought and order goes to rot." Blackmur in contrast outlines the "advance" in terms of new or fresh idiom: "language so twisted and posed in a form that it not only expresses the matter in hand but adds to the stock of available reality." In "Olympus" (1970) Berryman describes his coming across the Blackmur quotation during his last year at Columbia (1935–36): "I was never altogether the same man after *that*." In an early essay on Cummings (1930) Blackmur had denied to that poetic experimenter the value of "fresh idiom," branding the poet's use of Freudian wit and dream work "baby-talk." Berryman would appropriate the term for the language of his own dream songs as if to emphasize his respect for both figures. Roethke, who had similarly employed a dream language in *The Lost Son* (1948) and whose work Berryman taught along with that of Yeats and Whitman at the University of Iowa in 1954, seems also to have influenced Henry's creation. Less influential than some critics would maintain is the work of Joyce. Berryman refrains from portmanteau words and translingual punning and restricts his inventions to syntax rather than neologisms.

The stress that Berryman, by means of these writers, places on the language aspects of Freudian psychology in reconceiving characterization for *The Dream Songs* appears less arbitrary and eccentric in the light of the work Jacques Lacan was engaged in at approximately the same time. Acknowledging that creative writers had preceded him in many of his discoveries, Lacan proposes an interpretation of dream work based on the linguistic theories of Roman Jakobson and the anthropology of Lévi-Strauss. Lacan views Freudian dream theory as a grammar or phonology of the mind so that psychoanalysis becomes a kind of decoding device for condensed or displaced messages rather than a method of indicating disease. Using the metaphoric and metonymic poles of Jakobson to divide language into systems either of similarity and substitution or of contiguity and connection, Lacan sees dream in Straussean terms—as a network of symbolic exchanges where relationships between the exchangers rather than actual possession of objects are important. Pathology, in fact, occurs when one substitutes for this relation between persons a relation between body images and desires to accumulate that which is intended to serve only symbolically. In the matter of identity the linguistic "I" is not the subject except as a relation and becomes for Lacan "the ego" only as it assumes a body image or "false-self." Like Berryman he identifies this body image of self with a notion of mimesis based on mirror-ing. The image is constructed out of a series of identifications with or oppositions to another, and by being so constructed, it loses track of the fact that the conceptualzer or the "I" is never fully realized in the conception or, as Berryman says of himself in relation to Henry, Henry does not have the poet's advantages of supervision.

Dream interpretation becomes as a result for both Lacan and Berryman a form of masking based on syntactical translation, and Berryman is fond of relating the various structures of dreams that he has been able to determine. In song 327, for instance, he claims to have once taken a dream "to forty-three structures, that / accounted in each for each word." Jane Howard reports that another Berryman dream, perhaps the one in which "he was cast as the Pope, dispatched on a mission of critical importance to Eastern Europe to check up on a malcontent Polish cardinal," yielded "thirty-eight structures—not levels, structures." But, as Lacan suggests, the gap that exists in such translations between the subject and the form of his expression can never fully be resolved even by a multiplicity of structures. Speech or discourse which tries to overcome this difference merely confirms the impossibility of filling up the hole which language itself creates. Even the disjunctions of syntax to enlarge language to include new emotions lead merely to new blocks that, in Pascalian terms, act as obstacles toward that abyss of pure being. In the views of both Lacan and Berryman, one must give up this notion perpetuated by science and by poets like Eliot and Williams that through language one can become transparent and assume rather that in this world everything must be relational and that out of this social relativity must come characterization.

Thus, by reinterpreting the mutually subjective Yeatsian masks as syntactical structures, Berryman manages to do in *The Dream Songs* what Roethke never quite succeeded in accomplishing by "taking a cadence" from the Irish poet—namely to achieve identity by using a second active intelligence. Berryman needs to achieve an identity in such terms because, like Jarrell, writing had for him become a kind of self-analysis and he was put off by the determinism implicit in Freud's perpetual looking back. In song 384, when the characterization of Henry is over and the actual dissolution of personae begins, one can assume that Berryman's possession is over and that the rhetoric which was a tacit recognition of a split that inaugurated the characterization is resolved appropriately into a silence. Henry's now being one with the author eliminates any need for words, and this oneness is the "death" which Henry speaks of in song 26 as resolving his "original crime."

It involves no sacrifice of emotion to thought, merely the end of a relational existence by the end of relating. As in Rilke and Roethke this resolution is along the lines of a connaturality: one merges with what one contemplates because at a deep level there is an essential unity of all existence. Indeed *The Dream Songs* repeats the message of *Song of Myself:* one learns of all life's essential unity by feeling widely, and this wide feeling can best be accomplished by resisting glib conceptualizations. Readers of Berryman's volume are asked, as they are by Whitman, to confront individually a large number of incidents. These incidents are deeply moving, both for their pathos and their humor; and they work less to delineate dimensions in character than, like the extravagances of baroque music, to enlarge a reader's sensibilities. In their themes of survival they touch on Audenesque social concerns, and in their themes of alienation impinge on the Yeatsian outsider; but mainly by their stresses on fresh idiom, they emphasize the shift from biological to human relationships. "No ideas, but in things," Williams had insisted; and here Berryman adds: "No humanity, but in adequate language."

DAVID K. WEISER

Berryman's Sonnets:
In and Out of the Tradition

Published in 1967, about twenty years after their composition, *Berryman's Sonnets* were quickly recognized as more than a virtuoso performance. By reviving some long-dead conventions of the Renaissance love lyric, the poet expressed his own highly original personality. As WIlliam J. Martz pointed out, the hallmarks of that personality are "his energy, his humor and his exuberance." More recent critics have dealt with the sonnets as an anticipation of Berryman's concern for self-depiction, a task that was best fulfilled in his *Dream Songs*. Joel Conarroe, in the longest study so far, concludes that the sonnet sequence "is important in the development of Berryman's craft because for the first time . . . he drops the mask of neutral objectivity." Berryman's poetic speaker "emerges as a unique man who records his own sensibility in a voice that, at least in the strongest, truest sonnets, is recognizably his own."

But *Berryman's Sonnets* have intrinsic value, quite apart from the poet's later development. Like George Meredith's *Modern Love,* they illustrate the process of creative imitation, in which old forms are deliberately reshaped to express new attitudes. Berryman is far closer to the Renaissance model than was Meredith, who made no attempt to echo sixteenth-century style. Writing a century later, the American poet immersed himself in the past without excluding his present experience. His language can combine American slang with Elizabethan euphony in lines like "Snug, slim and supple-breasted girl for play" (sonnet 104), or "On a thousand greens the late slight rain is

From *American Literature* 55, no. 3 (October 1983). © 1983 by Duke University Press.

gleaming" (sonnet 11) and "Doomed cities loose and thirsty as a dune" (sonnet 46). Such intricate sound patterns attest to Berryman's familiarity with metrical techniques of the Renaissance. Joined with Elizabethan diction, in words like "toys" (sonnet 8), "roil" (sonnets 10 and 85), "lickerish" (sonnet 38), "rack" (sonnet 55) and "lusk" (sonnet 78), the iambic pentameter adds resonance to Berryman's Renaissance imitations.

Berryman's sonnets actually employ the theory of *inventio* that prevailed in the Renaissance. They are "imitations" in the sixteenth-century sense, deviating from their models much as the sonnets of Sidney and Shakespeare vary from those of Petrarch and Wyatt. By comparing Berryman's sonnets with their sources and analogues, we can discover how perfectly he assimilated old poetic forms but not their content. For all his technical prowess, the modern poet could not sustain belief in such postulates as right reason and natural law. A radical discrepancy thus separates his sonnets from their tradition.

The title *Berryman's Sonnets* boldly suggests a parallel with Shakespeare. Unlike the elusive Bard, this poet requires us to see his sonnets as a personal document; he defines himself through his uses of the past. When he echoes Shakespeare we are more impressed by deviations from the source than by fidelity to it. Sonnet 40 is a case in point: "Marble nor monuments whereof then we speak / We speak of more." The impersonal plural of "we spoke" and "we speak" implies a continuity of poetic voices from past to present. The speaker represents a consensus of poets, especially the moderns who are characterized by "our short songs." He contends at first that poetic immortality is an ideal for which "none hopes now." It is "a Renaissance fashion, not to be recalled." Moreover, an element of progress is implied: "We dinch 'eternal numbers' and go out. / We understand exactly what we are." Then the poet's individual voice enters the sonnet to complete it. He reverses the previous argument, making the *volta* coincide with his shift to a personal perspective:

> Do we? Argent I craft you as the star
> Of flower-shut evening: who stays on to doubt
> I sang true? ganger with trobador and scald!

The formative assertion of Shakespeare's sonnet 55 has now been vindicated. Yet Berryman never matches its confidence: "Not marble, nor the gilded monuments / Of princes, shall outlive this pow'rful rhyme." The appeal of his own sonnet lies in the unresolved conflict between the two opposing viewpoints, cynical and affirmative. In itself, his closing tercet is unconvincing because it ignores all that was said before. It reaffirms poetic immortality but unaccountably limits what Shakespeare had called "all posterity" to a small circle of poets. Similarly, the first eleven lines are unattractive in their cynicism. Their smug generalizations seem to cry out for refutation. The entire sonnet thus embodies the sustained tension characteristic of Berryman. Two contradictory sections actually complement each other, so that the complex whole most accurately reflects the poet's mind. Shakespeare's simpler and stronger expression of confidence in his art has been absorbed into a new complexity. Berryman, we find, has imitated a model only to represent himself.

Other Shakespearean echoes in *Berryman's Sonnets* are less conspicuous but equally effective. Sonnet 104 whimsically presents a darkly sensual "piece" who is dreamt of by the speaker, only to dismiss her scornfully when he wakes. Berryman's "dark lady" is merely an apparition. As a projection of forbidden impulses, she must be exorcized: "black dreams, / The dirty water to get off my chest." This introspective tendency continues in sonnet 105, where the final words "unman me" recall Lady Macbeth's plea: "Come, you spirits / That tend on mortal thoughts, unsex me here" (*Macbeth,* 1.5.40–41). Berryman's speaker invokes time rather than spirits: "Time, time that damns, disvexes. Unman me." In this way he ends a sonnet whose sense of guilt and weariness recalls that of Macbeth himself: "I grieve knee-down, I slack / Deeper in evil."

Again, in sonnet 100 the phrase "mock the time" is a concealed quotation from *Macbeth.* Berryman puts it in a broader context of dissimulation:

> Burnt cork, my leer, my Groucho crouch and rush,
> No more my nature than Cyrano's: we
> Are 'hindered characters' and mock the time.

Conarroe claims that "the poet is unable to make known his passion, and so puts on a comic mask." But mocking the time is derived from Macbeth's tragic acquiescence:

> Away, and mock the time with fairest show:
> False face must hide what the false heart doth know.
> (1.7.81–82)

Both echoes of *Macbeth,* in sonnets 105 and 100, are meant to brand the speaker's adultery as tragic and unnatural. Since guilt feelings are placed within a wider range of associations, some of them comic, the resulting tone is richly complex. Just as Berryman could not duplicate Shakespeare's boast of immortality, so in acknowledging his pangs of conscience he creates a further conflict. The allusions are instrumental in helping the reader define that interplay of opposing emotions, so that familiar meanings are ironically modified by the modern context that absorbs them.

Another example of this process is sonnet 20, whose background is the Princeton University bicentennial. Playing on the colloquialism "two bands are raising hell," Berryman modulates to a weightier tone: "O hell is empty and Knowlton Street is well, / The little devils shriek." What he means will become clear when we recognize his borrowing from *The Tempest:* "Hell is empty, / And all the devils are here!" (1.2.213–14). These words, spoken by Ferdinand during the shipwreck scene, are vital to Berryman; they enable him to transmute everyday reality. A public event, "the bicentennial of an affair with truth," seems unreal to the speaker who is obsessed with his own, much less truthful affair. The same clash is presented schematically in the sestet, where three lines parodying the ceremony are interwoven with parenthesized lines that relate the speaker's love-longing: "Two centuries here have been abused our youth: / (Your grey eyes pierce the miles to meet my eyes)." Ferdinand's exclamation is thus applied to the Princeton ceremony, registering the speaker's extreme dissociation from society. Shipwreck, being a conventional image of Petrarchan despair, forebodes even greater suffering than that caused here by the mistress' absence. At present, the speaker can endure and even enjoy his contradictory emotions: "an angelic tear / Falls somewhere, so (but I laugh) would mine."

A final example of how well Berryman converts Shakespearean material to his own purposes is sonnet 31, dealing with the lover's deceits. His relation with his wife becomes a series of mechanical pretences: "merely to lie still / In grand evasion." He exploits the double meaning of "lie" and concludes: "I am dreaming on the hour when I can hear / My last lie rattle, and then lie truly still." The analogous lines in Shakespeare are in sonnet 138: "Therefore I lie with her and she with me, / And in our faults by lies we flattered be." Here the two senses of lying are compatible, both being enacted by poet and mistress. Berryman's echo again points to a basic difference of outlook. Thinking of his wife rather than his mistress, he does not desire sex or even life itself but only to "lie truly still." He establishes an overriding sense of remorse, whereas the Shakespeare sonnet defends falsehood for pleasure's sake.

The form of *Berryman's Sonnets* is not Shakespearean, however, but Petrarchan; the inner lines of each quatrain make one rhyme and the outer lines another. Strictly following this pattern with a rhyme link between lines four and five, he allows himself only two rhyme sounds in the octet and three in the sestet. There are only five rhymes in these sonnets as against Shakespeare's seven. Moreover, in the chronological form of the sequence, with its specific dates and locations, we discern the direct influence of Petrarch rather than Shakespeare. The earlier poet had fused art and life in his sonnet-sequence instead of leaving their relation equivocal. Petrarch did not lend words for Berryman to echo but he supplied a structural model for individual sonnets and their arrangement. In addition, the familiar "conceits" derived from Petrarch and his imitators furnished a basis for Berryman's ironic variations.

Sonnet 75, for example, explicitly compares the two poets. Its first eight lines review main events in Petrarch's career, while the sestet contrasts his love for Laura with Berryman's passion for Lise: "He never touched her. Swirl our crimes and crimes." Although the historical facts are uncertain ("the old brume seldom clears"), Berryman is sure that his physicality compares unfavorably with Petrarch's ideal love. His mistress has nothing in common with Laura except her appearance, being "gold-haired (too)." He ends the poem by addressing her directly: "Two guilty and crepe-yellow months / Lise! be our bright surviving actual scene." The specific contrast is between two months and twenty-one years. But the difference in duration is less revealing than that in the quality of love. The key word, I believe, is "guilty" since the many descriptions of sensual delight throughout these sonnets rarely conceal their brooding remorse.

Berryman is constantly aware of the unbridgeable gap between his own practice and the Renaissance ideal of love. His use of Petrarchan conceits, like the borrowings from Shakespeare, highlights basic differences by means of superficial likeness. Sonnet 14 begins with one such conceit, "moths white as ghosts," but the speaker quickly puts this image at a distance by giving it another, less venerable source: "I am one of yours, / Doomed to a German song's stale metaphors." He then breaks down the compound image, dwelling on "ghost" in quatrain two: "I am your ghost. . . . on Denmark's moors / I loiter, and when you slide your eyes I swing." The allusion is to Lise's Danish ancestry as well as to the ghost in *Hamlet*. Moth and ghost are helplessly dependent, fitting the speaker's representation of himself. The Petrarchan conceit thus finds its place within an eclectic range of associations. In the sestet of this sonnet, love itself is epitomized in starkly colloquial language: "The billiard ball slammed in the kibitzer's mouth" and "this diamond meal to gag on." The impact of love receives a direct, objectified description, while the speaker's self-portrait is mockingly sentimental.

In sonnet 52 we note a Petrarchan theme, one that is used by Sidney in *Astrophel and Stella*. However, detachment from these sources is obtained through translation into German: "*Da ist meiner Liebstens Haus.*" Another parallel with Sidney, "the English Petrarke," is drawn explicitly in sonnet

16. Its rather convoluted opening explains that the poet had seen his lady three times before falling in love:

> Thrice, or I moved to sack, I saw you: how
> Without siege laid I can as simply tell
> As whether below the dreams of Astrophel.
> Lurks local truth some scholars would allow
> And others will deny in ours!

Undoubtedly, the first two lines employ the Petrarchan conceit of love as a conquering army. Berryman's deviation from this idea is complete; he wonders how he could have seen Lise without falling into the siege of love. However, an earlier sonnet, the second, explains that the poet had tried to resist temptation: "I said / A month since, 'I will see that cloud-gold head, / Those eyes lighten, and go by': then your thunder rolled." For that matter, Sidney himself had repudiated the convention: "Not at first sight, nor with a dribb'd shot, / Love gave the wound which while I breathe will bleed." Perhaps it is this resemblance which reminds Berryman of Astrophel. He compares his own uncertainty to that of scholars about the biographical element, the "local truth," in Sidney's sonnet-sequence. Anticipating future commentators on his own sequence, he uses an ambiguous construction in which the contrast "some scholars would allow / And others will deny" refers both to Sidney and to Berryman. There is also a hint that future readers, presumably "new critics," will play down the biographical background to these poems. The speaker thus enjoys the irony of having an experience whose living reality will be denied.

A subtler derivation from Sidney and Petrarchan tradition can be discerned in sonnet 51. Conarroe terms this of all the sonnets "perhaps the most calculated in its effects, playing on an aviary theme." The complexity lessens, I suggest, when the poem is placed in its tradition:

> A tongue there is wags, down in the dark wood O:
> Trust it not. It trills malice among friends,
> Irrelevant squibs and lies, to its own ends
> Or to no ends, simply because it would O.
> To us, us most I hear, it prinks no good O;
> Has its idea, Jamesian; apprehends
> Truth non-aviarian; meddles, and "defends"
> Honour free . . . that such a bill so wily should O!
> Who to my hand all year flew to be fed
> Makes up his doubts to dart at us . . . Ah well,
> Did you see the *green* of that catalpa tree?—

> A certain jackal will lose half its head
> For cheek, our keek, our hairy philomel.—
> How can you tell?—A little bird told me.

A distinctly ballad-like quality results from the "O" exclamation in the octet. This open vowel joins in compound rhymes conveying a sense of wonder at the strange behavior described. We learn that a malicious "tongue" threatens the lovers. Although the slanderer's name is not given, his actions are well delineated. Having caught on to the affair, he discusses it among his friends and pretends to justify the lovers. The gossiper is shown symbolically as "our hairy philomel," and proverbially as "a little bird." He has forgotten his obligations to the speaker, at whose hand he "flew to be fed." That phrase is a palpable echo of Wyatt's "They Flee From Me," in which faithless friends are characterized in animal, possible aviary, imagery:

> I have sene theim gentill tame and meke
> That nowe are wyld and do not remember
> That sometyme they put theimself in daunger
> To take bred at my hand.

But the immediate source of Berryman's imagery can be traced back to line eight, where the slanderer's name is suggested: "that such a bill so wily should O!" This is most probably the same Bill from whom the speaker wished to flee in sonnet 22: "No Bill comes by to cadge / A Scotch in Rector's, waving his loose tongue." He may also be the garrulous one mentioned in sonnet 78: "William and I sat hours and talked of you." What is most importnat, though is the way Berryman's imagination seizes on the name "Bill" and transforms it through a pun into a network of historically valid associations. The talkative Bill becomes a bill, hence a "tongue," which in the Renaissance is constantly an epithet for slanderers.

The sonnet's mode of discourse is strongly akin to that of Sidney's sonnet 78 in *Astrophel and Stella,* an emblematic description of jealousy. Sidney represents that emotion as a monster and comments on its jaws, feet, eyes and ears. Jealousy is endowed with all these features "by Nature's speciall grace." It is the "succour of lies" but self-destructive as well: "who his owne joy to his owne hurt applies." Berryman's aviary emblem is also given a distinctive quality of loving evil for its own sake, telling lies "simply because it would O." His sonnet's tone is more intimate than Sidney's, which excludes all first-person forms, yet its method is still iconic description for the sake of criticism. Sonnet 51 thus indicates the depth to which Berryman absorbed Renaissance modes of expression. Only several words, especially "Jamesian," betray the modern perspective that underlies the old techniques. Since the sonnet does

not depict the speaker directly, it can adhere to its model with compara-
tively few deviations.

Despite his extensive debts to the past, it is typical of Berryman to mock
the tradition that he writes in. Quite a few sonnets are openly self-critical.
They ask whether *Berryman's Sonnets* are not merely an antiquarian exercise.
Berryman's self-consciousness, his awareness of possible flaws in his method,
implies that he is not subservient to conventions but in control of them. In
sonnet 23 he asserts that he loves but "would not cloy your ear . . . / With
'love' and 'love,' " In fact, "love" appears frequently throughout the sequence
despite these strictures against the word, "pompous and vague on the stump
of his career." Loyal to the modern notion of authenticity, Berryman's speaker
continues his verbal blacklist:

> Also I fox "heart," striking a modern breast
> Hollow as a drum, and "beauty" I taboo;
> I want a verse as a bubble breaks,
> As little false.

The ideal of freshness within a Petrarchan framework may seem paradoxical.
Yet the resultant tension is a main source of the sonnets' appeal. Even if "love"
is a tasteless cliché, Berryman has no choice but to use it and its well-worn
Renaissance antithesis, "lust." He denies the possible charge that "I *loved*
you not, but blurred / *Lust* with strange images" (italics mine). We infer from
this argument that the poet will require traditional words and connotations
as long as he celebrates the idea of love. To redeem those words, he must
employ them sparingly and ironically. We find that linguistic predicament
at the end of sonnet 23: "I am in love with you— / Trapped in my rib-cage
something throes and aches!" Modern poetics forbids calling that something
the "heart" but the modern poet has not found an alternative. He turns to
the past, despite its inadequacy, for a context against which he can define
himself. In sonnet 97 the stock phrases, *"I laid siege—you enchanted me,"*
are italicized and labelled as "magic and warfare, faithful metaphors." The
value of such phrases seems exhausted until Berryman invests them with a
series of atavistic associations, imagining himself and his beloved as "the
hunter and the witchwife." This hackneyed imagery of magic and war,
presented hesitatingly at first, is finally justified by the keenly felt physical
contact that generates it, the core of sexuality then as now: "Abrupt as a
dogfight, the air full of / Tails and teeth."

The most thoroughly anti-Petrarchan sonnet is 103, which begins by
examining yet another catch-phrase: "A 'broken heart' . . . but *can* a heart
break, now?" The succeeding lines echo Rosalind's well-known remarks in

As You Like It: "The poor world is almost six thousand years old, and in all this time there was not any man died in his own person, videlicet, in a love cause" (4.1.91–94). Berryman's version mocks poetic conventions rather than the mythological lovers debunked by Rosalind:

> Lovers have stood bareheaded in love's "storm"
> Three thousand years, changed by their mistress' "charm,"
> Fitted their "torment" to a passive bow,
> Suffered the "darts" under a knitted brow,
> And has one heart *broken* for all this "harm?"

Admittedly, self-criticism is an integral part of the Petrarchan mode. The earlier poets had often berated their vanity and its terms of expression. But Berryman's contrast of old conceits with "something definite," his aching arm, shows his radical departure from tradition. He prefers a unique, physically demonstrable ailment as the symbol of his suffering. The arm, "a piece of pain joined to me," does not entirely ruin him but it spoils his tennis: "after fifteen minutes of / Serving, I can't serve more." This precise account contradicts the vague improbability of a "broken heart." It resembles Petrarchan tradition only in that the pain is mysterious, perhaps supernatural: "no doctor can find a thing." The sonnet's final words, "still, this is something," remind us that a limited area of pain corresponds better to the lover's state than do the extravagant figures of his predecessors.

These qualifications of thought and style, however, do not alter the basic premise of *Berryman's Sonnets*. The poet's decision to revive an outmoded structure with all its conventions implies a firm belief in the continuity of literary culture. He seems to have adopted quite literally what T. S. Eliot calls "the historical sense . . . a perception not only of the pastness of the past, but of its presence." In fact, Eliot himself is described in the fifth of these sonnets: "The poet hunched, so, whom the world admires." The lines that follow recall "Little Gidding" in the *Four Quartets*, so that this meeting with Eliot corresponds to the latter's own encounter with the Dantesque "dead master." The words "easy," "pyre" and "shore" all occur in the Eliot poem, so that Berryman's continuation is an act of homage:

> our discourse was easy,
> While he hid in his skin taut as a wire,
> Considerate as grace, a candid pyre
> Flaring some midday shore.

Another echo of Eliot will be heard in sonnet 101, whose opening lines recall

those of "Ash Wednesday" and create a subtle parody due to the difference
between the ladies addressed:

> Because I'd seen you not believe your lover,
> Because you scouted cries come from no cliff,
> Because to supplications you were stiff.

Eliot's influence (at its height in the late forties) clearly stimulated Berryman
toward revitalizing the past. Rather than founding a latter-day School of
Petrarch, he placed the old tradition squarely within the new. Such adaptation
occurs in the questioning of old concepts, in the broadening contexts of
quotations and allusions, in references to features of modern life (cars, planes
and frozen daiquiris) and in the frequent mention of contemporary poets.
Not only Eliot but Yeats, Thomas, Pound, Cummings and Stevens are also
alluded to. Perhaps the most surprising contemporary reference is a quotation
from book 2 of W. C. Williams's *Paterson,* wedged into sonnet 58: "Since
the corruption of the working classes / I am speaking of the Eighteenth
Century." The subject here is the speaker's rejection of a conventional life,
"sensible, coarse, and moral." This enables him to parody ordinary happiness
and its clichés: "the water's fine, come in and drown." But by the sonnet's
conclusion he admits his own complicity in the corruption that Williams had
noticed: "The Reno brothels boom, suddenly we writhe." The borrowing
from *Paterson* thus marks the speaker's exile from community mores and
his use of poetry as a source of value. His references to contemporary poets
only complete the literary continuum that begins with Pindar and Vergil and
includes writers as disparate as Donne, Hölderlin and Villon.

The speaker of *Berryman's Sonnets* identifies himself primarily as a poet
rather than a lover. It follows that love itself is neither castigated nor praised
as lavishly as in the Renaissance lyrics. It is a consistently sensual need that,
for a time, is shared and gratified. In this context, the figure of Lise remains
a real person with very real faults. Her name, on the analogy of Samuel
Daniel's "Delia," could be read as an anagram yielding "lies" rather than the
Renaissance poet's "ideal." Berryman's precise descriptions of lovemaking,
his acceptance of it as a good, brings him closer in spirit to Ovid's *Ars Amoris*
than to Shakespeare, let alone Petrarch or Dante. It is appropriate that
Sigmund Freud is referred to as "the Master," echoing Dante's epithet for
Aristotle. Nothing could better point out the contrast of world views between
Berryman and the poets whose forms he has borrowed. Like his master, he
stresses the individual's urges against social norms that restrain them. This
acceptance of irrational man weakens the basic tension inherent in the genre
that Berryman imitates. For if the Renaissance poets felt anguish and shame

for their supposed depravity, they could also transform love into a symbol of the divine. Since Berryman does not uphold the rational ideal, he has no basis for isolating in his mistress either the angelic or the animal elements that traditionally coexisted in human nature. There is, as we have seen, a persistent sense of guilt underlying the sequence. However, Berryman's guilt is no less irrational than his love.

A comparative reading of sonnet 15 will best demonstrate how the modern poet's intellectual distance from the Renaissance influences the form and style of his work. This is the only sonnet out of one hundred and fifteen that acknowledges a specific source, carrying the subscription: "after Petrarch and Wyatt." It is based on Petrarch's sonnet 189, as well as Sir Thomas Wyatt's sixteenth-century translation. Assimilating the content of the two earlier poems, Berryman extends their vision. Many words and phrases from the Wyatt poem, itself an imitation rather than an exact rendering, are retained. However, no line is repeated verbatim. At some points Berryman is more faithful to Petrarch's original than Wyatt had been, while at others he deviates from both his predecessors. On the level of auditory coherence he outdoes them by using only two rhyme-sounds in the sestet rather than three. The rhyme scheme is cddccc, with the last two lines yielding the half-rhyme "art" and "port." This sestet is closer to Petrarch than is Wyatt's, which divides into a third quatrain and a couplet: cddcee. As a result, Berryman's *volta* or change of thought is located where Petrarch had made it, in line twelve rather than line thirteen. Elsewhere, his sonnet tends to correspond with Wyatt's on a line-by-line basis, just as Wyatt had corresponded to Petrarch. However, in lines three, four, ten and twelve he breaks the pattern of lineation by substituting run-ons for the earlier poems' end-stopped lines.

Many of Berryman's alterations are skilfully rhetorical. Where Wyatt's "galy" passes "twene Rock and Rock," his "ship" sails "between whirlpool and rock." The contrast of two obstacles is more effective than Wyatt's repetition of one. It also alludes to but avoids mentioning the familiar image of Scylla and Charybdis, which Petrarch had cited explicitly. The modern poet, moreover, writes an irregular pentameter, allowing him to emphasize certain ideas more sharply. For example, Wyatt ends his octet with these perfectly regular lines:

> An endless wynd doeth tere the sayll a pase
> Of forced sighes and trusty ferefulness.

Berryman repeats "endless" and gives it initial position to stress the idea of perpetual suffering:

> Endless a wet wind wears my sail, dark swarm
> Endless of sighs and veering hopes, love's fret.

Not only is this a more forceful description of the lover's plight, it also comes much closer to Petrarch's original:

> *La vela rompe un vento umide, eterno,*
> *Di sospir, di esperanze, e di desio.*

Berryman retains the threefold division of sighs, hope and desire, even keeping them in the same order. Instead of Petrarch's "sighing" (*sospir*) and Wyatt's "sighes" he invents a more emphatic expression: "dark swarm / Endless of sighs." To "hopes" he adds the nautical term "veering" and for "desire" he writes "love's fret." These changes point to Berryman's dislike of abstract terms and his preference for sensuous language. Thus "sharp seas" and "winter nights" are fused into "a midnight winter storm." Where Wyatt merely lists "a rayne of teris, a clowde of derk disdain," Berryman makes a vivid contrast between two images: "rain of tears, real, mist of imagined scorn."

Berryman discards conventional images that do not suit his modern idiom. On this level, his changes are no longer rhetorical but substantive. Wyatt concurs with Petrarch in speaking of the "ennemy" and "lorde" who steers the ship. But Cupid finds no place in Berryman's poem, usurped by an image of the lady herself who "gleams at the wheel . . . her hair streams." Clearly, the modern poet knew how much artifice his reader could accept, and what kind. He omits the extraneous notion of dying for love, which Wyatt had introduced:

> And every owre a thought in rediness,
> As tho that deth were light in suche a case.

For this he substitutes a complex expression based loosely on Petrarch:

> When we met
> Seaward, Thought frank & guilty to each oar set
> Hands careless of port as of the waters' harm.

By inserting "when we met," Berryman bypasses the agency of Cupid and underscores the directly human encounter. Both Renaissance poets present a lonely speaker who is the prisoner of Love and his crew of evil thoughts. But in the modern sonnet the ship holds two lovers who have knowingly embarked on a destructive voyage together. The "Thought" that Berryman personifies in the singular marks their mutual deception. However, where Wyatt alludes to death, Berryman follows Petrarch in describing an indifference to the voyage's dangers and destination. This recklessness is internalized rather than projected into mythological symbols.

The most illuminating change made by Berryman occurs at the sonnet's end. The Renaissance poets, however enamoured, viewed courtly love as an unfortunate lapse of reason. As Wyatt put it:

> Drowned is reason that should me comfort
> And I remain dispering of the port.

The English poet placed an even greater burden on reason than did the Italian, for Petrarch had combined reason with art:

> *Celansi duo mei dolci usati segni;*
> *Morta fra l'onde e la ragion et l'arte*
> *Tal ch'i'ncomincio a desperar del porto.*

For Berryman, however, the ideal of reason does not exist. The contest of reason and passion, which pervaded the love poetry of the Middle Ages and the Renaissance, has been resolved in favor of the irrational. He is forced to make a major revision, therefore, when he describes the effects of love:

> Muffled in capes of waves my clear signs, torn,
> Hitherto most clear,—Loyalty and Art.
> And I begin now to despair of port.

The substitution of "Loyalty" for reason (*ragion*) reveals Berryman's departure from Renaissance thought. We are not told what sort of loyalty is meant, or to whom, but the term implies an emotional bond rather than a logically defined commitment. In this way, although Berryman intensifies the Petrarchan account of love as a perilous sea-voyage, he fundamentally alters its conclusion. As a psychological study of the lover's changing mood, his poem is the most effective of the three. As a juxtaposition of two radically opposed ideas, it is the least articulate.

A more typical example of Berryman's creative imitation, incorporating many Renaissance features but lacking a specific model, is sonnet 25. The poem is a striking expression of the turmoil that results when feelings of loyalty are pitted against stronger feelings of passion. It too employs the imagery of storm-tossed sailing to depict the speaker's state of mind. However, Berryman is now free to develop the image in his own way. He begins by setting forth his predicament:

> Sometimes the night echoes to prideless wailing
> Low as I hunch home late and fever-tired,

> Near you not, nearing the sharer I desired,
> Toward whom till now I sailed back.

The wailing must be his own, occasioned by his return to his wife and separation from his love. The former is "the sharer I desired," but the memory of his earlier passion does not diminish his current obsession. The basic change in the poem, then, lies in his attitude toward his wife. When he loved her, his homecoming had been a "sailing." The same return now "yaws," or strays from course. It declines into the melodramatic shipwreck that the rest of the poem describes. The scene, from line five on, is vintage Hollywood:

> The men are glaring, the mate has wired
> *Hopeless:* locked in, and humming, the Captain's nailing
> A false log to the lurching table.

This extended series of images for a single idea is a "Petrarchan conceit." The separate details, the men, the mate and captain, have no precise reference of their own. Together, they compose a single analogy to what the speaker feels. The figure of the captain, however, corresponds most closely with his own awareness of losing control. "Locked in, and humming," he is eccentric, isolated from others, and possibly mad.

As the sonnet ends, a subtle shift blends the captain's image with that of the poet-speaker: "Lies / And passion sing in the cabin on the voyage home." The voyage is both the speaker's reluctant homecoming and its symbolic equivalent, in which the "cabin" or controlroom stands for the speaker's mind. Finally, the madness suggested by the captain's behavior is explicitly endorsed:

> wind
> Madness like the tackle of a crane (outcries
> Ascend) around to heave him from the foam
> Irresponsible, since all the stars rain blind.

The last phrase, "since all the stars rain blind," is a description of the raging inner weather that the speaker endures. Madness is a consequence of his suffering, but also provides a means for accepting it. We can readily agree that a captain should not be blamed for the rainstorm that destroys his ship. But when we apply this image to its referent, we find it less than compelling. The speaker who abandoned one love for another has created the storm that ruins him. He is hardly "irresponsible." Berryman was indeed "nailing a false log" when he devised this metaphor, though surely not deliberately. His reference to madness constitutes an implicit plea for innocence. In addition, there is probably a pun intended in "rain," suggesting the misrule of blind fortune. This, too, should be seen as a desperate, guilt-ridden rationalization.

John Berryman did not write these sonnets, then, merely as a formal exercise but in order to explore, however inconclusively, a theme that would concern him throughout his career. Love was not for him the transcendent force that Renaissance poets had deified. But an illicit love affair brought out his awareness of an underlying conflict between inner impulses and outer norms. For Renaissance poets that clash had been internal, between a man's own powers of reason and passion. For Berryman, as with other American writers, it was another version of the conflict between the individual and society. He could not be reconciled to the seemingly arbitrary bonds that hindered his pleasure. Nor could he understand his mistress' refusal to give up her family. If we look ahead to the fourth *Dream Song,* we find the same problem represented with far greater discernment. Here "Henry" is attracted to a married woman whom he watches in a restaurant. He is dismayed by her lack of interest in him, as she sits and eats beside her husband. The situation is a paradigm for *Berryman's Sonnets,* except that the protagonist's desire is not requited. He comes to realize that the law is, after all, an inescapable reality:

> The restaurant buzzes. She might as well be in Mars.
> Where did it all go wrong? There ought to be a
> law against Henry.
> —Mr. Bones: there is.

ELIZABETH KASPAR ALDRICH

Berryman Saved from Drowning

Throughout the critical literature on John Berryman, including the poet's remarks on his own work, *Homage to Mistress Bradstreet* is identified as the breakthrough in his career. The term implies a view of the career which is roughly contained in William Martz's remark that with this poem "the early Berryman becomes the later Berryman," a man who has achieved "poetic maturity" and, above all, "found his own voice." The early Berryman had not, and had suffered from all the evils of a secondary poet, slave on the one hand to his strong precursors and on the other to an ideal of originality for its own sake, lacking in subject matter, and given over to mannered peculiarities of style. The breakthrough is especially impressive in Berryman's case since, as James Dickey once remarked, he was evidently a poet-made and not a poet-born. What sustained him through the long years of apprentice labor, when the poetry was often simply not good, was as much a commitment to poets as to poetry, a sense of shared calling and shared suffering which finds its supreme expression in the elegies of the *Dream Songs*. *Mistress Bradstreet,* suggesting many forms in the course of its fifty-seven verses—invocation, dialogue, narrative, meditation—ends as an elegy.

In the title of the poem we find stated, ostensibly, both its central subject, an historical figure embodying the origin of a poetic tradition, and the contemporary poet's relation to it. In this sense the poem is "about" its own origins and occasion: about the meaning to the poet of a poetic precursor,

From *On Poetry and Poetics: Swiss Papers in English Language and Literature,* no. 2, edited by Richard Waswo. © 1985 by Gunter Narr Verlag. Elizabeth Kaspar Aldrich was formerly Elizabeth Davis.

149

about the problematic burden of what I would suggest is a specifically American past. In several different interviews and commentaries Berryman gave his own account of the genesis and progress of *Mistress Bradstreet,* never substantially changed though often elaborated. One version, from the *Paris Review* interview of 1970:

> The situation with that poem was this. I invented the stanza in '48 and wrote the first stanza and the first three lines of the second stanza and then I stuck. . . . Then I stuck. I read and read and thought and collected notes and sketched for five years, until, although I was still in the second stanza, I had a mountain of notes and draftings—no whole stanzas, but passages as long as five lines. The whole poem was written in about two months, after which I was a ruin for two years.

Whereas he had been aware in beginning the *Dream Songs* that he was "embarked on an epic," Berryman says, "in the case of the Bradstreet poem I didn't know." This is something of a blueprint for "breakthrough": the beginning almost automatic, in unconsciousness, the arrest, the long and laborious gestation, the rush of creativity (or if you like, parturition) at the end, the all or nothing risk—two years of exhausted and depleted aftermath. The process is as much psychological as technical, and Berryman cited four "shocks" which set him going, two from life and two from literature. From his life: an operation undergone by his wife (he implies a hysterectomy; Eileen Simpson tells us otherwise), and a devastating experience in group therapy. From literature: a first reading of *The Adventures of Augie March,* which Berryman repeatedly called Bellow's "breakthrough," a rereading of Tolstoy's *Anna Karenina.*

What interests me in this description of what we might call a compositional context is what Berryman omits from it, that is, the work he was engaged in in 1948 when he wrote those initial eleven lines: the sequence, begun in 1947 but not published until twenty years later as *Berryman's Sonnets,* and—in this he was quite drastically blocked—the biography of Stephen Crane which he had been commissioned to write in 1945 and which was published in 1950. Each of these is of peculiar significance, I think, to *Mistress Bradstreet.*

The connection with the *Sonnets* is the more obvious and has been often remarked. We now know, what very few did in 1953, that in 1947 Berryman had an adulterous love affair with a woman named by him "Lise" and wrote a sonnet sequence commemorating it: eroticism, rebellion, defiance, a peculiarly Catholic sense of guilt, longing, a continuing suggestion, evidently picked up by the lady herself, that the whole enterprise exists in order to allow the poet occasion for his sonnets (the last lines of the final 115th announce their own dependence on the beloved's departure) and entry into the often-evoked literary tradition of Petrarch, Sidney, Spenser, Shakespeare, and so on. Technically, the sonnets prepared Berryman for the new stanza invented for *Bradstreet* and sustained through great length: they were, in Martz's words, "good practice." But the connection is closer: lines attributed to Lise are now given to Anne Bradstreet (for instance, in 32.5, "I *want* to take you for my lover"). More important, this *secret* fact of the poet's personal and literary life adds special resonance to the title of his public work. A living mistress has departed and has been replaced by a dead poet, Mistress Bradstreet. The poet's relation to the latter is of wooing, really seduction, and in this sense the transformation of Anne Bradstreet in the poem includes the transformation of poet, "historical figure embodying the origin of a tradition," to adulteress.

The connections between the poem and the biography of Crane are subtler but actually, I think, closer. First, the prose work provided as much technical preparation of another sort as the sonnet sequence. It is, after all, a biography of a dead writer (a fiction writer occasionally a poet; Berryman is a poet occasionally a fiction writer): *Mistress Bradstreet* is, largely, a poetic biography of a dead writer presented as autobiography, or autobiographical monologue. And just as Berryman's poetic style was greatly influenced by Crane's prose (we recall his mention of other prose works as sources of poetic inspiration), so the prose of his own biography, in its occasionally circular or inverted syntax, in its imagery as well, can be heard in the poetic lines. Second, Berryman's personal identification with Crane was, according to all evidence and accounts, extreme and traumatic, and we will have occasion to consider an even greater identification realized in the Bradstreet poem. Finally, Berryman used his biography as an occasion to make his own, assertive revision of the American literary canon: Crane was in eclipse at this time, and the claims Berryman makes for his value and importance are so great as to have been ridiculed by contemporary reviewers as the most mindless kind of hyperbole. This project also has something to do with Berryman's choice of Bradstreet as subject; or if, as he claimed, Bradstreet rather chose *him,* then with her service to him as subject.

Before turning to the critical question of the choice of subject, however, I should mention the intersections that exist between these two projects— the sonnets and the biography—since they do anticipate the central *temporal* "intersection" in the long poem. In sonnet 22 the poet imagines his mistress Lise "If not in white shorts," then in another age, the age and milieu of Crane's

youth and more particularly, it seems to me, of his youthful novel *Maggie*.
The final two lines contain a reference to "the *Red Badge* / Stevie's becoming
known for" and end with the living lovers' return to their own time and place:
"We drive home." Sonnet 99 begins: "A murmuration of the shallow,
Crane / Sees us," and ends with the question, "Does his wraith watch?" In
other words, in the first instance the lovers "visit" the time of Crane; in the
second, Crane—both wraith and, in an obvious implicit pun, water-bird—
"visits" theirs. Berryman's imagination of the past (of his literary past, we
might say) seems spatial; he thinks in terms of visits, of the *exchange* of visits.
The mirror-numbers 22 and 99 cannot, I think, be accidental.

To resume the question of choice: "the question," as Berryman wrote
in 1965, "most put to me about the poem [of] why I chose to write about
this boring high-minded Puritan woman who may have been our first
American poet but is not a good one." Perhaps the answers are suggested
by these words. First of all, the Puritans *were* of historical interest to
Berryman, and his own role as their historian was of crucial importance to
him. (The term "historian," Whitman's designation of the poet, is one which
Berryman cites with high approval at the expense of Eliot.) He was disgusted
that "most critics" failed to recognize this dimension of his work and gratified
when Robert Lowell pronounced it "the most resourceful historical poem
in our literature." And the facts of Bradstreet's history are convenient. The
first edition of her poems published in England in 1650 was entitled *The
Tenth Muse Lately Sprung Up in America;* evidently presenting the author
as her own Muse, the title is peculiar for its time, but for Berryman's it seems
a delightful anticipation: she is there, a point of origin, for the later poet
to invoke.

First and late: here, I would suggest, is a crux in Berryman's choice of
Bradstreet and in his relationship to her. Bradstreet's position in the American
literary canon is as firmly fixed as Crane's was unstable. In terms of this canon
she has what no other American poet can enjoy, that is, absolute priority.
The priority has little or nothing to do with stature or quality: it is based
on what one might call the peculiarly American standard of having got there
first. It is worth noting that had Berryman wished to discover an historical
figure of greater literary stature he had a ready opportunity in Edward Taylor:
excitement over the discovery of Taylor's manuscripts was a bare ten years
old when Berryman began work, in a milieu where the event itself was of
immediate impact. This is not what he wished.

We may speculate, as some critics have already done, that what Berryman
wished was, indeed, a bad poet. "The endearing incompetence of her verse"
Carol Johnson saw as a major part of her qualification as Muse. "All this

bald / abstract didactic rime I read appalled" the poet interrupts his Mistress in stanza 12. What, then, appeals? The weakness of Bradstreet as poet tends to some useful displacements of the homage itself. To pay homage to what is an essentially "academic" status of *first* American poet is, considered in a certain light, to *embrace* a burden, the poverty of the American tradition, the raw lowness of its origin, and in celebrating it to render it a blessing. This is in fact a characteristically Puritan strategy which could be applied to everything from religious persecution to the weather, from God's scourges of his chosen to the term Puritan itself. In a powerful sense homage may fill a vacuum or even, as it were, reverse a judgment. Homage is of course also displaced from poetic to other achievement, to the sheer physical survival of a pioneer woman, and more particularly, to that woman's person. She is from across the centuries the object of a sexual conquest which wins her away from her husband and her God and into the role of Muse/mistress. Sexual and literary mastery blend here: the twentieth-century poet's voice has priority in this poem, and from it emerges Bradstreet's, the "sourcing" of his own. Her stature comes from what Johnson has called "her subjection to superior praise," what I would elaborate as containment within a mastering voice which celebrates her priority—historical, hence negligible—while demonstrating its own—poetic, hence central.

This of course is an achievement of the entire poem, but the first "modulation" of the poet's voice into Bradstreet's (identified in Berryman's notes at 4.8) tells much about the initial move towards mastery. From stanza 4:

> When the mouth dies, who misses you?
> Your master never died,
> Simon ah thirty years past you—
> Pockmarkt & westward staring on a haggard deck
> it seems I find you, young. I come to check,
> I come to stay with you,
> and the Governor, & Father, & Simon, & the huddled
> men.

The modulation is evident in the single term "Father," which can only be Anne's; although the "I" of line 7 refers to the poet, the modulation creates some retrospectively ambiguous reverberations: whereas "I come to stay with you" announces the poet's movement back in time to Anne, it may also echo and answer his earlier address to her (3.4), "I think you won't stay," one which follows his first summons of Anne to *his* time. Throughout the poem, indistinct shiftings of reference in the "I . . . you" relationship create a sort of undertone of variations on the very theme of priority. And there are further ambiguities in this stanza directly related to the theme of mastery. "Your master never died" is peculiar. "Simon ah thirty years past you," in apposition to master, echoes the reference to Simon in 1.1—"The Governor your husband lived so long"—but it also seems to repudiate it: the Governor did, finally, die. Here the timeless or out-of-time poet seems to "enter" the term master (crowding Simon out, as it were); or perhaps to join a series of those who have mastered the early poet by virtue of their aesthetic "care"—to fill a role that has never died. In the end "your Master" may be poetry itself, embodied in the present text.

The replacement of Simon by the poet (and poetry) has earlier begun. The assurance of 1.8—"Simon will listen while you read a Song"—is doubtfully contradicted in the following stanza, which we must cite in full.

> Outside the New World winters in grand dark
> White air lashing high thro' the virgin stands
> foxes down foxholes sigh,
> surely the English heart quails, stunned.
> I doubt if Simon than this blast, that sea,
> spares from his rigour for your poetry
> more. We are on each other's hands
> who care. Both of our worlds unhanded us. Lie stark.

The identification of Simon with the New England winter goes further than the rigorous deafness 'of each. We cannot ignore the strongly sexual overtones of lines 2–4: an evocation of winter; a suggestion of the shock of a ravished bride. There is also another sort of sexual possibility, that is, of castration, in "Both of our worlds unhanded us" to which I should like to return later. What I would suggest here is that literary mastery, apparently distinguished from the sexual in these lines (or, as in "Lie stark," frankly equated with it) is covertly associated with a different, somehow maimed sexuality that is shared by both true master and mastered.

To return to the modulating line of stanza 4: the trio of authority in "the Governor, & Father, & Simon" contains peculiarities which anticipate a major aspect of Anne's narrative. The Governor, we know from both logic and history, can only be Winthrop, but the term is abstract and the only previous reference to The Governor has been to Simon (1.1). Curiously enough, Anne's father Thomas Dudley was also (after Winthrop, before Simon) Governor of Massachusetts. In other words, although the title in this context refers to one individual, it might refer to the other two named. Again, the abstraction of the reference to Father—admittedly, an intimate form of address which serves to distinguish the daughter/speaker—nevertheless permits a suggestion of the divine Father, as it also extends our sense of an interchangeability, or at least changeability, of title. The effect is rather of a *mélange*, from which emerges one image of thrice-fortified (patriarchal) Authority whose loftiness is accentuated further (even typographically) by the presence of "the huddled men."

One other telling example of this effect as it is sustained in the poem: in stanza 12 the poet interrupts Anne's description of her tireless "Versing" to question her motive (line 5)—"To please your wintry father?" The lower case would suggest Thomas Dudley; the nature of the "abstract didactic rime," indeed of all Puritan verse, would suggest the Lord; the adjective "wintry" is Simon's. In fact, some reproach of Simon for being more a wintry father than a lover/husband may be implicit in the poet's rather testy attack on Anne as artist: "mistress neither of fiery nor velvet verse, on your knees/hopeful & shamefast, chaste, laborious, odd" (12.8, 13.1), if we take mistress in a double sense and chaste in an anachronistically narrow (e.g. virginal) one—both possibilities of the poet's "modern" voice. In this instance Anne replies with an admission of past repinings, carried forward into present rebellion, against her God (13.8: "I found my heart more carnal and sitting loose from God"), her husband (14.4: "so-much-older Simon"), and her father (14.5: "so Father smiled"), united in the collective entity suggested in her phrase "Their will be done."

The "mastery" which Berryman's poem enacts depends, I would suggest, on the continuing presence, and subversion, of such a trinitarian "master-figure" combining the Puritan God (or such earthly agents of Divine power as John Cotton), the human father (or such public agents of patriarchal authority as the Governor), and the husband. And from the latter figure the expected sexual power or authority is eventually removed—appropriated, as I suggested above, by the seducer/poet who simultaneously transforms the nature of sexual mastery and identifies it with the explicitly *poetic*.

The nature of the appropriation is itself extremely complex. As we noticed of stanza 2, the traditionally virile or aggressive sexual imagery associated with Simon is apparently left intact, while the poet appears associated with images perhaps emasculated or "feminized"; later, he comes forth "weak as a child, / tender & empty, doomed, quick to no tryst" (25.4–5). Such images of the poet suggest not just the child, I think, but the child victimized, doomed by the Father to annihilation. I am intrigued by the climactic detail Berryman selected for Anne's opening (and historically accurate) narrative of stanzas 5 and 6, that is, the drowning of "young Henry Winthrop," son of the Governor of 4.8. Although one could argue that the proleptic appearance of a Henry in Berryman's work can only be coincidental, the poet's later lament, which occurs during the central dialogue with Anne wherein he likens himself to a child—"I am drowning in this past"—seems to me to point squarely to identification with the drowned son. Berryman's life-long obsession with a (possibly apocryphal) incident when his own suicidal father threatened to drown him may lie behind the association. Let us consider entire this crucial section of the poem, the stanzas following on Anne's bidding the poet to "Sing a concord of our thought," which conclude their final dialogue.

> —Wan dolls in indigo on gold: refrain
> my western lust. I am drowning in this past.
> I lose sight of you
> who mistress me from air. Unbraced
> in delirium of the grand depths, giving away
> haunters what kept me, I breathe solid spray.
> —I am losing you.
> Straiten me on.—I suffered living like a stain:
>
> I trundle the bodies, on the iron bars,
> over that fire backward & forth; they burn—
> bits fall. I wonder if
> I killed them. Women serve my turn.
> —Dreams! You are good.—No.—Dense with
> hardihood
> the wicked are dislodged, and lodged the good.
> In green space we are safe.
> God awaits us (but I am yielding) who Hell wars.

Stanzas 33 and 34 are composed not of "concord," but of symbolic oppositions among the elements (earth, air, fire, and water) and between the temporal realms of history and eternity or, if we like, of the secular and the Divine. Again, in subtle contradiction of concord, the poet's associations seem as much private and personal as traditional. In the timeless realm of air, the mistress / Muse Anne is joined to the Virgin Mother evoked by the Byzantine dolls (see Berryman's note to 33.1). "Drowning in this past" he prays to her for rescue. The "grand depths," both formless and yet "solid," suggest here a contrastingly secular and annihilating world of history. Like a delirious diver (see note to 33.5–6) he divests himself of "what kept me"— the female Spirit evoked above. Thus Anne's interruption "—I am losing you!" The depths are also implicitly masculine, for "*this* past" in which the poet is drowning is not, we realize in the end, the past of Anne who is losing him, from whom he is slipping away. Just as the drowning-image contains a seminal element of Berryman's autobiographical myth, so the poet's admission prepares the way for the sole, strictly self-referential or "autobiographical" confession in the long poem: "I suffered living like a stain." Whereas the simple past tense here places the poet in a "posthumous" mode (reviewing a life completed), the present tense in which he continues (34.1–4) calls forth the obsessive repetition of *dream*. (The subtle irony of Anne's consoling "Dreams! You are good" depends on an alteration of meaning, from dream as psychic reality to dream as idle phantom, which must be incomplete.) Interior and exterior histories merge here. The infernal image of 34.1–4 is at once radically interior and personal, in this dream sense, and wholly appropriate to the mid-century experience of war and holocaust. The strangely effective "Women serve my turn," both confession and threat, operates in a different sort of present. A seeming shift of reference from the dream-world to the ongoing circumstances of the "actual" life, the line jolts us into a revision of this poem, of the poet's relation to his subject. The emphatic opposition of the poet to the general "women" underlines, I think, a major aspect of the confession. Guilty within all these masculine spheres, of private and public history, of literary act, he is in a more fundamental sense *guilty* of the masculine. The poet's ventriloquist-identification with the Puritan woman is a self-rescue from the annihilating depths of the personal (time- and gender-bound) self and to its limitations as poetic subject.

Anne's answering image of consolation weds the eternal realm of faith with the spatial particularity ("dislodged . . . lodged") of the "green space" earth. But her consolation or absolution of the poet must be imperfect "(but I am yielding)" and it calls forth his own final confession of no-faith.

> —I cannot feel myself God waits. He flies
> nearer a kindly world; or he is flown.
> One Saturday's rescue
> won't show. Man is entirely alone
> may be. I am a man of griefs & fits
> trying to be my friend. And the brown smock splits,
> down the pale flesh a gash
> broadens and Time holds up your heart against my eyes.

The sky—the realm of air—is empty, God is flown. But the earth, which is the woman's body, contains its own eternal spirit, which is joined to the poet's. The effect of the stanza's final three lines is multiple. In "Time holds up your heart *against* my eyes" we sense not so much a hungering vision filled as rather a blank one *screened*. The image is of shielding: the sky may remain as empty and godless as ever "in the present," but the poet has transformed time, consciousness, "heart," and is protected from that void. The image also recalls to me strongly the childbirth-stanza 19, "inverted" as it were. In this sense the poet is more than shielded by the mother-figure; he is able to "enter" her, not as lover but as offspring returned to its source. Poetically, identification is complete, and the voice of Anne continues uninterrupted through the close (stanza 53) of the narrative part of the poem.

Such a reading of *Mistress Bradstreet,* wherein the poet usurps and replaces the father-husband, drowns or is emasculated as the son, and *becomes* the mother, may approach "intra-poetic relationships as parallels of family romance" in a manner rather too literal for criticism. But Berryman's own invitations to such readings remain provocative, even imperative.

> The idea was not to take Anne Bradstreet as a poetess—I was not interested in that. I was interested in her as a pioneer heroine, a sort of mother to the artists and intellectuals who would follow her and play a large role in the development of the nation. People like Jefferson, Poe, and me.

This is the hindsight of Berryman post *Dream Songs,* supplemented by the now heart-wrenching note of March, 1971 (after the final phrase quoted above) "Get the delusion." As he and his various biographers tell us, Berryman evidently organized his own, let's say psychoanalytic, version of his life—and of its poetic record *The Dream Songs* (his *Song of Myself*)—in relation to the fact of his father's suicide. According to Kenneth Connelly,

> This fact hangs like a fatal curse over the poem from beginning to end, dramatizing Henry's sense of rootlessness and confusion, heightening the temptation of death, and confronting him with the challenge not to betray his children as he has been betrayed.

With the benefit of our own hindsight we might view the poet's strategy in *Mistress Bradstreet,* to identify with or become the mother, as an earlier, somehow liberating response to this parental challenge. In so becoming, the poet enables himself to rectify or reverse whatever inadequacies the maternal figure may suffer (or inflict) as precursor—a term we may take, I believe, in both familial and literary senses. To view Berryman's strategy in this way is, however, to render still more problematic the very notion of "mastery" which I've sought to explore.

Let us return to the point of identification with Bradstreet with which Berryman himself begins:

> We are on each others' hands
> who care. Both of our worlds unhanded us.

"One point of connection" between himself and his subject, as Berryman remarked, "being the almost insuperable difficulty of writing high verse in a land that cared and cares so little for it," the hint of emasculation in "unhanded" which I mentioned above is in keeping with the attitude of weakness and rejection in which each poet stands in relation to his community and culture. And the suggestion is equally appropriate to the different and opposite ways the two are unhanded by their respective worlds. In Puritan New England Bradstreet's writing was unwomanly, masculine. In Berryman's twentieth-century America, to be a poet—he had occasion to deplore this himself—was to be unmanned, feminized. Given such sexual reversal, implicit in the very figure of the American poet, the seventeenth-century mother appears a kind of "weak father" to the twentieth-century offspring. It is the complex fate of the latter, the drama which *Mistress Bradstreet* enacts, that he must master, embrace, become, "complete" such a problematic precursor.

"A poem's force," Berryman wrote in 1965 (placing himself, to my mind, somewhere between Ernest Hemingway and Harold Bloom) "may be pivoted on a missing or misrepresented element in an agreed-upon or imposed design." Having begun my account of his breakthrough-poem by examining some elements missing from the poet's own account of its origins, let me conclude by proposing—in the spirit of Bloom's call for an "antithetical criticism"— an alternative, only superficially absent "strong" father to the work: that is, the Hawthorne of *The Scarlet Letter*. According to Bloom, the American poet differs notably from the British in his relation to the father:

> It seems true that British poets swerve from their precursors while American poets labor rather to "complete" their fathers. The British are more genuinely revisionists of one another, but we (or at least most of our post-Emersonian poets) tend to see our fathers as not having dared enough.

Berryman, in the course of his acknowledgment of a Russian novelist's immediate influence on *Mistress Bradstreet,* remarks in passing on his "own" literary tradition:

> The only woman in American literature is Hester Prynne, and she is very good. I have great respect for her and the book, but Mistress Bradstreet is much more ambitious. It is very unlikely that it is better, but it attempts more.

Hawthorne, in his ironically truthful, seriously fictive account of himself and the origins of his Romance, "The Custom House":

> While thus perplexed,—and cogitating, among other hypotheses, whether the letter might not have been one of those decorations which the white men used to contrive, in order to take the eyes of Indians,—I happened to place it on my breast. It seemed to me,—the reader may smile but must not doubt my word,—it seemed to me, then, that I experienced a sensation not altogether physical, yet almost so, as of burning heat; and as if the letter were not of red cloth, but red-hot iron. I shuddered, and involuntarily let it fall upon the floor.

And Berryman's poetic "reply," which we have already had occasion to consider:

> And the brown smock splits,
> down the pale flesh a gash
> broadens and Time holds up your heart against my eyes.

The surface connections between Berryman's Bradstreet and Hester Prynne are clear enough. I do not believe it is possible to link the terms "Puritan" and "adulteress" and *not* to think of Hawthorne's character: she is, as it were, the original. The "series of rebellions" which Berryman described as marking the theme of the poem—"each rebellion, of course . . . succeeded by a submission"—is very much the pattern of Hester's career. Indeed, the character described in chapter 13, "Another View of Hester," who, had it not been for her child, "might have come down to us in history, hand in hand with Anne Hutchinson, as the foundress of a religious sect . . . [who] might, and not improbably would, have suffered death from the stern tribunals of the period, for attempting to undermine the foundations of the Puritan establishment" carries rebellion, albeit speculative, to what would seem to be its limit. Inventing, Berryman makes Anne Hutchinson a friend of his Anne. Given such links, Berryman's reference to Hester Prynne in the *Paris Review* interview seems inevitable.

But there are other, deeper connections which I think his more enthusiastic concern in that interview with Augie March and Anna Karenina may actively work to obscure. *The Scarlet Letter* is, after all, a fiction "about" its own and its author's precursors, about the burden of its American past. It represents in Hawthorne's work—in addition to being what we might call his own "breakthrough"—the synthesis of his active involvement with history with his great theme of inherited guilt, of the nature of good and evil *in historical time,* of the problematic relation of son to father explored in terms equally ambiguous of progress or declension. In one sense Hawthorne confronts or comes to terms with the "stern and black-browed Puritans" evoked in "The Custom House" by assuming the badge or brand of the woman they victimized. It may be that the "Custom House" narrator's involuntary dropping of that brand symbolized for Berryman, as it has for other readers, a failure on Hawthorne's part of full, sympathetic identification with his heroine; his own ambition to "attempt more" seems to lie in this area. Berryman, as we've seen, enters or becomes the person of a woman doubly victimized: in the past by the hostile new world (which still victimizes him, through indifference and neglect); in the present by the poet himself, whose turn women serve.

What we must ask ourselves in the end is what is the nature of this second victimization: what turn *is* served for the poet? And here I think the perspective of *The Scarlet Letter* as precursor is most valuable, for from that perspective we can see, what may otherwise be less clear, the extent to which *Mistress Bradstreet* expresses, if not a yearning for religious faith, then a piercing lament at its loss and an attempt, through poetry, somehow to overcome it.

Let us recall briefly the trinitarian master-figure whose presence in *Mistress Bradstreet* serves the purpose of Anne's mild rebellion and the poet's subtler subversion. In a rather curious note on the composition of the poem Berryman, recalling "three occasions of special heat," mentions finally the "pleasant moment . . . when one night, hugging myself, I decided that her fierce dogmatic old father was going to die blaspheming, in delirium." A clear enough gesture, it seems to me, of oedipal rebellion (the image of Berryman hugging himself is mischievous and *boyish*), and an interesting conjunction of this conflict with the very issue of faith. But there is also, I would hazard, an element of self-identification with the old man dying in delirium by the poet "Unbraced / in delirium of the grand depths, giving away / haunters what kept me." In this sense the death is a kind of appropriation: I (poet) shall deprive you of your proper death and you (Father) shall suffer the death to which *I* am doomed.

But what we notice almost immediately in the poem, especially of the climactic confession of stanza 35 and those that follow, is that such processes as rebellion and subversion are incomplete; indeed, they are ultimately reversed. The woman's "submission" is rather a triumph of achieved or *re*achieved faith (stanzas 37–39) which emphasizes as much as it cures the gulf between her and her modern suitor. The interest of Anne's "bald/abstract didactic rime" must in the end be for him, more than its historical priority, its motivating subject: a "real" God who is at the ontological center of her world and work. The dilemma of the modern poet of no-faith is that the motivating subject of his work must either be the self-swallowing abyss of his personal past or—if external to him—then lie in the faith of *another*. In so far as *Homage to Mistress Bradstreet* celebrates the faith of the subject, it acknowledges a doubly secondary quality in itself. And against this secondary status the poet's strategy again seems to be one of appropriation. By making Anne Bradstreet the object of *his* faith and worship (and the subject of his poem) the poet empties the sky of her own God.

> O all your ages at the mercy of my loves
> together lie at once, forever or
> so long as I happen.

During the composition of *Mistress Bradstreet*, Eileen Simpson writes, Berryman, "in a state of manic excitement," was convinced that "he was having a religious experience, was on the point of conversion." He rid himself of the delusion, it seems, during a visit to the devoutly Catholic poet Robert Fitzgerald. Afterwards, the work went on in an atmosphere of even greater "nightmare."

It may be that we gain some insight into the quality of this nightmare through contrast. In chapter 5 of *The Scarlet Letter*, "Hester at Her Needle," we find a long passage on the effects on Hester's imagination of the "strange and solitary anguish of her life" in which our sense of an authorial self-reflexion is particularly strong. The effects themselves touch on Hawthorne's central themes—the evil of isolation from the community of men, the very different evils, of which Hester's "new sense" has given her appalled revelation, of the community of guilt which all men share. The "loss of faith [which] is ever one of the saddest results of sin" is here, for Hester, a loss of faith not in God but in her fellow men; and it is a threatened or remembered loss, we sense, which the author himself struggles through by means of his character. It is at this point in the text that we are reminded of the symbolic moment recounted in "The Custom House":

> The vulgar, who, in those dreary old times, were always contributing a grotesque horror to what interested their imaginations, had a story about the scarlet letter which we might readily work up into a terrific legend. They averred, that the symbol was not mere scarlet cloth, tinged in an earthly dyepot, but was red-hot with infernal fire, and could be seen glowing all alight, whenever Hester Prynne walked abroad in the night-time. And we must

needs say, it seared Hester's bosom so deeply, that perhaps there was more truth in the rumor than our modern incredulity may be inclined to admit.

Just as his reference to the *"dreary* old times" is decidedly ironic, so the author's apparent participation in "our modern incredulity" must be read aslant. In his relation to this incredulity or lack of faith, *and to the heroine who anticipates it,* it may well be that Hawthorne enjoyed a greater freedom of the poet than his "dispossessed" literary descendant. His actual possession of the Puritan past (strong traits of his ancestors' nature have intertwined themselves with his) permits him a rather privileged balance in the nineteenth-century present vis-à-vis both the past and the future. In feeling the former as a solid and weighty burden, in both participating in and liberating himself from it through Hester, Hawthorne permits himself an anticipation of the future which, if tainted with skepticism and irony, is nevertheless genuine and genuinely earned.

The "more" that Berryman's poem attempts seems to me, finally, a foredoomed willing-into-being of a burdensome past (the "present" of Anne's world against which she rebels, to which she finally submits) the real burden of which is its quality of absence. Thus, extreme identification with his heroine represents an attempted appropriation of a past from which he is—by the very fact of a literary ancestor like Hawthorne—all the more displaced. But the very hopelessness of the effort is the extraordinary power of *Homage to Mistress Bradstreet.* This is a poem which celebrates impossibilities. The impossibility of living in the faithless void of the present time, the impossibility of being an American poet at all—these are celebrated in this most American of poems in verse Berryman equalled but never surpassed. And it is the nearly impossible intensity of the poet's emotion—need, rage, longing, grief—that this verse contains, and that his Muse / mistress / subject is able to embody. Anne Bradstreet could, paradoxically, embody for Berryman the very weaknesses and absences from which his poetic effort had hitherto suffered— his breakthrough, at what he described as enormous cost; thereafter, *The Dream Songs* and Henry.

Chronology

1914   John Berryman is born on October 25, 1914 in McAlester, Oklahoma to John Allyn Smith, a bank-worker, and Martha Little Smith. The poet is named John Allyn Smith, after his father, and is the elder of two sons. Berryman's family life is turbulent, due in part to his father's insecurities about his marriage. The family moves to Tampa, Florida in 1925.

1926   Berryman's father commits suicide. Berryman's mother marries John Angus McAlpin Berryman, who legally adopts the two boys. The poet's name is changed to John Allyn McAlpin Berryman. The family moves to New York City.

1932–36   After attending prep school at South Kent in Connecticut, Berryman attends Columbia College, where he befriends Mark Van Doren and decides to become a poet. He graduates Phi Beta Kappa in 1936 and is awarded the Euretta J. Kellett scholarship to study in England.

1936–38   Berryman attends Clare College in Cambridge. During this period, he meets W. H. Auden, Dylan Thomas, and W. B. Yeats and wins the Oldham Shakespeare Scholarship for 1937. He becomes engaged for the first time, but the relationship breaks off before the marriage. He returns to New York with his second Bachelor of Arts degree.

1939   In New York, Berryman meets Delmore Schwartz. Later in the year, he becomes an instructor of English at Wayne State University, Detroit.

1940–43   Berryman teaches English at Harvard University. He meets Eileen Patricia Mulligan and marries her in 1942. He publishes

"Twenty Poems" in *Five Young American Poets* in 1940, and his first book, *Poems,* in 1942.

1943–45   For one year (1943–44), Berryman teaches English at Princeton University, where he works with R. P. Blackmur. He meets Robert Lowell and Edmund Wilson, who become close friends. The Rockefeller Foundation awards him a Foundation Research Fellowship for 1944–45, and he records his poetry for the Library of Congress (1945). His short story "The Imaginary Jew" wins a contest sponsored by *Kenyon Review.*

1946–47   Berryman teaches Creative Writing at Princeton. He has an adulterous love affair with the woman he names "Lise" in *Berryman's Sonnets,* written in 1947 but not published until 1967. He begins psychiatric treatment.

1948–51   Berryman becomes a fellow at Princeton. He begins writing *Homage to Mistress Bradstreet* and publishes *The Dispossessed,* his second book of poems, in 1948 and *Stephen Crane,* a critical biography, in 1950. He meets Saul Bellow, Ezra Pound, and Randall Jarrell and continues to receive awards for his poetry. He teaches one semester at the University of Washington.

1952–54   Berryman teaches one semester as the Elliston Professor of Poetry at the University of Cincinnati, before winning a Guggenheim Fellowship (1952–53) and travelling to Europe. In 1953, Berryman is separated from Eileen. He moves back to the United States to teach poetry for a semester at the University of Iowa, and for a summer session at Harvard.

1954–56   Berryman becomes a teacher in Humanities at the University of Minnesota, where he teaches until the time of his death. He begins writing *The Dream Songs.* In 1956, he is divorced from Eileen and marries Elizabeth Ann Levine. He publishes *Homage to Mistress Bradstreet* (1956). *Partisan Review* awards Berryman his second Rockefeller Fellowship.

1957–58   Berryman is awarded the Harriet Monroe Poetry Prize. His first son, Paul, is born. Berryman lectures for two months in India for the U.S. State Department. He publishes *His Thought Made Pockets & The Plane Buckt* (1958).

1959–63   Berryman is divorced from Ann. He is awarded the Brandeis University Creative Arts Award, and he publishes (with Ralph

Ross and Allen Tate) *The Arts of Reading* (1960), an anthology with commentary. Berryman teaches at the University of Utah (1959), the University of California at Berkeley (1960), Indiana University (1961), the Bread Loaf School of English, Middlebury, Vermont (1962), and Brown University (1962–63). He marries Kathleen (Kate) Donahue in 1961. He participates in the National Poetry Festival in Washington, D.C. and is awarded a grant from the Ingram Merrill Foundation. His first daughter, Martha, is born.

1964–65 Berryman publishes *77 Dream Songs,* which wins the Pulitzer Prize. He also receives the Russell Loines Award from the National Institute of Arts and Letters, and is awarded a Guggenheim Fellowship for 1966–67.

1966–67 Using the money from the Guggenheim Fellowship, Berryman and his family live in Dublin, where Berryman writes most of what is to become book 7 of *The Dream Songs.* He receives a $5,000 fellowship from the Academy of American Poets, and a $10,000 award from the National Endowment for the Arts. He publishes *Berryman's Sonnets* and *Short Poems* (both 1967).

1968–69 Berryman publishes *His Toy, His Dream, His Rest* (1968), which wins the National Book Award and the Bollingen Prize. He then publishes *The Dream Songs* (the complete edition) in 1969. He is named a Regents' Professor at the University of Minnesota. He begins treatment for alcoholism.

1970–71 Berryman publishes *Love & Fame,* but it gets bad initial reviews. Berryman continues to be treated for alcoholism. His second daughter, Sarah Rebecca, is born.

1972 John Berryman commits suicide on January 7, 1972. *Delusions, etc.,* a book of poetry, is published posthumously.

1973 *Recovery,* a novel, is published.

1976 *The Freedom of the Poet,* a collection of critical essays and stories, is published.

1977 *Henry's Fate & Other Poems, 1967–1972* (edited by John Haffenden) is published.

Contributors

HAROLD BLOOM, Sterling Professor of the Humanities at Yale University, is the author of *The Anxiety of Influence, Poetry and Repression,* and many other volumes of literary criticism. His forthcoming study, *Freud: Transference and Authority,* attempts a full-scale reading of all of Freud's major writings. A MacArthur Prize Fellow, he is general editor of five series of literary criticism published by Chelsea House. During 1987–88, he served as the Charles Eliot Norton Professor of Poetry at Harvard University.

WILLIAM WASSERSTROM was Professor of Creative Writing at Syracuse University from 1960–1978, before leaving academia to work on his research and writing. His books include *The Ironies of Progress: Henry Adams & the American Dream* and *The Legacy of Van Wyck Brooks: A Study of Maladies & Motives.*

DENIS DONOGHUE is Henry James Professor of English and American Literature at New York University. His books include *Thieves of Fire* and *Ferocious Alphabets.*

ERNEST C. STEFANIK is the author of *John Berryman: A Descriptive Bibliography* and was the co-editor of the *John Berryman Studies* journal.

DAVID KALSTONE was Professor of English at Rutgers University. He has published extensively on poets from Sir Philip Sidney to James Merrill and John Ashbery.

EDWARD MENDELSON is Professor of English at Columbia University. He is the author of several studies on W. H. Auden and is the literary executor of the Auden estate.

JOHN BAYLEY is Wharton Professor of English Literature at Oxford University. His books include *The Uses of Division, Selected Essays,*

Romantic Survival, Shakespeare and Tragedy and *Pushkin: A Comparative Commentary.*

JOEL CONARROE is Professor of English at New York University and president of the John Simon Guggenheim Memorial Foundation. He is the author of *John Berryman: An Introduction to the Poetry.*

DIANE ACKERMAN is Assistant Professor of English at the University of Pittsburgh and a poet. Her books include *Planets, Wife of Light,* and *On Extended Wings.*

JEROME MAZZARO, Professor of English at the State University of New York, Buffalo, has written extensively on Renaissance and modern poetry.

DAVID K. WEISER is a professor at Tel-Aviv University. He is the author of *The Prose Style of John Jewel.*

ELIZABETH KASPAR ALDRICH is a Professor of English at the University of Geneva. She is the author of articles on American fiction and autobiography and is currently at work on a book entitled *American Hagiography,* secular saints' lives from William Bradford to Marilyn Monroe.

Bibliography

Alvarez, A. "John Berryman." In *Beyond All This Fiddle,* 88–90. London: Allen Lane/Penguin Press, 1968.

——. Review of *Delusions, etc. New York Times Book Review* (June 25, 1972): 1, 12, 14.

Arpin, Gary Q. *John Berryman: A Reference Guide.* (Boston: G. K. Hall, 1976.

——. "Mistress Bradstreet's Discontents." *John Berryman Studies* 1, no. 3 (1975): 2–7.

——. *The Poetry of John Berryman.* Port Washington, N.Y.: Kennikat Press, 1978.

Barbera, Jack Vincent. "Shape and Flow in *The Dream Songs.*" *Twentieth Century Literature* 22 (1976): 146–62.

——. "Under the Influence." *John Berryman Studies* 2, no. 2 (1976): 56–65.

Bawer, Bruce. *The Middle Generation.* Hamden, Conn.: Archon, 1986.

Bloom, James D. *The Stock of Available Reality: R. P. Blackmur and John Berryman.* Lewisburg, Pa.: Bucknell University Press, 1984.

Blum, Morgan. "Berryman as Biographer, Stephen Crane as Poet." *Poetry* 78 (1951): 298–307.

Browne, Michael Dennis. "Henry Fermenting: Debts to *The Dream Songs.*" *Ohio Review* 15, no. 2 (1974): 75–87.

Butscher, Edward, "John Berryman: In Memorial Perspective." *Georgia Review* 27 (1973): 518–25.

Carruth, Hayden. "Declining Occasions." *Poetry* 112 (1968): 119–21.

——. "Love, Art and Money." *Nation* (November 2, 1970): 437–38.

Ciardi, John. "The Researched Mistress." *Saturday Review* (March 23, 1957): 36–37.

Conarroe, Joel. *John Berryman: An Introduction to the Poetry.* New York: Columbia University Press, 1977.

Cott, Jonathan. "Theodore Roethke and John Berryman: Two Dream Poets." In *On Contemporary Literature,* edited by Richard Kostelanetz. New York: Avon, 1964.

Davie, Donald. "Problems of Decorum." Review of *Recovery. New York Times Book Review* (April 25, 1976): 3–4.

Dickey, James. "John Berryman." In *Babel to Byzantium,* 198–99. New York: Farrar, Straus, & Giroux, 1968.

Dodsworth, Martin. "John Berryman: An Introduction." In *The Survival of Poetry,* 100–132. London: Faber & Faber, 1970.

Dunn, Douglas. "Gaiety and Lamentation: The Defeat of John Berryman." *Encounter* 43 (August 1974): 72–77.

Evans, Arthur and Catherine. "Pieter Bruegel and John Berryman: Two Winter Landscapes." *Texas Studies in Literature and Language* 5 (1963): 309–18.

Fitts, Dudley. "Deep in the Unfriendly City." *New York Times Book Review* (June 20, 1948): 4.

Fitzgerald, Robert. "Poetry and Perfection." *Sewanee Review* 56 (1948): 690–93.

Flint, R. W. "A Romantic on Early New England." *New Republic* (May 27, 1957): 28.

Galassi, Jonathan. "Sorrows and Passions of His Majesty the Ego." *Poetry Nation* no. 2 (1974): 117–24.

Gelpi, Albert. "Homage to Berryman's *Homage*." *Harvard Advocate* 103 (1969): 14–17.

Gilman, Milton. "Berryman and the Sonnets." *Chelsea* 22/23 (1968): 158–69.

Haas, Joseph. "Who Killed Henry Pussy-cat? I did, says John Berryman, with love and a poem, and for freedom, O." *Chicago Daily News* (February 6, 1971) 4–5.

Haffenden, John. *John Berryman: A Critical Commentary.* London: Macmillan, 1980.

———. *The Life of John Berryman.* London: Routledge & Kegan Paul, 1982.

Hamilton, Ian. "John Berryman." *London Magazine* 4 (February 1965): 93–100.

Harris, Marguerite, ed. *A Tumult for John Berryman.* San Francisco: Dryad Press, 1976.

Heyen, William. "John Berryman: A Memoir and an Interview." *Ohio Review* 15, no. 2 (1974): 46–65.

Hoffman, Daniel. "John Berryman." In *Contemporary Poets of the English Language,* edited by Rosalie Murphy, 85–87. Chicago: St. James Press, 1970.

Holder, Alan. "Anne Bradstreet Resurrected." *Concerning Poetry* 2 (1969): 11–18.

Howard, Jane. "Whiskey and Ink, Whiskey and Ink." *Life* 63 (July 21, 1967): 66–76.

Hudgins, Andrew. " 'I am Fleeing Double': Duality and Dialectric in *The Dream Songs*." *Missouri Review* 4 (1980–81): 93–110.

Hughes, Daniel. "The Dream Songs: Spells for Survival." *Southern Review* (Australia) 2 (1966).

Hyde, Lewis. "Alcohol & Poetry: John Berryman and the Booze Talking." *American Poetry Review*, 4 (July–August 1975): 7–12.

Jarrell, Randall. Review of *The Dispossessed. Nation* (July 17, 1948): 80–81.

Johnson, Carol. "John Berryman and Mistress Bradstreet: A Relation of Reason." *Essays in Criticism* 14 (1964): 388–96.

Kelly, Richard J. *John Berryman: A Checklist.* Metuchen, N.J.: Scarecrow Press, 1972.

———. "Scholarship & Poetry: Berryman's Prose." *John Berryman Studies* 2, no. 3 (1976): 63–65.

Kostelanetz, Richard. "Conversation with Berryman." *Massachusetts Review* 11 (1970): 340–47.

Kunitz, Stanley. "No Middle Flight." *Poetry* 90 (July 1957): 244–49.

Lieberman, Laurence. "Hold the Audience!—A Brief Memoir of John Berryman." *Eigo Seinen* 118 (1972): 68–70.

"The Life of the Modern Poet." Review of *Delusions, etc. Times Literary Supplement* (February 23, 1973): 193–95.

Linebarger, J. M. *John Berryman.* New York: Twayne, 1974.

Lowell, Robert. "The Poetry of John Berryman." *New York Review of Books* (May 28, 1964):3–4.

Martz, William J. *John Berryman*. University of Minnesota Pamphlets on American Writers. University of Minnesota Press, 1969.

Mazzocco, Robert. "Harlequin in Hell." *New York Review of Books* (June 29, 1967): 12–16.

McBride, Margaret M. "Berryman's 'World's Fair.' " *Explicator* 34, no. 3 (1975): Item 22.

McClatchy, J. D. "John Berryman: The Impediments to Salvation." *Modern Poetry Studies* 6 (1975): 246–77.

McGuire, Jerry. "John Berryman: Making a Poet of the Self." *Modern Poetry Studies* 10 (1981): 174–89.

Meredith, William. "A Bright Surviving Actual Scene: *Berryman's Sonnets*." *Harvard Advocate* 103 (1969): 19–22.

———. "Henry Tasting All the Secret Bits of Life: Berryman's Dream Songs." *Wisconsin Studies in Contemporary Literature* 6 (1965): 27–33.

———. "In Loving Memory of the Late Author of *The Dream Songs*." Foreword to *John Berryman: A Checklist*, edited by Richard J. Kelly, xi–xx. Metuchen, N.J.: Scarecrow Press, 1972.

Mills, Ralph J., Jr. *Creation's Very Self: On the Personal Element in Recent American Poetry*. Fort Worth: Texas Christian University Press, 1969.

Molesworth, Charles. "Shining the Start." *John Berryman Studies* 1, no. 4 (1975): 17–22.

Neill, Edward, "Ambivalence of Berryman: An Interim Report." *Critical Quarterly* 15 (1974): 267–76.

Nims, John Frederick. " 'The Dispossessed,' 'World's Fair,' and 'The Traveler.' " *Poetry: A Critical Supplement* (1948): 1–6.

———. "Homage in Measure to Mr. Berryman." *Prairie Schooner* 32 (1958): 1–7.

North, Michael. "The Public Monument and Public Poetry: Stevens, Berryman, and Lowell." *Contemporary Literature* 21 (1980): 267–85.

Oberg, Arthur. "John Berryman: *The Dream Songs* and the Horror of Unlove." *University of Windsor Review* 6 (1970): 1–11.

———. *Modern American Lyric*. New Brunswick, N.J.: Rutgers University Press, 1977.

Pearson, Gabriel, "John Berryman—Poet as Medium." *the Review* (1965): 3–17.

Perosa, Sergio. "A Commentary on *Homage to Mistress Bradstreet*." *John Berryman Studies* 2, no. 1 (1976): 4–25.

Pinsky, Robert. *The Situation of Poetry*. Princeton: Princeton University Press, 1976.

Porterfield, Jo R. "The Melding of a Man: Berryman, Henry, and the Ornery Mr. Bones." *Southwest Review* 58 (1973): 30–46.

Rich, Adrienne. "Mr. Bones, He Lives." *Nation* (May 25, 1964): 538, 540.

Ricks, Christopher. "Recent American Poetry." *Massachusetts Review* 11 (1970): 313–38.

Seidel, Frederick. "Berryman's Dream Songs." *Poetry* 105 (1965): 257–59.

Shapiro, Karl. "Major Poets of the Ex-English Language." *Tribune Book World* (January 26, 1969): 4.

Sheehan, Donald. "The Silver Sensibility: Five Recent Books of American Poetry." *Contemporary Literature* 12 (1971): 98–121.

Siegel, Muffy E. A. " 'The Original Crime': John Berryman's Iconic Grammar." *Poetics Today* 2 (1980): 163–88.

Simpson, Eileen. *The Maze.* New York: Simon & Schuster, 1975.

——. *Poets in Their Youth.* New York: Random House, 1982.

Simpson, Louis. "On Berryman's *Recovery.*" *Ohio Review* 15, no. 2 (1974): 112–14.

Sisson, Jonathan. "My Whiskers Fly: An Interview with John Berryman." *Ivory Tower* 14 (October 3, 1966): 14–18, 34–35.

Stefanik, Ernest C. "An Entrance." *John Berryman Studies* 1, no. 4 (1975): 52–53.

——. *John Berryman: A Descriptive Bibliography.* Pittsburgh: University of Pittsburgh Press, 1974.

Stitt, Peter A. "The Art of Poetry XVI." *Paris Review* no. 53 (1972): 117–207.

——. "Berryman's Last Poems." *Concerning Poetry* 6 (1973): 5–12.

——. "John Berryman: The Dispossessed Poet." *Ohio Review* 15, no. 2 (1974): 66–74.

——. "John Berryman's Literary Criticism." *Southern Review* 14 (1978): 368–74.

Thompson, John. "An Alphabet of Poets." *New York Review of Books* (August 1, 1968): 34–36.

Vendler, Helen. "Savage, Rueful, Irrepressible Henry." *New York Times Book Review* (November 3, 1968): 1, 58–59.

Vonalt, Larry. "Berryman's Most Bright Candle." *Parnassus: Poetry in Review* 1 (1972): 180–87.

Wallace, Ronald. "John Berryman: Me, Wag." In *God Be with the Clown: Humor in American Poetry,* 171–201. Columbia, Missouri: University of Missouri Press, 1984.

Warner, Anne B. "Berryman's Elegies: One Approach to *The Dream Songs.*" *John Berryman Studies* 2, no. 3 (Summer 1976): 5–22.

Wilson, Edmund. "Stephen Crane—Hannah Whitall Smith." *New Yorker* 26 (January 6, 1951): 77–85.

Wyatt, David M. "Completing the Picture: Williams, Berryman, and 'Spatial Form.'" *Colby Library Quarterly* 13 (1977): 246–62.

Acknowledgments

"Cagey John: Berryman as Medicine Man" by William Wasserstrom from *The Centennial Review* 12, no. 3 (Summer 1968), © 1968 by *The Centennial Review*. Reprinted with permission.

"Berryman's Long Dream" by Denis Donoghue from *Art International* 13, no. 3 (March 20, 1969), © 1969 by Denis Donaghue. Reprinted with permission.

"A Cursing Glory: John Berryman's *Love & Fame*" by Ernest C. Stefanik from *Renascence* 25, no. 3 (Spring 1973), © 1973 by the Catholic Renascence Society, Inc. Reprinted with permission of *Renascence: Essays on Values in Literature* (Marquette University Press).

"*Recovery:* The Struggle between Prose and Life" (originally entitled "Review of *Recovery*") by David Kalstone from *The New York Times Book Review* (May 27, 1973), © 1973 by The New York Times Company. Reprinted with permission.

"How to Read Berryman's *Dream Songs*" by Edward Mendelson from *American Poetry since 1960*, edited by Robert B. Shaw, © 1973 by Edward Mendelson. Reprinted with permission.

"John Berryman: A Question of Imperial Sway" by John Bayley from *Contemporary Poetry in America*, edited by Robert Boyers, © 1973 by Skidmore College, © 1974 by Schocken Books, Inc. Reprinted with permission of Robert Boyers.

"After Mr. Bones: John Berryman's Last Poems" by Joel Conarroe from *The Hollins Critic* 13, no. 4 (October 1976), © 1976 by Hollins College, Virginia. Reprinted with permission.

"Near the Top a Bad Turn Dared" by Diane Ackerman from *Parnassus: Poetry in Review* 7, no. 2 (Spring–Summer 1979), © 1979 by Poetry in Review Foundation. Reprinted with permission.

"The Yeatsian Mask: John Berryman" by Jerome Mazzaro from *Postmodern American Poetry* by Jerome Mazzaro, © 1980 by the Board of Trustees of the University of Illinois. Reprinted with permission of University of Illinois Press and the author.

"Berryman's Sonnets: In and Out of the Tradition" by David K. Weiser from *American*

176

Index

Adams, John, 15
"After a Journey" (Hardy), 84
Age of Anxiety, The (Auden), 82
Aiken, Conrad, 122
Alastor (Shelley), 2
Aldrich, Elizabeth Kaspar, 2–3
Alvarez, A., 1, 5, 95, 101, 122–23
American poetry: problems of, 3–6,
    15, 66, 73, 159, 163
"Among School Children" (Yeats), 76
Amours jaunes, Les (Corbière), 37
Andrewes, Lancelot, Bishop, 41, 44
Anne Bradstreet and Her Time
    (Campbell), 121
"Anne Bradstreet Resurrected"
    (Holder), 121–22
Aristotle, 46, 142
Ashbery, John, 89
Asolando (Browning), 2
Astrophel and Stella (Sidney), 138–39
As You Like It (Shakespeare), 140–41
"At Chinese Checkers," 115
Auden, W. H., 1–2, 54, 56, 61, 75,
    78–79, 80–83, 90–91, 107,
    112–16, 118–20, 132
Aurelius, Marcus, 103

Bailey, Philip James, 2
Baldwin, James, 15
Baraka, Imamu Amiri (LeRoi Jones),
    10–11
Barth, John, 88
Bayley, John, 1, 111
Beats, the, 20
Beckett, Samuel, 7, 72, 87, 94
Beethoven, Ludwig van, 96–98, 129

"Beethoven Triumphant," 97
Bellow, Saul, 90, 121, 150, 160
Benn, Gottfried, 25
Berryman, John: on Anne Bradstreet,
    102, 158; and confessional
    poetry, 54, 79, 95; on *Dream
    Songs*, 53–54, 74, 112; and func-
    tion of autobiography in his
    poems, 35, 38–48, 71–88; on
    Henry, 54, 74–75, 112; on in-
    fluence of Auden and Yeats, 1,
    56; on long poems, 21; on metre,
    71; on *Homage to Mistress
    Bradstreet*, 102, 150, 158; and
    poet as victim, 25, 35; and prob-
    lems of American poetry, 3–6,
    15, 66, 73, 159, 163; and
    suicide, 5, 68–69, 89–90
Berryman's Sonnets, 57, 72, 78, 91,
    98, 120, 122, 124, 128, 150; ar-
    tificial language, 117–19; Lise,
    117, 137–38, 142, 150–151;
    traditional elements, 133–47
Bible, the, 7–8, 13–14, 19, 124–25
"Big Buttons, Cornets: The Advance,"
    9
Biographia Literaria (Coleridge), 73
Bishop, Elizabeth, 72, 88
Black Mountain poets, the, 20
Blackmur, R. P., 28, 62, 73, 129–30
Blake, William, 2
Bloom, Harold, 159
Bloom, Leopold (*Ulysses*), 72
Bones, Mr. (*Dream Songs*), 9–13, 15,
    19, 22–23, 52–53, 59, 62, 64,
    74, 82, 90, 102, 112, 123, 147
Boroff, Edith, 55

Bradstreet, Anne (*Homage to Mistress Bradstreet*), 3, 7, 23, 57–58, 61, 78, 91, 102–5, 120–22, 151–63; and female experience, 104, 120, 123; function of, 104–5, 120, 151, 158–63

Bradstreet, Simon (*Homage to Mistress Bradstreet*), 103, 154–55

Brahma, 18

Bridges, Robert, 94, 120

Bridge, The (Crane), 21

Brodsky, Joseph, 19–20

Brown, Norman O., 6

Browning, Robert, 2, 31

Burroughs, William S., 6, 71, 88

Byron, George Gordon, Lord, 71, 74, 84, 87

Cage, John, 16

Cagey John (*Dream Songs*), 16–17, 19

Campbell, Helen, 121

Cantos (Pound), 21, 55, 73, 75, 91

"Care and Feeding of Long Poems, The," 21

Carew, Thomas, 108

Carruth, Hayden, 117, 123

Ciardi, John, 120, 122–23

Civilization and Its Discontents (Freud), 116

Clarke, Austin, 31

Coleridge, Samuel Taylor, 73

Conarroe, Joel, 133, 135, 138

confessional poetry, 54, 79, 95

Confessional Poets, The (Phillips), 95

Connelly, Kenneth, 158

Corbière, Tristan, 37

Corvo, Baron, 30

Cotton, John (*Homage to Mistress Bradstreet*), 103

Cowley, Abraham, 102, 108

Crane, Hart, 19, 21, 96

Crane, Stephen, 14–16, 18–19, 119, 150–52

Crazy Jane, 3, 117, 124

"Crisis," 85

cummings, e.e., 54, 101, 129–30, 142

Dante Alighieri, 32, 49, 141

Darwin, Charles, 112–23

Davie, Donald, 89

Delusions, etc.: and *Angst*, 108; rela-

tionship to *Recovery*, 49; and search for faith; structure of, 95–98, 108

Desire and Pursuit of the Whole, The (Corvo), 30

Diamond, Stanley, 17

Dickey, James, 123, 149

Dickinson, Emily, 94, 96

Dispossessed, The, 57, 61, 91, 115, 117, 119, 121

Don Juan (Byron), 84

Don Quixote (Cervantes), 55–56, 117–18

Donne, John, 78, 102, 114, 121, 127, 142

Dream Songs, The; 77 *Dreams Songs* (1964), then added *His Toy, His Dream, His Rest* (Songs 78–385), 1969, 1–4, 6–20, 36, 38, 50, 52, 53–69, 71, 74–75, 77, 86–88, 91–99, 102, 111–18, 124–32, 133, 147, 149–50, 158, 163: and dreams, 7–8, 55, 60–62, 129–31; epigraphs of, 6–8, 11; and minstrelsy, 9–13; and mysticism, 18–20; "Nervous Songs, The," 57, 91, 115–17; numerology in, 8–9, 54; paratactic method in, 67; structure of, 21–33, 54–55, 60–69, 102, 124–32; syntax in, 25–32, 57, 113–15, 130–31

Dreams (Schreiner), 7–8, 13

Dreiser, Theodore, 90

"Drunks," 39–40

Du Bartas, Guillaume, 121

Ego and the Id, The (Freud), 15

Eisenhower, Dwight David, 28

"Eleven Addresses to the Lord," 44, 94

Eliot, T. S., 1, 21, 30–32, 36, 46, 68, 72, 85, 90, 113, 115, 121, 131, 141–42, 152

"Eloisa to Abelard" (Pope), 65

Empson, William, 123

Estrangement (Yeats), 29

Eugene Onegin (Pushkin), 74–75, 80

"Eve of St. Agnes, The" (Keats), 80

Fearing, Kenneth, 82

Fenollosa, Ernest, 129

Fiedler, Leslie A., 12
"Fifty Years of American Poetry" (Jarrell), 123
Finnegans Wake (Joyce), 129
Fitts, Dudley, 115, 122
Fitzgerald, Robert, 91, 122, 162
Fitzwilliam Virginal Book, 54
Five-Finger Exercises (Eliot), 32
Flaubert, Gustave, 80
Ford, Ford Madox, 96
"Four Monarchs, The" (Bradstreet), 121
Four Quartets (Eliot), 21, 141–42
Frank, Anne, 117
Freedom of the Poet, The, 89–90
"Freshman Blues," 39
Freud, Sigmund, 14–15, 19, 42, 45, 60, 112, 115–16, 120, 129–31, 142
Frost, Robert, 24, 28

Genet, Jean, 11
Ginsberg, Allen, 20
Giroux, Robert, 90
"Go, Lovely Rose" (Waller), 30
Graves, Robert, 18–19, 61–62
Gray, Thomas, 87

Haffendon, John, 90
Hamlet (Shakespeare), 28, 137
Hardy, Thomas, 84, 88
Hawthorne, Nathaniel, 3, 159–63
Hazlitt, William, 24
"He Reigns," 96–97
Heisenberg, Werner Karl, 106
"Hell Poem, The," 86
Hemans, Felicia Dorothea, 2
Hemingway, Ernest, 2
Henry (*Dream Songs*), 9–20, 22–33, 50, 52–55, 59–69, 74–75, 78, 80, 82, 86–87, 91–93, 98, 102, 123–31, 147, 156, 158: as Berryman, 29–33, 102; a disguise, not a mask, 29–33; function of, 15–20; 21–33; *Henriad*, in a, 32; as a mask, 123–32; sources for, 14–15
Henry's Fate & Other Poems, 90
"Her & It," 38
Herbert, George 108
"Heroes, The," 83, 85

His Toy, His Dream, His Rest, 21, 55, 63–64
Hodgson, Ralph, 31–32, 68
Holder, Alan, 121–22
Hölderlin, Friedrich, 142
Homage to Mistress Bradstreet, 1, 3, 20, 23, 30, 36, 57, 61, 65, 77–79, 91, 101–9, 119–24, 149–63: and female experience, 104, 120, 123; function of Anne Bradstreet in, 104–5, 120, 151, 158–63; as historical poem, 121, 149, 151; as polyphonic tour de force, 102–3; and Puritanism, 153–163; structure of, 124, 158–63
"Home Ballad, The," 43
Hopkins, Gerard Manley, 48, 54, 57, 91, 94, 101, 107, 120, 127
Housman, A. E., 119–20
Howard, Jane, 114, 119, 131
Hugh Selwyn Mauberley (Pound), 29

Iliad (Homer), 125
"Imaginary Jew, The," 23
"In Memory of Major Robert Gregory" (Yeats), 115, 120
In the Penal Colony (Kafka), 24
Interpretation of Dreams, The (Freud), 129

Jakobson, Roman, 130
James, Henry, 14, 26, 73, 76, 90, 138–39
James, William, 125
Jarrell, Randall, 5, 28, 41, 62, 66, 112, 114–15, 120, 122–23, 131
Jefferson, Thomas, 15
Jim Crow, 9–10, 16–17
Job, 46, 112
Johnson, Carol, 152
Johnson, Henry, 14–15
Johnson, Lyndon Baines, 21
Jolson, Al, 23
Jones, LeRoi. *See* Baraka, Imamu Amiri
Jonson, Ben, 118
Joyce, James, 16–17, 31, 46, 72, 80, 85, 95, 116, 129–130
Jung, Carl Gustav, 116

Kafka, Franz, 24
Kavanagh, Patrick, 31
Keats, John, 31, 35, 37, 44, 84, 93,
    97, 113, 126
Keeler, Christine, 28, 125
Kennedy, John F., 28, 61
Kierkegaard, Søren, 41, 44
King Lear (Shakespeare), 82
Kipling, Rudyard, 123
Koch, Ilse, 117
Kora in Hell (Williams), 111
Kunitz, Stanley, 122–23

Lacan, Jacques, 130–31
Lamb, Charles, 13
Lamentations, Book of, 7–8, 13, 19,
    124–25
Lawrence, D. H., 80
"Lay of Ike, The," 80
Lazarus, 22, 63
Leacock, Stephen, 129
Leadbetter, Huddie, 13
Leaves of Grass (Whitman), 73
Lévi-Strauss, Claude, 17, 19, 126,
    130
Lewis, Matthew Gregory, 90
Life Drama, A (Smith), 2
Life Studies (Lowell), 71, 76, 95
Lise (*Berryman's Sonnets*), 137, 142,
    150–51
Lonely Crowd, The (Riesman), 125
"Long Way to MacDiarmid, The,"
    118
Lorenz, Konrad, 17
Lost Son, The (Roethke), 130
Love & Fame, 2, 35–48, 51, 65, 68,
    71, 80–81, 86, 90, 92–99: and
    the dedication, 37–38; and place
    in oeuvre, 90, 94–95, 98; and
    structure as narrative self-portrait,
    35, 38–48; and title source, 37,
    93
Lowell, Robert, 1, 9, 12, 61, 71–73,
    76–81, 83, 85, 88–89, 94–95,
    119, 122–23, 152
Luther, Martin, 20, 41

Macbeth (Shakespeare), 135
MacNeice, Louis, 60
McCarthy, Mary, 73
Maggie (Crane), 17, 152

Mailer, Norman, 15, 71, 74
Mallarmé, Stéphane, 73, 87
Marcuse, Herbert, 87
Maritain, Jacques, 117
Martz, William J., 118, 133, 149,
    151
Marvell, Andrew, 30
Marx, Groucho, 82, 135
Marx, Karl, 112
Marxism, 113
Mason, William, 2
Meditations (Bradstreet), 103
Men and Women (Browning), 2
Mendelson, Edward, 2
Meredith, George, 74–75, 133
Meredith, William, 14, 97, 119, 124
Metamorphosis, The (Kafka), 24
Miller, Henry, 71
Milton, John, 118
Minstrels, Virginia, the, 10
Modern Love (Meredith), 74–75, 133
"Monkhood," 39
Monster, The (Crane), 14, 16
Moore, Marianne, 16, 88
Mozart, Wolfgang Amadeus, 2, 95
Muni, Paul, 24

Nabokov Vladimir, 94
Nash, Ogden, 90
negative capability, 35, 113
"Nervous Songs, The," 57, 91,
    115–17
New Critics, the, 122
"Not to Live," 106
"Note on Poetry, A," 113, 120
Notebook (Lowell), 71, 77
Notes of a Son and Brother (James),
    26

O'Casey, Sean, 31
Olson, Charles, 20
"Olympus," 130
"On the London Train," 113–15, 118,
    122
Op. posth. series, 15, 19, 54, 125
Ovid, 142

Paradise Lost (Milton), 126
Paradiso (Dante), 59
Pascal, Blaise, 131

Pater, Walter, 102
Paterson (Williams), 21, 72, 91, 142
Petrarch, 57, 117, 134, 136–38,
  140–47, 150
Picasso, Pablo, 80
Pindar, 142
Plath, Sylvia, 1–2, 62, 75, 123
Plato, 126
"Plato and the Definition of the
  Primitive" (Diamond), 17
Poems, 61
"Poetry of Confession, The" (Rosen-
  thal), 79
"Poetry of Ezra Pound, The," 118
"Poetry of John Berryman, The"
  (Lowell), 122
Pope, Alexander, 65
Pound, Ezra, 21, 29, 54–55, 72–73,
  85, 89–90, 95, 101, 118–19,
  129–30, 142
"Professor's Song, A," 2
Prynne, Hester: and relation to Anne
  Bradstreet, 160–63
psychoanalysis, 14–15, 42, 120, 130,
  158
Puritanism, 74–75
Pynchon, Thomas, 89

Quarles, Francis, 121

Ramsey, Frederic, 13
Ransom, John Crowe, 90
Recluse, The (Wordsworth), 55
Recovery, 49–52, 89–90, 116, and
  Delusions, etc., 49; and dreams,
  50–51; and role of Alan
  Severance, 49–52, 116, 118
Red Badge of Courage, The (Crane),
  14
"Regents' Professor Berryman's Crack
  on Race," 68
religion, 17–19, 41–48, 52, 94–95,
  107; Christianity in *Love &
  Fame*, 35, 41–48; Puritanism,
  153–63
Renaissance, the, 133–34, 139–47
Renault, Mary, 6
"Researched Mistress, The" (Ciardi),
  120
"Resolution and Independence"
  (Wordsworth), 73

Rice, Thomas Dartmouth: and 77
  Dream Songs, 9; as Daddy Rice,
  9–11, 17
Richards, I. A., 122
Rilke, Rainer Maria, 11, 80, 132
Roethke, Theodore, 1, 12, 28, 62,
  66, 115, 129–32
Romantic Survival, The (Bayley), 80
Rosenthal, M. L., 79
Roth, Philip, 89

"Sailing to Byzantium" (Yeats), 79
Santayana, George, 31
Sartre, Jean Paul, 85
Scarlet Letter, The (Hawthorne),
  159–63
Schreiner, Olive, 7, 13–14, 16, 19,
  126
Schwartz, Delmore, 5, 28, 62–63, 89,
  96, 115, 127, 129
"Sea and the Mirror, The" (Auden),
  81
Sealdah Station, the, 25
"Search, The," 41
77 *Dream Songs*, 6, 21–22, 24, 54,
  59, 124: and *Dream Songs*, 21
Severance, Alan (*Recovery*), 49–52,
  116, 118
Sexton, Anne, 1, 82
Shakespear, Olivia, 116
Shakespeare, William, 24, 32, 37, 75,
  90, 117, 134–37, 151
"Shakespeare's Reality," 90
Shapiro, Karl, 5, 66, 112
Shelley, Percy Bysshe, 2
Short Poems, 90
Shiva, 17–18
Sidney, Sir Philip, 57, 117, 134,
  137–39, 158
Simpson, Eileen, 150, 162
Simpson, Louis, 89, 94
Smith, Alexander, 2
"So Long? Stevens," 61
Song of Myself (Whitman), 1, 22, 91,
  112, 132, 158
"Song of the Tortured Girl, The," 117
Soviet poets, 61
Spender, Stephen, 83
Spenser, Edmund, 78, 118, 151
Stanley, Henry, 14
Stephen Crane, 14, 16, 18

Stevens, Wallace, 1, 26, 60–61, 72–73, 101, 142
Stitt, Peter, 119
"Sunlight Lay Across My Bed, The," 7–8
"Sur un portrait de Corbière" (Corbière), 37
Swift, Jonathan, 28, 31
Synge, John Millington, 31

Tambo and Bones (Wittke), 7, 9–10
Tate, Allen, 1, 3, 6
Taylor, Edward, 152
Tempest, The (Shakespeare), 136
Tenth Muse Lately Sprung Up in America, The (Bradstreet), 152
Tertz, Abram, 7
Testament of Beauty, The (Bridges), 75
Thomas, Dudley (Homage to Mistress Bradstreet), 153–55
Thomas, Dylan, 77–78, 90, 96, 119, 142
Thoreau, Henry David, 72, 118
Tolstoy, Leo, 150, 160
Tom the Lunatic, 3
Toynbee, Philip, 6, 12
"Translator, The—I, II," 19
Tristram Shandy (Sterne), 88
Trollope, Anthony, 80
Twelfth Night (Shakespeare), 117
Twenty Poems, 38
"Two Organs," 81, 86

Ulysses (Joyce), 32
Under Pressure (Alvarez), 122

Valéry, Paul, 73, 80
Van Doren, Mark, 85, 90, 92, 113

Vendler, Helen, 96
Vietnam, 28
"View of Myself," 42
Villon, François, 142
Virgil, 142
Vita nuova (Dante), 49
Vonnegut, Kurt, 88

"Waiting for the End, Boys," 114
Waller, Edmund, 30
Warhol, Andy, 6
Washington, George, 96
Wasserstrom, William, 124–25
Waste Land, The (Eliot), 91, 121, 127
Whitman, Walt, 26–31, 73, 76, 112, 130, 132, 152, 158
Wilbur, Richard, 92
Williams, William Carlos, 1, 21, 28, 98, 111, 118, 129, 131–32, 142
Wilson, Edmund, 80, 91–92
"Winter Landscape," 1, 61
Winters, Yvor, 28
Winthrop, John, Governor (Homage to Mistress Bradstreet), 153–55
Wittgenstein, Ludwig, 106
Wittke, Carl, 7
Wolfe, Thomas, 79
Words for Music Perhaps (Yeats), 116–17, 124
Wordsworth, William, 26, 31, 55, 60, 72–73, 87, 126
Wyatt, Sir Thomas, 113–14, 134, 139, 143–45

Yeats, W. B., 1–4, 28–29, 31, 36, 40, 56, 61, 64, 72, 74, 76, 78–82, 85, 90–91, 98, 111, 113–18, 120, 122, 124, 126–30, 132, 142
"Young Woman's Song," 117